POTATO

POTATO

The definitive guide to potatoes and potato cooking

ALEX BARKER WITH RECIPES BY SALLY MANSFIELD

LORENZ BOOKS

Paperback edition published in 1999 by Lorenz Books

© Anness Publishing Limited 1999

Lorenz Books is an imprint of
Anness Publishing Limited
Hermes House
88-89 Blackfriars Road
London SE1 8HA

This edition distributed in Canada by Raincoast Books,
8680 Cambie Street, Vancouver, British Columbia V6P 6M9

ISBN 0 7548 0404 6

A CIP catalogue record for this book is available from the British Library

Publisher: Joanna Lorenz
Senior Editors: Linda Fraser and Toria Leitch
Copy Editor: Leslie Mandel-Viney
Indexer: Hilary Bird
Editorial Reader: Diane Ashmore
Production Controller: Ann Childers
Designer: Margaret Sadler
Photography: Steve Moss (potatoes) and Sam Stowell (recipes)
Food for Photography: Alex Barker (techniques), Eliza Baird (recipes)
Additional Recipes: Roz Denny, Jacks Clarke, Joanna Farrow, Shirley Gill, Sarah Gates, Steven Wheeler, Hilaire Walden,
Christine France, Rosamund Grant, Sheila Kimberley, Liz Trigg, Carla Capalbo, Carole Clements, Judy Jackson, Ruby Le Bois,
Chris Ingram, Matthew Drennan, Elizabeth Wolfe-Cohen, Shehzad Hussain, Rafi Fernandez, Manisha Kanini, Laura Washburn,
Andi Clevely, Katherine Richmond, Jennie Shapter

Printed and bound in Singapore

3 5 7 9 10 8 6 4 2

NOTES
For all recipes, quantities are given in both metric and imperial measures and,
where appropriate, measures are also given in standard cups and spoons. Follow one set, but not a mixture
because they are not interchangeable.

Standard spoon and cup measures are level.
1 tsp = 5ml, 1 tbsp = 15ml, 1 cup = 250ml/8fl oz

Australian standard teaspoons are 20ml. Australian readers should
use 3 tsp in place of 1 tbsp for measuring small quantities of gelatine, cornflour, salt etc.

Medium potatoes and eggs are used unless otherwise stated.

CONTENTS

THE POTATO – ITS HISTORY

THERE ARE FEW more important foods in the world than the potato. Its history goes back to the early days of man – a past spanning feast and famine. It has long played a vital role as the best all-round source of nutrition for mankind, and will continue to do so in the future.

The potato was discovered by pre-Inca Indians in the foothills of the Andes Mountains in South America. Archaeological remains have been found dating from 400 BC on the shores of Lake Titicaca, in ruins near Bolivia, and on the coast of Peru. Cultivated by the Incas, it influenced their whole lives. The Peruvian potato goddess was depicted holding a potato plant in each hand. The South American Indians measured time by the length of time it took to cook potatoes to various consistencies. Potato designs were found in Nazca and Chimu pottery. Raw slices of potato placed on broken bones were thought to prevent rheumatism.

The original potatoes, ranging from the size of a nut to a small apple, and ranging in colour from red and gold to blue and black, flourished in these temperate mountain plateaux. The first recorded information about the potato

was written in 1553 by the Spanish conquistador Pedro Cieza de Leon and soon potatoes joined the treasures carried away by these Spanish invaders. They became standard food on Spanish ships, and people began to notice that the sailors who ate them did not suffer from scurvy.

The first known purchase of the potato was by a hospital in Seville in 1573. Its cultivation spread quickly throughout Europe via explorers such as

Above: A ceramic plate made by the Incas, which typically would have been used for serving potatoes

Sir Francis Drake, who is reputed to have brought potatoes back to Britain. These are thought to have been cultivated on Sir Walter Raleigh's estate in Ireland, 40,000 acres of land given to him by Queen Elizabeth I expressly to grow potatoes and tobacco. Botanists and scientists were fascinated by this novel plant – it was mentioned in John Gerard's herbal list in 1597 – and potatoes may first have been grown mainly for botanical research. During Charles II's reign, the Royal Society recognized the potato as being nutritional and inexpensive and, with the ever-present fear of famine and war, governments in Europe tried to persuade their farmers to start growing this valuable crop in quantity.

However the potato also carried with it a reputation. As part of the nightshade family, it was thought to be poisonous or to cause leprosy and syphilis and to be a dangerous aphrodisiac. In France, a young chemist, Antoine Augustin Parmentier, set about converting the French and their King Louis XVI with his potato delicacies (hence his name is now used often in connection with potato dishes), and Marie Antoinette was persuaded to wear potato blossoms in her hair. But in some cases it took more than just

Above: The Golden Hind *in which Sir Francis Drake brought potatoes back to Britain*

Above: The potato flower

persuasion. King Frederick of Prussia ordered his people to plant potatoes to prevent famine but had to enforce these orders by threatening to cut off the noses and ears of those who refused. European immigrants introduced potatoes to North America but it was not until Irish immigrants took the potato to Londoncerry, New Hampshire in 1719, that it began to be grown in any quantity. Early in the 19th century, Lord Selkirk also emigrated with a group from the Isle of Skye in Scotland to settle in an area known as Orwell Point on Prince Edward Island, Canada. With him he took potatoes and the community survived on potatoes and cod for many years.

By the end of the 18th century, the potato was becoming a major crop, particularly in Germany and Britain. The Irish peasants were eating a daily average of ten potatoes per person, 80 per cent of their diet. In addition, potatoes were fodder for their animals who provided their milk, meat and eggs. This total dependence proved to be disastrous for the Irish when the blight of *Phytophthora infestans* struck the potato harvest in three successive years in the 1840s. Over a million people died and it is hardly surprising that the potato became known as the white or Irish potato, to distinguish it from the sweet potato.

The Irish took their love of the potato with them when they moved in large numbers to the north of England, as well as to Europe and America to escape the famine. The British government had by now accepted the potato as a nutritious, cheap and easily grown food and were encouraging the use of allotments for potato growing; "potato patches" as they became known in the Victorian era. The fear of another potato crop disaster through disease, along with the new-found appreciation of its table value caused intense interest in improving potato varieties throughout Europe. At the International Potato Show at London's Alexandra Palace in 1879 there were reputed to have been several hundred varieties on show. By the turn of the century the potato was the accepted main vegetable crop and was exported throughout Europe.

POTATOES IN THE WORLD TODAY

Now the potato is the staple food for two-thirds of the world's population and our third most important food crop. It is the best all-round source of nutrition known to man, second only to eggs for protein and better even than soya beans, the protein food of the second half of the 20th century. Growing potatoes is also the world's most efficient means of converting land, water and labour into an edible product – a field of potatoes produces more energy per acre per day than a field of any other crop.

Above: The great exhibition hall at London's Alexandra Palace

*Above: The sweet potato or yam flower (*Ipomoea batatas*)*

surrato, *pompiterre*, *bombiderre*, *castanhola* (chestnut from Spain) are some of the European ones. Chinese names include *shanyao* (mountain medicine), *didan* (ground egg), *fanzaishu* (potato with many children) and *aierlanshu* (Irish potato), to mention but a few.

THE POTATO PLANT CYCLE

The potato is related to both the tomato and the tobacco plant. Its botanical name is *Solanum tuberosum*, from the *Solanaceae* family, and the only edible part is the tuber. The plant is bushy and sprawling with clusters of dark green leaves. It produces flowers which range in colour from white to purple or striped and occasionally grows yellow-green fruits which contain anything from 100 to 300 kidney-shaped seeds. When grown from seed (or seed potato) it sprouts upwards producing a shoot, and downwards producing a root. The shoot first forms leaves, then flowers and as they die back the excess energy is stored as starch below ground in tubers at the ends of the roots. These tubers, the potatoes, grow larger as more and more starch is produced.

Potato tubers have several small indentations or external buds (as consumers we call them eyes and cut them out before eating them) which, when allowed to grow, form new stems or sprouts. Some of these will successfully grow into new plants using the stored food in the tuber. This original tuber is known as a seed potato which home growers and most commercial growers buy every year. In fact, you only need a piece of potato with one bud in, not even the whole potato, to produce one potato plant.

Producing the plant from seed is a much more complex process. The flower grown from this seed needs pollinating and it is only when this occurs in a controlled environment that you can be sure what the resultant plant will be like. In all the major potato growing countries there are seed potato producers and breeding centres where researchers are constantly developing

Statistics for potato production around the world show up many interesting factors. Russia is still the world's largest potato producer with Poland, China and the USA not far behind them.

Consumption trends, however, are now changing the demands which are put upon potato growers. This is due mainly to the trend towards Mediterranean eating which is heavily based on alternative starch foods, such as pasta and rice. Although potatoes are still a major seller the bulk of those sold

are pre-packed, many in the form of chips. Part of this consumption of chips is in a frozen form, and is worldwide, with America and the Far East setting the trend. Freezing potatoes is certainly not new, however. The early Incas, 2,000 years ago, turned potatoes into a form of convenience food called chuno, by a process of natural freezing and drying which meant they could be kept for much longer.

Throughout the world the potato goes under many other names: *pomme de terre*, *kartoffel*, *patata*, *batateirs*, *batala*

FROM FIELD TO TABLE

The potato grows in over 180 countries, from an altitude of sea level to 14,000 feet, under a wider range of climatic conditions than any other staple food. It matures faster too, taking from 90 to 140 days. Yet much still depends on the grower knowing his or her potato, finding the right potato for the market and then making the most of the environment – a technology on its own.

Large scale potato production is highly mechanized, from planting to harvesting. Rows of furrows are made in the field by machines, ready for mechanical planters to drop in the seed potatoes. Machines aided by computer determine the depth of the troughs, the spacing of seed potatoes and soil fertilization, monitoring for pests and diseases and crop spraying as well. In good time for harvesting, the plant is left to finally mature and be ready for picking, which is done by machine, several rows at a time. The potatoes, separated from soil and stones by machines and briefly air dried, are stored in insulated boxes in controlled ventilation warehouses. Those going to local market are graded by size or riddled before being bagged or put into sacks.

Above: A selection of rare potatoes, clockwise from top, Mr Bressee, International Kidney, Blue Catriona, Champion, Edgecote Purple, Arran Victory

new breeds. The Netherlands, the USA, Peru and the UK are key centres and, as with rare breeds of animals, the researchers log those that go out of favour or fashion, endeavouring to keep these breeds going for future reference and genetic research. Their main aim, however, is to develop new breeds which will enable more efficient potato production for the various climates throughout the world. These include breeds that can resist viruses and diseases or ones that will store better for longer, and breeds which provide the culinary qualities that certain markets demand, such as being good for chipping and processing. It is rare, of course, that all the desired qualities are found in one plant – in fact on average only one in 100,000 seedlings ever becomes registered as a cultivar (a possible new breed).

Only then does a seed go into field trials and it could be at least another 3–4 years before it is seen on the commercial market. There are several thousand varieties in existence throughout the world therefore, although only a fraction of those are in regular production. Countries with seed potato research centres provide key information annually for their seed producers. In Britain there are about 700 varieties held at the Department of Agriculture and Fisheries for Scotland listed in the Douglas M MacDonald collection. The Potato Association of America classifies up to 4,000 varieties but the International Potato Centre in Peru (CIP) has the largest gene bank, holding 3,694 cultivars.

Although varieties such as Blue Don, Elephant King Kidney, Perthshire Red, The Howard and Victoria – some dating as far back as the 16th century – have become extinct, other more famous names are in various collections for posterity. These include Congo, a bright blue potato from pre-1900, Edgecote Purple and Champion. Other aged varieties are being revived, through the success of research and supermarket innovation. Names such as Mr Bressee, Blue Catriona and Arran Victory are returning to our shops. Home growers, buying from seed catalogues, now have an even more exciting wealth of new varieties to experiment with.

Above: Grading potatoes by size using a riddling machine

After harvesting, potatoes are stored or cured at a temperature of 15–18°C/ 59–65°F before being put into long-term storage at a temperature just above freezing. This helps to prevent sprouting but potatoes going into storage for up to ten months may also be sprayed. At these temperatures the potato starch can be affected and turn to sugar, so before processing the potatoes go back into short-term storage at the curing temperature to convert the sugars back to starch. On smaller farms and in areas where farm workers are readily available, many of these jobs are still done partially by hand. In more rural regions potatoes can still sometimes be found stored in clamps where the potatoes are stacked up under piles of soil and straw to keep them dry and frost-free.

Above: The Yanaimilla and the Compis (see below) are descendants of the original South American potatoes

Potatoes are classified by the length of time they take to mature although this can be affected by the weather and the climate. First earlies, also called new potatoes, are planted in early spring for harvesting, after some 100–110 days, in early summer. Second earlies, as the name implies, are planted in late spring and harvested, after 110–120 days, from mid to late summer as late new potatoes. Maincrop potatoes are planted in the spring but not harvested for at least 125–140 days in late summer. These are the potatoes which go into long-term storage for sale in the next season, whilst earlies go straight into the shops.

When a young potato is dug up it has fragile, flaky skin. As it matures the skin sets and after a certain length of time will no longer flake and the flesh becomes much more starchy. Maincrop potatoes have to be kept in the ground maturing as long as possible to produce skins which are thick enough to survive in long-term storage. You will now find that you can buy a young, new Maris Piper for instance, which is small and flaky, at the same time as you can buy the large, firm maincrop Maris Piper, since each may be grown in different areas by different producers.

NUTRITION

The potato is the single most important source of vitamin C for much of the world, in particular the poorer countries where there is little fruit and certainly no other dietary supplements. We all need vitamin C to help fight off infections and to keep muscle, skin and bones healthy. Unlike many vegetables, the entire potato is edible and nutritious, providing important amounts of protein, vitamins and minerals, and it can be cooked in ways to suit most climates, ethnic traditions and cooking abilities. More than that, for the Western societies which are suffering from the excesses of good food, potatoes can provide a useful amount of one of the key elements needed in our modern healthy diet – fibre.

Above: The Compis, like the Yanaimilla, are only grown by local Andean Farmers

The bulk of the potato, about 75 per cent or more according to how you cook it, is made up of water. The largest

Above: Baked potatoes are a valuable source of protein, fibre and vitamin C

amount of the rest – 17 per cent – is starch, known also as complex carbohydrate. Current recommendations for the Western diet suggest that we should get at least 40 per cent of our food energy – our total calorie consumption per day – from starchy foods such as potatoes. One large baked potato, approximately 300g/11oz, will provide about 250 calories. Potatoes also contain 2.1 per cent protein, 1.3 per cent fibre, good quantities of vitamin C, almost no fat and other important trace elements such as foliate (for red blood cells), potassium (which helps calm the nerves) and iron (which helps oxygen travel easily around the body). New potatoes have a particularly high vitamin C content and a 100g/3¾oz serving can provide 23 per cent of our daily requirement.

The way potatoes are stored and cooked also affects their nutritional content. Vitamin C can be lost during long storage in too much light and it can also be lost whilst they are soaking in water before and during the cooking process. Chips, surprisingly, are not such a bad way of cooking potatoes as they are often portrayed. They manage to retain more of the vitamin C because the method of cooking involves less soaking in water and, if oven-baked, 100g/3¾oz chips will actually have fewer calories than 100g/3¾oz of fruit and nut mix.

GROWING YOUR OWN POTATOES

Potatoes usually grow well in most soils, and whether you have a small corner or a large plot, whether you have years of experience or are a novice gardener, they will produce a worthwhile result for relatively little effort. Just 9C0g/2lb of seed potatoes can give around 23kg/50lb potatoes, so unless you have plenty of storage space or have a large family you may only need to plant a small amount or stagger the harvesting. Early potatoes produce a smaller crop than maincrop potatoes so they also require less space.

PREPARATION

Prepare the ground in the autumn before it gets too hard, clearing the weeds and digging in a good compost or manure, about one bucketful to 1sq m/1.2sq yds. A couple of weeks before planting, dig over the ground adding fertilizers as recommended. Potatoes need a lot of space; a 900g/2lb seed bag will require 0.9–1.2sq m/3–4sq ft of soil for instance. Seed potatoes can be put in trays at the end of January in a cool room or warmed greenhouse, to encourage the sprouts to grow earlier and give a better crop.

PLANTING

In most climates first earlies can be planted from mid-spring; in colder regions wait until late spring.

1 Make drills or shallow trenches about 10cm/4in deep and 45cm/18in apart with a hoe, or up to 60cm/2ft apart for maincrop potatoes, Place the seed potatoes, sprouts uppermost, into them.

2 Fill in the drills with soil, increasing the height of soil over the potato seed for protection.

3 For easier, weed-free growth and frost protection, plant the seeds under black plastic. Secure the edges of the plastic under soil.

4 Make several cross-shaped slits where the potatoes will be planted, making sure they are covered with at least 5cm/2in of soil.

PROTECTING

As the shoots start to appear, draw up more soil over the seed potato into a ridge, giving protection against frost, and continue this earthing-up process every two weeks until the foliage meets between the rows or you have soil mounds about 15cm/6in high. Water occasionally in a very dry spring or more frequently for earlies.

HARVESTING

Early potatoes should be ready for harvesting from early summer in milder climates – as a rough guide after about 12–14 weeks. You could start by carefully pushing away earth from the higher part of the ridges to remove any that are ready. Replace the soil if they are still too small.

Maincrop potatoes, on the other hand, have to be held in the ground until the foliage dies down, so the tubers can keep growing and the skin sets firmly for longer storage. To be sure, lift one or two potatoes, as above, and try rubbing the skin. If it rubs off easily the potatoes are not ready.

1 Dig up the potatoes with a large fork and sort them into groups by size. Leave them on the ground for an hour or two to dry off.

2 Store them in large sacks made of hessian if you can find them, or in string bags. Slatted boxes are suitable too, but use straw to both protect the potatoes from bruising and keep them frost-free and dry. Keep in a dark, cool but not damp place such as a garage, as long as it does not get too cold.

PREPARATION TECHNIQUES

The method you use to prepare your potatoes affects the mineral and vitamin content, and the cooking technique.

CLEANING POTATOES

Most potatoes you buy today are very clean, especially those from supermarkets and pre-packed potatoes, so giving them a light wash will probably be sufficient before boiling them. Locally grown potatoes, farm shop or home-grown potatoes may still have some earth attached to them, so give them a light scrub before cooking. If you are not going to cook them immediately avoid scrubbing the potatoes with water as they can start to go mouldy in warm or damp weather.

1 If the potatoes are very dirty, use a small scrubbing brush or a gentle scourer to clean and remove the peel of the new potatoes.

2 Remove any green or discoloured patches or black eyes carefully, using a pointed knife or potato peeler, unless you are going to peel them after cooking, at which stage they will come out of their skins easily.

PEELING POTATOES

It is well known that much of the goodness and flavour of a potato is in the skin and just below it. You can boil the potatoes and then peel them afterwards when they are cool enough to handle. The taste is much fresher and earthier if they are prepared this way and perfect for eating plain or simply garnished. Leave the skins on occasionally, which gives more taste and added texture, plus a vital source of roughage and fibre to the diet. Save any peelings you have left over for a very healthy version of crisps.

To peel potatoes use a very sharp potato peeler (there are many different varieties to choose from) to remove the thinnest layer possible in long even strips. Place the potatoes in a saucepan of water so they are just covered until ready to cook, but preferably cook them immediately to avoid any loss of vitamin C.

If you cook potatoes in their skins and want to peel them whilst hot ready for eating immediately, hold the hot potato with a fork and then gently peel off the skin – the skin tends to peel more easily while the potatoes are still hot.

SCRAPING POTATOES

Really new potatoes peel very easily, often just by rubbing them in your hands. You can tell a good new potato, when buying them, by how easily the skin rubs or flakes off.

With a small sharp knife scrape away the flaky skin and place in just enough water to cover.

RUMBLING

This wonderfully old-fashioned word refers to a catering machine with a large revolving bowl and rough, grater-like sides. The potatoes rumble around until the skins are eventually scratched or scraped off. There is one product available for the domestic market which peels the potatoes in the same way.

Wash the potatoes, place in the peeler drum with water as directed, then turn on to speed 2–3 and leave for several minutes. Remove any that are peeled and then continue until the rest are ready. Transfer to a pan of cold water ready for cooking. Don't put in more potatoes than recommended or they may come out misshapen.

GRATING BY HAND

Potatoes can be grated before or after cooking, depending on how you will be using them. They are easier to grate after cooking, when they have had time to cool, and can be grated on a large blade straight into the cooking dish or frying pan. Be sure you don't overcook the potatoes, especially if they are floury, as they will just fall to pieces. Floury potatoes are ideal for mashing, while waxy potatoes are a good choice for making rösti or hash.

Raw potatoes exude a surprising amount of starchy liquid that is vital to helping some dishes stick together. Check before you start whether you need to keep this liquid. The recipe should also tell you whether to rinse off the starchy liquid or just dry the potatoes on kitchen paper. Don't grate the potatoes too soon as the flesh quickly begins to turn brown.

Using a standard grater, grate raw potatoes on a board.

Or if you need the liquid, grate into a medium bowl using either the medium or large blade. Squeeze the liquid from the potatoes by hand.

CHOPPING

Potatoes are often required to be chopped for recipes such as salads and dishes using leftovers. If you are cooking them first the best potatoes to choose are the waxy ones which stay nice and firm. They chop most easily when they are cold and peeled.

To chop, cut the potato in half, then half again and again until it is cut up evenly, as small as is required.

DICING

If the recipe calls for dice this means you have to be much more precise and cut the potato into even shaped cubes. This is usually so that all the sides brown neatly or the pieces cook through evenly.

1 To dice, trim the potato into a neat rectangle first (keep the outside pieces for mash, or to add to a soup), then cut the rectangles into thick, even slices.

2 Turn the stack of slices over and cut into thick batons and finally into even cubes of the size needed for the recipe you are using.

SLICING BY HAND

It may not always matter how neatly and evenly you slice your potatoes, but for some dishes it will affect both the appearance of the finished dish and the cooking time. Try to cut all slices the same thickness so that they cook evenly. Use a large knife for the best results, and make sure that it is sharp otherwise it may slip and cause a nasty cut. To make rounder slices cut across the width of the potato, for longer slices cut along the length of the potato. If you need to slice cooked potatoes for a recipe, be sure to slightly undercook them so they don't fall to pieces either in the dish or when slicing, and let them get really cold before handling them. For most casseroles and toppings cut them about 3mm/⅛in thick.

Put the tip of the knife on the work surface or board first, then press the heel of the knife down firmly to create nice even slices.

SLICING WITH A MANDOLINE

A relative of the musical instrument of the same name, the mandoline has several different cutting blades which vary both the size and shape of the cut potato. The blades are fitted into a metal, plastic or wooden framework for ease of use. It can produce slices from very thin to very thick, as well as fluted slices for crinkle-cut style crisps. It's quite a dangerous gadget, and needs handling with respect because of its very sharp blades. You can cut different thicknesses as required, such as, medium thick (about 2–3mm/¹⁄₁₆–¹⁄₈in) for sautéed potato slices and very thin for crisps.

Plain Slices

Fix the blade to the required thickness, then holding the potato carefully slide it firmly up and down or across the blade. Use the handle or gadget that is provided with some versions to hold on to whenever possible.

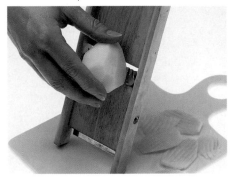

Crinkle-cut

For crinkle-cut slices cut the potato horizontally down the fluted blade. Take particular care when the potato gets smaller as it is easy to cut one's fingers

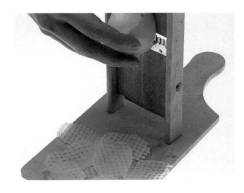

Waffled Crisps

For the fancy waffled crisps (*pomme gaufrettes*), cut horizontally down the blade, rotating each time you slice to get a lattice effect.

MAKING CRISPS BY HAND

Home-made crisps are the best, but they can be very fiddly if you do not have the right tools for making them. For a large batch slice the potatoes in a food processor, but for a small batch the slicing blade on a standard grater should give thin enough potato slices if you use it carefully. You can also use a sharp knife to make crisps, but you need to be very careful.

Grating Crisps

To make thin crisps, hold a standard grater firmly on a chopping board, placing a damp cloth on the board to anchor the grater to it and prevent it from sliding. Slide the potato down over the slicing blade carefully. Be sure the grater or mandoline has a very sharp blade. Adjust it to the right thickness or, if it's not adjustable, you will find that the harder you press, the thicker the

Slicing Crisps

This method is best if you want to make small quantites of thick crisps. Hold one end of the potato firmly in your hand and cut thin slices – 3mm/¹⁄₈in thick – with a sharp knife, on a chopping board. Slicing crisps with a knife means that it is easier to adjust the thickness. Remember that the thicker the slice, the less oil will be absorbed by the potato during cooking.

MAKING RIBBONS BY HAND

Thin ribbons, which also deep fry into delicious crisps, can be simply cut with a potato peeler. (Any leftover odd shapes can go into the stockpot.)

To make ribbons, peel the potato like an apple to give very long strips. Work quickly, or put the ribbons in a bowl of cold water as you go, to prevent them turning brown.

CHIPS

The French give their chips various names, depending on how thin or thick they are cut. The larger you cut them the healthier they will be, since they will absorb less fat during the cooking. You can also make chips with their skins on, giving additional fibre.

Traditional English Chips

Use the largest chipping potatoes and cut the potatoes into 1.5cm/⅝in thick slices, or thicker if you wish.

Turn the slices on their side and cut into 1.5cm/⅝in batons, or slightly thicker or thinner if you prefer.

Chip Wedges

For a healthier alternative cut your chips, extra thick, into wedge shapes. First cut the potatoes in half lengthwise, then into long thin wedges.

Pommes Frites

Cut as for chips but slice again into neat, even batons about 5mm/⅓in thick, either by hand or machine.

Pommes Allumettes

Cut the potato into a neat rectangle by removing the rounded sides, then into thin slices and julienne strips about half the thickness of *pommes frites*.

Pommes Pailles (Straw Chips)

Cut the potatoes as for *pommes allumettes* into even finer julienne strips. They are usually pan fried.

Chip-cutter Chips

Chips can be cut with a special chip cutter (see equipment section) and some mandolins. Cut the potatoes to a suitable size to fit.

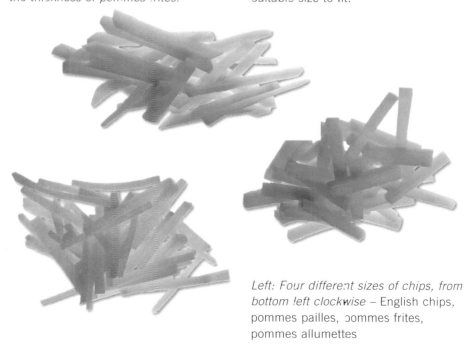

Left: Four different sizes of chips, from bottom left clockwise – English chips, pommes pailles, pommes frites, pommes allumettes

HASSELBACK AND FAN POTATOES

Children often refer to these as hedgehogs as they look quite spiky when roasted to a crispy, golden brown. Peel and dry the potatoes then slice as shown, brush with oil and then put them to roast as soon as possible before they begin to discolour.

To make hasselback potatoes, cut large potatoes in half and place cut side down on a board. With a sharp knife, cut very thin slices across the potato from end to end, slicing deep but not quite through the potato.

To make potato fans, use medium potatoes of long or oval shape and cut them at a slight angle, slicing almost but not quite through the potato, keeping the back section still attached. Press the potato gently on the top until it flattens and fans out at the same time. If you have not cut far enough through it will not fan very much, but if you have cut too far it will split into sections. The best way to cook both these potatoes is to cook them with melted butter and oil and roast them in the oven, preheated to 190°C/375°F/ Gas 5, for 40–50 minutes.

SHAPED POTATOES

Occasionally it is fun to spend the time making potatoes into an artistic creation. You might try these out with children when you are encouraging them to get more involved with preparing and cooking family meals. Use the offcuts for making mash or to thicken soups.

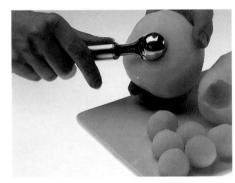

To make potato balls use large firm potatoes for the best results. Peel them and then using a large round or shaped melon baller push it firmly into the potato, twist, and ease out the potato shape. Keep in water until ready to cook, pat dry on kitchen paper and roast or sauté as usual.

To make turned potatoes, first peel small to medium firm potatoes (or quartered large potatoes), trim the ends flat and then cut or trim with a small knife into rugby ball shapes 2.5–5cm/ 1–2in long.

To make potato wedges, cut potatoes in half lengthways, then into quarters and then into eighths. Brush with oil and oven roast or deep fry. The larger the pieces of potato the less fat they will absorb.

PREPARING POTATOES BY MACHINE

Some machines will do many of the jobs already mentioned, such as peeling, grating, slicing, chipping and puréeing, with great speed but not with the precision of your own hands. To get the best results, always cut the potatoes to the same size, use the slowest speed or pulse so you can control the results, and cook the cut potatoes immediately or rinse and dry on kitchen paper to prevent browning.

Home-cooked chips are always the best kind, and cutting them by hand can be time consuming. So use a machine to prepare them for cooking. Fit the correct blade attachment and pack sufficient potatoes in the tube of the food processor so they can be pushed down. Turn on to the slowest speed and press the potato down with the plunger. The harder you press the plunger the thicker the chips will be.

They may turn out slightly bent but that won't affect the taste. For nice evenly sliced potatoes change the attachment on the machine and pack the potatoes so that they will remain facing the same direction and continue as above.

COOKING TECHNIQUES

There are endless different ways of cooking potatoes. However, the best technique depends on both the potato variety and the dish you are cooking.

BLANCHING

Potatoes are blanched (part-cooked) to soften the skin for easy peeling, to remove excess starch for certain recipes and to par-cook before roasting. Use a draining spoon or basket to remove large pieces of potato but when cooking smaller potatoes, place the potatoes in a chip basket for easy removal.

Place the prepared potatoes in a pan of cold water. Bring slowly to the boil and boil gently for 2–5 minutes depending on their size, then drain and use or leave in the cooling water until required.

BOILING

This is the simplest way of cooking potatoes. Place potatoes of a similar size, either whole or cut into chunks, with or without skins (sweet potatoes are best cooked in their skins to retain their bright colour) in a pan with sufficient water just to cover them. Sprinkle on 5–10ml/1–2 tsp salt or to taste, and bring slowly to the boil. Floury potatoes need very gentle boiling or you may find the outside is cooked before the inside is ready and they will become mushy or fall apart in the pan. New potatoes, which have a higher vitamin C content, should be put straight into boiling water and cooked for about 15 minutes and not left soaking. Very firm salad potatoes can be put into boiling water, simmered for

5–10 minutes and then left to stand in the hot water for another 10 minutes until required.

1 Place the potatoes in a large pan and just cover with salted water and a tight-fitting lid. Bring to the boil and leave to gently boil for 15–20 minutes depending on the size and type of potato. Boiling too fast tends to cook the potato on the outside first so it becomes mushy and falls apart before the middle is cooked.

2 When they are finished cooking, drain the potatoes through a colander and then return them to the pan to dry off, as wet or soggy potatoes are not very appetizing.

3 For really dry, peeled potatoes (for mashing for instance), leave them over a very low heat so any moisture can escape. In the north of England they sprinkle the potatoes with salt and shake occasionally until the potatoes stick to the sides of the pan.

4 In Ireland the potatoes are wrapped in a clean tea towel until ready to serve dry and fluffy.

STEAMING

All potatoes steam well but this gentle way of cooking is particularly good for very floury potatoes and those which fall apart easily. Small potatoes, such as new potatoes, steamed in their skins taste really delicious. Make sure potatoes are cut quite small, in even-size chunks or thick slices. Leaving cooked potatoes over a steaming pan of water is also a good way to keep them warm for several minutes.

1 Place prepared potatoes in a sieve, colander or steamer over a deep pan of boiling salted water. Cover as tightly as possible and steam for 5–7 minutes if sliced or cut small, increasing the time to 20 minutes or more if the potatoes are quite large.

2 Towards the end of the cooking time, test a few of the potatoes with a sharp knife, and when cooked, turn off the heat and leave until you are ready to serve them.

3 As an alternative, place a handful of fresh mint leaves in the bottom of the steamer before cooking. The flavour of the mint will penetrate during cooking.

FRYING

The key to successful frying is good fat. A mixture of butter and oil gives good flavour yet allows a higher cooking temperature than just butter.

Shallow Frying

Use a heavy-based large frying pan to allow an even distribution of heat and sufficient room to turn the food.

1 Heat about 25g/1oz/2 tbsp butter and 30ml/2 tbsp oil until bubbling. Put an even layer of cooked or par-cooked potatoes in the hot fat taking care not to splash yourself. Leave for 4–5 minutes until the undersides turn golden.

2 Turn the potatoes over gently with a large fish slice once or twice during cooking until golden brown all over.

Deep Frying

When deep frying, whether you use oil or solid fat, be sure it is fresh and clean. The chips must be well dried as water can cause the fat to bubble up dangerously. Always fry in small batches so the temperature does not drop too much when you add the food and it can cook and brown evenly. Remove any burnt pieces after each batch as this can taint the fat.

To deep fry chips, fill either a chip pan, a deep heavy saucepan with tight-fitting lid, or a deep-fat fryer, about half full with clean fat. Heat to the required temperature by setting the thermostat or test if the oil is hot enough by dropping in a piece of bread; it should turn golden in one minute.

When making chips they are best "blanched" first in hot fat to cook through and seal them without browning. These can then be removed, drained and frozen when cool. Give them a final cooking when you are almost ready to eat, to crisp them up and turn them golden brown.

1 Before frying, dry the chips very thoroughly in a cloth or kitchen paper. Any water or moisture will make the fat splash and spit.

2 Heat the basket in the fat first, then add the chips to the basket (don't overfill or they will not cook evenly), and lower slowly into the pan. If the fat appears to bubble up too much remove the basket and cool the fat slightly.

3 Shake the pan of chips occasionally to allow even cooking, and cook until they are crisp and golden. Remove with a draining spoon or chip basket and drain well against the side of the pan first.

4 Tip the chips on to kitchen paper to get rid of the excess fat before serving, sprinkled with salt.

Potato Baskets

1 Cut potatoes into thin, even slices and dry on kitchen paper without rinsing. You will need two wire potato baskets or ladles. Line the larger one evenly with overlapping slices, covering the base well, then clamp the smaller basket inside this one.

2 Slowly immerse in very hot fat for 3–4 minutes until starting to turn golden brown.

3 Remove from the heat, separate the ladles and ease out the basket. Drop back into the fat for another 1–2 minutes until golden.

4 Serve filled with vegetables, stir-fried meat, or sweet and sour prawns.

BAKING

One of the most comforting and economical meals is a salt-crusted potato baked in its jacket with a fluffy centre that is golden with melted butter and cheese.

Sweet potatoes can be cooked in exactly the same way, sprinkled with a little demerara sugar and topped with soured cream and crispy bacon.

Allow a 275–350g/10–12oz potato for a good size portion and choose the ones recommended for baking, such as Marfona, Maris Piper, Cara or King Edward. Cook in the middle of a hot oven at 220°C/425°F/Gas 7 for 1–1½ hours for very large potatoes or 40–60 minutes for medium potatoes. To test that they are cooked, squeeze the sides gently to make sure that they are sufficiently soft.

1 Wash and dry baking potatoes thoroughly then rub with good oil and add a generous sprinkling of salt. Cook on a baking tray as above.

2 To speed up cooking time and to ensure even cooking throughout, cook the baking potatoes on a skewer, or on special potato baking racks.

3 When really tender cut a cross in the top of each potato and set aside to cool slightly.

4 Hold the hot potato in a clean cloth and squeeze gently from underneath to open up.

5 Place the open potatoes on individual serving plates and pop a lump of butter in each one.

6 For a quick and simple topping, add a little grated tangy Cheddar or similar hard cheese, or a dollop of soured cream and some chopped fresh herbs, such as chives, parsley or coriander. Season with plenty of salt and ground black pepper.

Baked Potato Skins

Bake the potatoes at 220°C/425°F/Gas 7 for 1–1½ hours for large potatoes and 40–60 minutes for medium. Cut in half and scoop out the soft centres. (Mash for a supper or a pie topping.)

Brush the skins with melted butter, margarine or a mixture of butter and oil and return to the top of the oven, at the same temperature, for 20 minutes or until really crisp and golden.

Potato Parcels

Baking a potato in a foil or greaseproof paper parcel, or in a roasting bag, makes for a very tasty potato with no mess and no dirty dishes, if you're careful. If you leave the potatoes in their skins you could prepare them well in advance and put them in to cook in an automatic oven before you get home.

Wash or scrub and dry small potatoes, then wrap them up in a parcel with several knobs of butter, a sprinkle of seasoning and a sprig or two of mint, tarragon or chives. Bake at 190°C/ 375°F/Gas 5 for about 40–50 minutes for 450g/1lb potatoes.

COOKING IN A CLAY POT

This is most like cooking in a bonfire or under a pile of earth – but here the potatoes take on a deep woody aroma and intense flavour without all the charring and smoke. The terracotta potato pot takes a generous 450g/1lb of potatoes easily. As with all clay pot utensils it should be soaked for 10–20 minutes before using. Use small, even-size potatoes, preferably in their skins. Always place the pot in a cold oven and let the temperature gradually increase to 200°C/400°F/Gas 6. Cook for 40–50 minutes and then test with a pointed knife to see if they are ready.

1 Put the prepared potatoes in the clay pot, toss in 30–45ml/2–3 tbsp of good, preferably extra virgin olive oil or melted butter and sprinkle with roughly ground salt from a mill and pepper. Add your favourite flavourings, such as one large unpeeled clove of garlic, a thick piece of streaky smoked bacon, chopped, or fresh herbs.

2 Put the covered pot in the cold oven and allow to heat to 200°C/400°F/Gas 6. After 40–50 minutes test with a knife. Serve straight from the pot.

MICROWAVED POTATOES

Baking potatoes in the microwave is an enormous time saver, as long as you don't expect the crunchy crust of oven-cooked potatoes. New potatoes and potato pieces can be cooked very quickly and easily. In both cases prick the potato skins first, to prevent bursting. To bake, allow 4–6 minutes per potato, with the setting on a high temperature, increasing by 2–4 minutes for every additional potato. As a guide for smaller boiled potatoes, allow 10–12 minutes per 450g/1lb of cut potatoes on high, or follow the manufacturer's instructions.

Place large potatoes in a circle on kitchen paper on the microwave tray, make cuts around the middle so the skins don't burst and turn once during the cooking process.

Place small potatoes in a microwave bowl with 30–45ml/2–3 tbsp boiling water. Cover tightly with microwave film and pierce two or three times to allow steam to escape during cooking. Leave for 3–5 minutes before draining, adding a knob or two of butter, seasoning and a sprig of mint.

Alternatively, cover the potatoes with a close-fitting microwave lid and cook them using the same method as for the microwave film covered bowl.

Standing time

Allow sufficient standing time afterwards so the potatoes are evenly cooked. Large, baked potatoes should be left to stand for 10 minutes wrapped in serviettes. This will keep them warm before serving and ensure even cooking.

PRESSURE-COOKING

If you want baked potatoes or large potatoes to be cooked in a hurry, or if you want to make a quick and easy mash, this is an ideal cooking method, but it's important to make sure you do not to overcook them, otherwise the potatoes will become dry and floury. Follow the instructions in your manual and allow up to 12 minutes cooking time for large whole potatoes; less for smaller ones. You can cook the potatoes in their skins, which speeds up the process further. Once the potatoes are ready, carefully reduce steam pressure so that they do not overcook.

ROASTING

Melt-in-the-mouth crisp roasties are
what Sundays were meant for, so here
are some pointers to make sure you get
them right every time.

For soft, fluffy-centred roast potatoes,
you need to use large baking potatoes –
Wilja, Maris Piper, Record, Désirée and
Kerr's Pink all give excellent results.
Peel (you can roast potatoes in their
skins but you won't get the crunchy
result most people love), and cut into
even-size pieces. Blanch for 5 minutes,
then leave in the cooling water for a
further 5 minutes to par-cook evenly.
Drain well and return to the pan to dry
off completely. Well-drained potatoes
with roughed up surfaces produce the
crispiest results.

A successful roast potato also
depends on the fat you cook them in
and the temperature. Beef dripping
gives the best flavour, although goose
fat, if you are lucky enough to find
some, is delicious and gives a very light,
crisp result. With other roasts you can
use lard or, where possible, drain off
enough dripping from the joint. A
vegetarian alternative is a light olive oil,
or olive and sunflower oils mixed.

The fat in the tin must be hot
enough to seal the potato surfaces
immediately. Use a large enough
roasting pan so that you have room to
turn the potatoes at least once. Don't
leave the almost cooked potatoes in too
much fat as they will become soggy.
Serve as soon as they are ready for
maximum crispness.

1 Blanch the peeled chunks of potato
and drain, then shake in the pan or fork
over the surfaces to rough them up.

2 Pour a shallow layer of your chosen
fat into a good heavy roasting tin and
place it in the oven, heating it to a
temperature of 220°C/425°F/Gas 7. Add
the dry, forked potatoes and toss
immediately in the hot oil. Return to the
top shelf of the oven and roast for up to
one hour.

3 Once or twice during cooking remove
the roasting tin from the oven and,
using a spatula, turn the potatoes over
to evenly coat them in fat. Then drain
off any excess fat so they can crisp up
and brown more easily.

Healthy Wedges

As a healthier alternative to deep-fried
chips and roasties, serve wedges of dry-
roasted potatoes sprinkled with various
seasonings. Bake at 190°C/375°F/Gas 5,
turning often until golden and crisp.

1 Cut large baking potatoes into long
thin wedges. Toss in a small amount of
very hot sunflower oil in a roasting tin.

2 Sprinkle on seasonings, turn the
wedges over several times and bake for
30–40 minutes, turning and testing
once or twice.

Flavourings

Flavourings you could try are:
- Curry powder mixes.
- Ground hazelnuts or other
  nuts.
- Dry seasoning mixes such
  as Italian Garlic Seasoning
  or Cajun Seasoning.
- Sesame seeds.
- Garlic and herb
  breadcrumbs.
- Grated Parmesan cheese.

MASHING AND PURÉEING

The ubiquitous mashed potato has seen a revival in recent years, from a favourite comfort food into a fashion food purely by the addition of olive oil or Parmesan cheese. Every chef and every trendy restaurant today produces their own version. It shows what can be done with a simple ingredient, but you've got to start with good mash. When choosing your potatoes remember that floury potatoes produce a light fluffy mash, while waxy potatoes will result in a dense, rather gluey purée which needs lots of loosening up. Boil even-size potatoes until very well cooked but not falling apart and dry them well, as watery potatoes will give a soggy, heavy mixture. Cold potatoes mash best of all. Sweet potatoes also mash well, to serve as a savoury or sweet dish.

You can mash potatoes in several ways: using a hand masher, which gives a very smooth result; pressing the potatoes through a ricer, sieve or mouli grater, which gives a very light and fluffy result; using a fork, which can result in a slightly lumpy, uneven mixture; or using a pestle-type basher. An electric hand-held mixer can be used but don't be tempted to blend or purée them in the food processor as the end product will be a very solid, gluey mixture, ideal for turning into soup.

Making Mash

There are a number of different hand mashers available for sale but the best ones are those that have a strong but open cutting grid. Simply push down on the cooked potatoes, making sure you cover every area in the pan and you will get a smooth, yet textured result.

Press potatoes through a ricer for an easy way to prepare light and fluffy mash. For a low-calorie side dish, press the potatoes straight into a heated bowl.

Alternatively beat in a generous knob of butter, some creamy milk and seasoning to taste, then continue mashing until you have a creamy, fluffy mixture.

Quick Mash Toppings

There are many simple ways to make mashed potatoes look more exciting and even tempt youngsters to try something new and unusual.

Rough up the topping on a shepherd's pie by running a fork through it.

An alternative decorative effect can be created using the back of a spoon to gently swirl the potato into soft hollows and peaks.

For a more chunky topping, use two matching spoons to make scoops or quenelle shapes, carefully moulding the potato around the sides of the spoons.

A quick and easy pattern to achieve is a lattice design. Run with a fork up and down the pie topping, before brushing with egg and then placing under a pre-heated grill to brown.

Piping Mashed Potatoes

Smooth and creamy mashed potatoes will pipe beautifully, and your results can look professional with very little practice. But it does have to be really smooth mash, since any lumps will ruin your efforts and may clog up the piping bag and nozzle. Place a large, star nozzle in a large clean piping bag and using a spoon fill the bag two-thirds with mash. Use your left hand to hold and guide the nozzle and your right hand to squeeze the potato down the bag. Practise a few times on a board, doing it slowly at first.

Duchesse Potatoes and Rosettes

These are the fancy portions which are often served in hotels. Rosettes are piped on to baking trays, brushed with beaten egg and baked until just golden to serve as a vegetable accompaniment to a main meal. They are very easy to make at home, however, if you want to impress your friends at a dinner party. You will need to use a firmer mashed potato than normal. To do this simply add egg yolks instead of milk to the potatoes in the pan and combine well. Brush with an egg glaze: 1 small egg, beaten with 15–30ml/1–2 tbsp water will give a thin mixture. Bake at 190°C/375°F/Gas 5 until golden brown.

1 Place a large, clean piping bag, fitted with a star nozzle, in a jug to hold it steady. Spoon in the thickened mashed potato until the bag is two-thirds full.

2 Start by squeezing out a small circle of potato, moving the nozzle slowly in one direction.

3 Then, still squeezing gently, fill in the centre and lift the bag up to make a cone shape.

Piped Topping

1 The same shape as above, made with a smaller nozzle, can be used to give a pie a very professional topping.

2 Bake the topping in the oven, preheated to 190°C/375°F/Gas 5 for 10-15 minutes, or grill for 5 minutes.

Potato Nests

These make a great meal for young children or an attractive dish for dinner. Fill with asparagus spears, fresh peas, sweetcorn, baked beans, soft cheese, chicken, fish or mushrooms in a creamy sauce and heat through.

1 Using the same nozzle as for duchesse potatoes pipe a large circle, or oval, on to a baking sheet or on to greaseproof paper

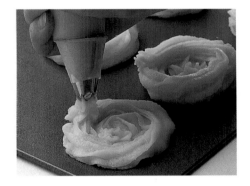

2 Then fill in the base and pipe over the outer circle again to give height to the sides. Glaze and bake as for duchesse potatoes.

Piped Edgings

Many dishes can have piped potato edges. Most well known is the individual starter Coquilles St Jacques, where the potato holds the fish and creamy sauce safely in the scallop shell.

Pipe a circle, just like the potato nests, but around the edge of a cleaned scallop shell or a china version of this. Brush with egg, fill with fish mixture and then grill until golden.

Mash Flavours

To make a Mediterranean version beat in salt, pepper and good quality olive oil to give a smooth soft mixture. Serve sprinkled with plenty of finely grated Parmesan cheese.

To make a wickedly rich mash, add thick cream or crème fraîche and grated fresh nutmeg. Mix thoroughly and serve with more grated nutmeg.

To make a lovely creamy mixture, beat in good, preferably extra virgin olive oil, and enough hot milk to make a smooth, thick purée. Then flavour to taste with salt and ground black pepper and stir in a few fresh basil leaves or parsley sprigs, chopped.

Chopped, cooked cabbage, spring onions and leeks are all regional favourites which add lots of flavour to a family supper dish.

Try a spicy mixture of chilli powder, or very finely chopped chilli and chives to sprinkle over a creamy mash.

To make a crunchy texture, place a few bacon rashers under a hot grill and once they are nice and crispy, chop them up and sprinkle over the potato.

To make a nutty mash, try toasted, flaked almonds or roughly chopped nuts of your choice.

USING COOKED POTATOES

Potatoes are one of the most versatile leftovers to have in the fridge, so it is well worth cooking extra when you make them, especially if a member of the family cannot tolerate wheat or cereals. You can use mashed potatoes in fish cakes, to thicken soups or stews, to make breads and scones and for a very light pastry to use in traditional savoury dishes or quiches. Grated, cooked potato can be used for rösti, hashes, omelettes, tortillas, and even to beef up a salad.

Potato Pastry

1 Rub 100g/4oz/8 tbsp dripping, lard or butter into 450g/1lb/4 cups sifted plain flour and add 450g/1lb mashed potatoes, 10ml/2 tsp salt, 1 beaten egg and sufficient milk so that when you draw the mixture together it is smooth but firm. Chill the pastry in the fridge for 10 minutes before use.

2 Roll the pastry out on a floured surface to an even thickness and use to line a suitable dish or tin. Chill the pastry in the dish again for 1 hour before pricking the bottom and filling as wished.

Potato Croquettes

1 Enrich a firm mash with egg, as for duchesse potatoes, season or add flavourings to taste, then shape into small cylinders, rolling out with a little flour or cornflour to prevent sticking.

2 Brush lightly with beaten egg, then coat or dip into any favourite mixture, like nibbed or flaked almonds or grated cheese mixed with breadcrumbs.

3 Shallow fry in butter and oil, turning occasionally until golden brown and warmed through. Croquettes can also be deep fried, or baked until golden brown. (Try putting a nugget of cheese in the middle before cooking for a delicious starter or supper dish.)

Rösti

1 Grate cold, par-cooked, waxy potatoes, on the largest side of a grater into a bowl and season to taste.

2 Heat a mixture of butter and oil in a heavy-based non-stick pan and, when bubbling, put in spoonfuls of the grated potato and flatten down neatly. Cook over low to medium heat until the rösti are golden and crisp underneath, which takes about 7–10 minutes.

3 Turn each of the rösti over with a fish slice, taking care that they do not fall apart and continue cooking for another 5 minutes or until really crisp.

4 To prepare one large rösti, spoon the potato mixture into the bubbling fat, flatten out evenly and leave to cook over a medium heat for about 10 minutes or until turning golden underneath. To turn the rösti over easily invert it on to a large plate – use a plate that fits right into the pan over the potato.

5 Turn the pan and plate over carefully so that the rösti slips on to the plate without breaking up.

6 Gently slide it back into the pan, with an extra knob of butter if necessary. Continue cooking for another 10 minutes or until crisp underneath. Serve cut into generous slices

BUYING AND STORING

Now that there is such a variety of potatoes to choose from, suited for every kind of cooking, it is important to think about how you plan to use your potatoes before you shop for them. Being tempted by some lovely little creamy International Kidneys or pale Pink Fir Apple potatoes, when what you want to make is a velvety thick soup or the topping for a shepherd's pie, won't give you complete success. Look at the Potato Index so that next time you go shopping you can choose the right varieties of potatoes to suit your menu ideas. If you always like to eat the skins and are concerned about what may be sprayed on them, then you would be well-advised to buy organic potatoes. Or grow your own – a very easy and rewarding task if you have the space.

When buying new potatoes check that they are really young and fresh by scraping the skin, which should peel off easily. New potatoes have a high vitamin C content so buy and eat them as fresh as possible for maximum goodness.

Maincrop potatoes should be firm. Avoid any which are soft, flabby, sprouting or have a white dusty mould.

Check for any green patches. These are a sign that the potatoes have been stored in the light and, although the rest of the potato is fine to eat, you do need to cut out these poisonous patches.

STORING

Potatoes have come from the dark and like to stay in the dark, and they do not keep too well unless carefully stored. In the warmth of a centrally heated kitchen they can start sprouting; the dampness of a cold fridge will make them sweaty and mouldy, and in too much light they begin to lose their nutritional value and start turning green. New potatoes in particular should be eaten within two or three days, to prevent mould forming on the surface. Unless they can be kept in the dark, it is better to buy in small quantities, a few pounds at a time, so that they are used quickly.

If you prefer to buy your potatoes in bulk, by the sack or in a large paper bag, then you need to find a dark, dry larder or garage, where they won't freeze in cold weather but the temperature is low enough not to encourage the growth of any sprouts.

If you are storing your potatoes in the house, put them into an open storage rack or basket or a well aerated bin in a dry, dark room.

When you buy potatoes in plastic bags remove them from the bags immediately you get them. Then store them in a suitable place.

Read the storage and keeping times of pre-packed potatoes, since these come in many varieties. Some are ready to cook, and others are already peeled or cleaned. You can even buy potatoes with seasonings or flavoured butter nowadays, but these are best consumed soon after purchasing, again read the packet for correct storage times.

PLANNING AHEAD

If you like to be organised and peel potatoes in advance – don't. Storing peeled potatoes in water will remove almost every trace of vitamin C. Even storing them tightly covered but without water in the fridge will result in nasty black potatoes.

A much better option is to almost fully cook the potatoes in their skins, leaving them very firm. They can be refrigerated like this, covered, for 2–3 days. Then when you come to use them, peel and chop the potatoes and reheat in the microwave or cook for a further 3–5 minutes with mint, or use as you would normally in a recipe. You should also find that they have far more flavour.

You can store already mashed potato covered with cling-film ready to make into rissoles or toppings.

FREEZING POTATOES

Raw potato does not freeze at all well as it goes mushy, but cooked potato freezes quite well, although it has a tendency to go watery, so make sure it is very well dried before freezing.

Pipe duchesse potatoes or rosettes on to a baking tray, freeze until hard and store in a container. Cook from frozen.

Croquettes, rissoles, potato cakes and rösti should be individually wrapped or separated by greaseproof paper and then packed in fours or eights. Partly defrost them if they contain any meat or fish, then cook as for the original recipe.

Chips can be cooked but not browned, ready for a last minute really hot fry to crisp them. Freeze them on trays and then transfer to bags. Partly defrost on kitchen paper to remove any particles of ice before deep frying in small batches.

POTATO PRODUCTS

There are many forms of prepared potato available in the shops today. Instant mashed potato, in powder or flake form, is very easy to use and now comes with popular flavour additions; potato flour makes a healthy alternative to wheat, and canned new potatoes mean a salad is made in seconds. Foil pouches contain ready-to-fry potato suppers with a very long shelf life, and an array of seasonings could give your baked potatoes, slices or wedges a welcome spark of flavour.

EQUIPMENT

The right piece of equipment for the job always makes life easier and you may find that there are now gadgets available that you haven't come across. Some tools, like potato peelers, become old friends too. If you are used to using one particular style you will be loath to change. Just glancing at the selection of equipment now available, it's difficult to know where to start. If you could try out a gadget before buying it, like trying on a dress, you would have an easier time choosing the right one. This list is designed to help.

The horizontal-angled blades are fast and easy to use on large potatoes.

Peeler with brush For dirty work you could try a swivel-blade peeler with brush attached.

Thick-grip peeler Many peelers now have good, thick grips which make light work of any peeling job and are much easier on the muscles for those with arthritic problems.

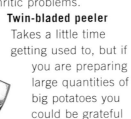

Left: Peeler with brush

Twin-bladed peeler Takes a little time getting used to, but if you are preparing large quantities of big potatoes you could be grateful for this efficiency.

Coloured peeler Modern kitchen colours are now echoed in the design of kitchen equipment such as peelers, but following the trend doesn't always produce quality products. Enjoy them for what they are, a touch of fun in the kitchen, and hope that they also work well.

Above: Lancashire peelers

Peelers

Lancashire peeler This is the most traditional peeler, with a solid handle, often made from wood and string, and a rigid blade. They are firm and last well and also double up as a corer.

Stainless steel peeler Lightweight and inexpensive. The sharpest ones will give the thinnest peel. Beware the very cheap ones with stainless steel blades that bend, snap or blunt very quickly.

Above: Thick-grip peelers

Above: Stainless steel peeler

Swivel-blade peeler These are for left- or right-handed people, but they are not very strong for heavy-duty work.

Above: Twin-bladed peeler

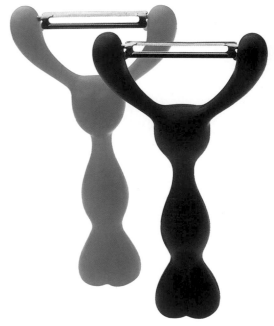

Above: Coloured peelers

Above: A selection of graters, including single-sided, box and standard shapes

Graters

The sturdier the better is the only approach if you want a grater for heavy-duty work, like grating large, raw potatoes. Standard or box graters are ideal and can have four or more sides with several different size blades, often including a slicer which acts like a mandoline. Some have simple removable base trays or come in their own box container, making it unnecessary to dirty a board or plate and leaving no messy trail. Single-sided graters can be difficult to hold unless you steady them with a damp cloth, but they are ideal to place over a bowl so that you can grate straight in. If you plan to put your grater in the dishwasher, look for a stainless steel one without too much plastic.

Paring Knives

These are one of the most important items in the kitchen, especially for small fiddly jobs. Choose a knife with a short enough blade to allow you to use your thumb as well, but not too short or you won't be able to use it for small chopping jobs. The knife should be curved but not serrated and it should have a sharp point. Don't be tempted by those with removable peeler blades, as these are easily lost and remove too much skin.

Above: Paring knives

Mandolines

The original mandoline was a simple wooden implement with adjustable flat or fluted blades. It was designed for chefs to cut wafer-thin slices of potato, or other hard foods like carrots, for making crisps and game chips and for shredding and chipping. Take care, as they can give your hands a nasty cut.

Modern mandolines These now often come in their own supporting plastic frame or box, sometimes with a shredder or chipper blade as well. They can have two or three blades which are adjustable to give variable thicknesses, and these are flat or fluted. Some of the plastic ones are machine washable and come with a gadget for holding the last part of the vegetable to protect you from slicing your fingertips.

For large quantities of chips and crisps where the thickness needs to be exact, a more professional mandoline is available, but it is very expensive.

Left: Mandoline

Long-handled wire baskets For blanching or frying chips in, these come in various sizes. Be sure to choose one that fits your pan almost exactly.
Small baskets Used for removing small quantities or pieces of potato when blanching or frying. There is a special attached pair for making potato nests.

Wire Baskets

Using a wire basket is the easiest way to remove a batch of chips quickly from hot fat or quantities of potato from boiling water. When putting potatoes into hot fat do be sure the basket is heated in the fat first or the potatoes will stick to it.

Steamers

Steaming gives a very light potato and has nutritional benefits since it allows far less of the vitamins to be lost during cooking. Electric steamers are excellent for large quantities of potatoes. Chinese steamer baskets, which have their own lids,

are also good, especially as you can stack them up and steam several different foods at once. Clean steamers well to remove the potato starch – this is easiest done whilst they are warm.
Stainless steel steamer Can be bought with its matching pan, or separately to stand over a similar sized pan. It should

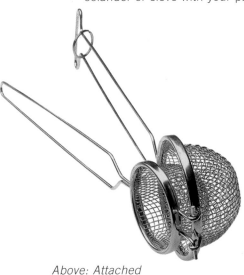

Above: Stainless steel steamer

also have a lid which makes it very useful for keeping cooked potatoes warm until needed.
Collapsible steamer These will fit into most sizes of pan. Alternatively, use a colander or sieve with your pan lid.

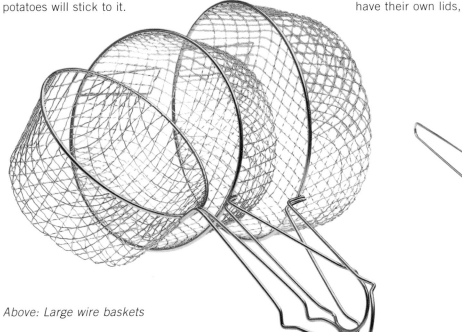

Above: Large wire baskets

Above: Attached baskets

Below: Metal ricer

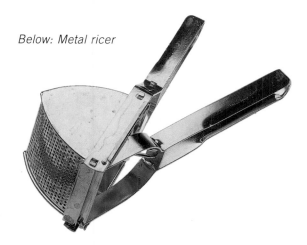

Below: Mouli grater

Ricers and Mashers

A ricer is a small rigid sieve with a pusher that makes the cooked potato come through looking like grains of rice.

Potato was often served like this, riced directly into a warmed serving dish without any butter or milk added – a much healthier version

of mash. It is also a very easy way to prepare mash so that it is ready to fork in the other ingredients. You can also use a basher or wooden implement to bash the potatoes around the pan in the old-fashioned way or just to help let off some steam.

Original metal ricer This has a triangular shaped bowl and is very sturdy. The round ricer doesn't take quite so much potato in the bowl.

Plastic ricer These are machine washable. They can have two sizes of blades, for smooth or textured results.

Mashers These come in various shapes and with different size holes, so you can choose accordingly if you prefer a smooth or rough mash. Some, but not all mashers, are machine washable.

Wooden basher A strong tool, which can give a chunky or fine result.

Large mouli grater This gives a very smooth result, and is suitable for puréeing or preparing a baby's dinner.

Left: Mashers

Electrical Equipment

Food processor If you frequently slice, shred or chip potatoes then a processor with these attachments could be a great time-saver. Different models have different attachments so research well before you buy. Most will have one slicer and one shredder blade, some will have additional sizes of blades and shredders and some also have chipper attachments.

Potato peeler It only takes a few minutes to peel the potatoes, whilst you are doing other things. It does leave a slightly rough surface on the potatoes which is good for roasting, but don't put too many in the machine at one time.

Deep-fat Fryers

Chip frying is one of the greatest causes of house fires so if you are a chip-loving family, it is essential that you buy an efficient deep-fat fryer (electric or not). Check the size before you buy as some can be quite small. Cooking chips in smaller quantities gives better results, and you should never be tempted to put in too many chips as the fat may bubble over. Don't buy a cheap fryer thinking it is saving you money because it won't last as long and will probably not be as safe. For the most efficient results be sure to keep the fryer well cleaned, change the oil frequently and preferably after each use. A good non-electric deep-fat fryer should be quite heavy, with a strong heatproof handle or handles and good-fitting basket and lid.

Electric deep-fat fryers

These have a thermostatically controlled temperature gauge so you fry at the right temperature, giving the crispest results. They often include specified temperature guides or controls for certain frying tasks. The fat and chips are in a sealed container which avoids smells and spitting fat and removes much of the danger. Most can be taken to pieces for easy cleaning or have removable electric cords and some have Perspex lids so that you can see the chips cooking.

Above: Food processor

Above: Deep-fat fryer

Potato Bake Stands

To speed up baking you can push your potatoes on to skewers, or stand them upright on a special potato bake stand, which can save up to one-third of the cooking time.

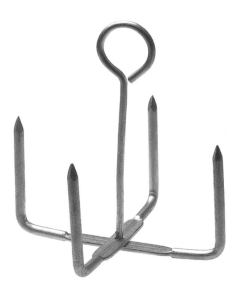

Above: Potato bake stand

Chip Cutters

Manual chip cutters can certainly take the time out of chip making but you will always have to cut the potato to fit the model before you start cutting chips. It really would be good if you could try these out first though, as they rely entirely on brute force. Blades should be removable for easy washing and the rest of the machine should also be easily washable.

Flat chip cutter This gives very neat, if small, chips, but is hard work.

Upright chip cutter Slightly easier to push down, this cutter has two sizes of blade but is very limited on the size of potato it can take.

Above: Scrubbing brushes

Above: Upright chip cutter

Scrubbing brushes

For easily cleaning mud off potatoes, a small brush is ideal. The bristles should be firm without being too hard on the skins as you do not want to remove then while you are scrubbing.

Potato Pots

The two terracotta and clay pots illustrated are designed specifically for potatoes, giving an earthy taste and an easy method of cooking. Remember to soak the pots in water before using, as it is this moisture which is important in the cooking.

Potato Ballers

To make potato garnishes or shapes, the large side of a potato baller is ideal if you have a firm wrist.

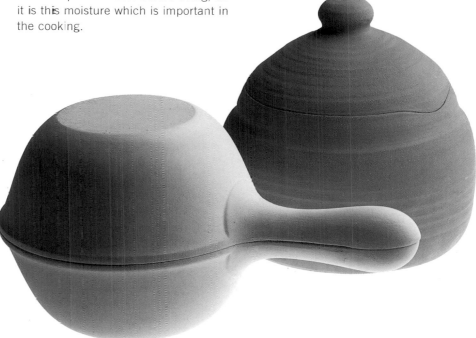

Right: Potato pots

Potatoes of the World

WITH THE REVIVAL OF OLD POTATO BREEDS and the creation of many new and unusual breeds, potatoes are fast becoming a hot fashion food. We can now choose from small, flaky new potatoes with their buttery sweet flavour; traditional maincrops with soft earthy tasting floury centres; waxy golden maincrop potatoes with velvety firm texture, small misshapen speciality potatoes which give delicious crunch to salads, omelettes and casseroles; and a growing collection of vivid red or pink, purple and blue potatoes trendy enough to grace many a London or New York restaurant menu.

This resumé includes a description of each potato along with details of origin, availability, suitability for cooking and, where relevant, for home growing. The potatoes are listed alphabetically in their most familiar name. Their seasonal details, classified according to how early in the season they are ready for digging up, are listed as: First Early, Second Early, Maincrop (early and late). This simply means that, anywhere in the world, the first earlies are the first new potatoes on the market ready for eating fresh and young, the second earlies are still theoretically a new potato although the skin will have begun to set so they will not be scrapers, whilst the maincrop potatoes which are on the market throughout most of the year are the ones that can be picked and stored for many months. However, the consumer may be even more confused by the fact that some potatoes are now being picked young for the early market as well as at full size for the maincrop market and others, which are transported from around the world, arrive labelled as new during the maincrop season! The label (if any) and the retailer may be able to help you but this index should be your best guide.

Ajax

Second Early

Origin: Netherlands

Availability: Netherlands, Pakistan, Vietnam

Suitability for cooking: Boiling, Chipping, Roasting

Description: Oval, with smooth yellow skin, pale yellow firm flesh, slightly bland in flavour

Alcmaria

First Early

Origin: Netherlands, 1970

Availability: Italy, United Kingdom

Suitability for cooking: Baking, Boiling and most other methods

Description: Long, oval, with yellow skin and firm flesh, and shallow eyes

Above: Ailsa
Above left: Alcmaria
Below: Alex

Accent

First Early

Origin: Netherlands, 1994

Availability: Netherlands, United Kingdom (not widely available yet)

Suitability for cooking: Boiling, Salad

Description: Uniform oval or round shape, light yellow smooth skin, waxy flesh which holds its shape, and bland taste. Scrapes easily and good for sautéeing

Home growing: Available

Agria

Maincrop

Origin: West Germany, 1985

Availability: Canada, New Zealand, Switzerland, United Kingdom

Suitability for cooking: Baking, Boiling, Chipping, Processing, Roasting

Description: Good size oval shape, deep yellow flesh and good flavour

Ailsa

Maincrop

Origin: Scotland, 1984

Availability: United Kingdom

Suitability for cooking: Boiling, Chipping, Processing

Description: Round or oval medium potato, white skinned with light, creamy-coloured flesh and pleasant flavour, with a floury texture

Home growing: Available

Alex

Second Early

Origin: Denmark, 1995

Availability: Europe, United Kingdom

Suitability for cooking: Salad and most other methods

Description: Splash of blue on the skin, creamy waxy texture and good mild flavour

Home growing: Good

Anna

Maincrop
Origin: Irish Republic, 1996
Availability: Irish Republic,
United Kingdom
Suitability for cooking: Baking and boiling
Description: Uniform shape with smooth
white skin and creamy while floury flesh;
often sold pre-packed

Anya

Second Early
Origin: Scotland, 1997
Availability: United Kingdom
Suitability for cooking: Boiling, Salad and
speciality uses
Description: Small finger potato, knobbly
long oval shape with pale
pink beige skin, white
flesh, a waxy
texture and
pleasant nutty
flavour

Ambo

Above: Ambo

Maincrop
Origin: Irish Republic, 1993
Availability: Irish Republic, New Zealand,
Switzerland, United Kingdom
Suitability for cooking: Baking, Boiling
and quite good all-round variety
Description: Creamy skin with
large pink eye patches
and very white, bland
floury flesh

Aminca

First Early
Origin: Netherlands,
1977
Availability: Denmark,
Italy, United Kingdom
Suitability for cooking:
Baking, Boiling, Chipping
Description: Oval, medium
to large potato, with light
yellow skin and cream or
light yellow flesh, medium
deep eyes, and dry
texture. Often used for
crisp production

Above: Anya
Top right: Aminca

Arran Banner
Maincrop – early
Origin: Scotland, 1927
Availability: Cyprus, New Zealand,
Portugal, United Kingdom
Suitability for cooking: Boiling
Description: Round potato with quite
deep eyes and white skin and a firm,
creamy flesh

Arran Comet
First early
Origin: Scotland, 1957
Availability: United Kingdom
Suitability for cooking: Boiling, Chipping
Description: Round to oval with white
skin and creamy flesh. Excellent early
season new potato, not quite so easily
found now

Arran Consul
Maincrop – early
Origin: Scotland, 1925
Availability: United Kingdom

Suitability for cooking: Boiling, Baking,
Mashing, Roasting and generally good
all-round variety
Description: Round with white skin and
creamy flesh. Reputed to be "the potato
that helped win the war", as it provided
good food for little money

Arran Victory *Irish Blues*
Maincrop – late
Origin: Scotland, 1918
Availability: United Kingdom (now rare in
England and limited in Scotland and
Northern Ireland)
Suitability for cooking: Baking, Boiling,
Roasting and other methods
Description: Oval shape with deep purple
skin and bright white flesh. This is the
oldest Arran variety still available, it is a
very tasty potato with a floury texture and
though not easy to find it is having a
revival of interest so it is well worth
looking out for
Home growing: Available

*Above: Arran Victory
Below from left to right: Arran Banner,
Arran Comet, Arran Consul (top right)*

Atlantic

Maincrop – early/mid-season
Origin: USA, 1978
Availability: Australia, Canada, New Zealand, USA (North Carolina)
Suitability for cooking: Baking, Boiling, Chipping, Mashing, Processing, Roasting
Description: Oval to round shape with light, scaly, buff skin and white flesh. Used largely for chips and crisps
Home growing: Available

Ausonia

Second Early
Origin: Netherlands, 1981
Availability: Greece, Netherlands, United Kingdom
Suitability for cooking: Baking, Boiling and most other methods
Description: Oval shape with white skin and light yellow mealy flesh. It is susceptible to discolouring after cooking. Predominantly sold in various pre-packed forms
Home growing: Available

Avalanche

Maincrop – early
Origin: Northern Ireland, 1989
Availability: United Kingdom (still rare)
Suitability for cooking: Boiling, Mashing
Description: Round or oval, medium potatoes, with white skin, firm, creamy flesh and good, slightly sweet flavour
Home growing: Available

Avondale

Maincrop
Origin: Irish Republic, 1982
Availability: Canary Isles, Egypt, Hungary, Israel, Morocco, Pakistan, Portugal, Spain, Sri Lanka, United Kingdom (but still rare)
Suitability for cooking: Quite good all-round variety
Description: Round or oval with pale, beige skin and creamy flesh. It has a moist waxy texture and mellow flavour

Barna

Maincrop – late
Origin: Irish Republic, 1993
Availability: Irish Republic, United Kingdom
Suitability for cooking: Boiling, Roasting
Description: Uniform, oval red-skinned potato with white slightly waxy flesh and warm, nutty taste
Home growing: Available

Above: Atlantic
Left: From top to bottom, Avalanche, Avondale, Barna

Belle de Fontenay *Boulangère Henaut*
Maincrop – early
Origin: France, 1885
Availability: Australia, France,
United Kingdom (occasionally)
Suitability for cooking: Boiling,
Mashing, Salad
Description: Long, slightly bent shape
with pale yellow skin, yellow flesh, firm
and waxy with an excellent buttery
flavour. One of the old classic potatoes of
French cuisine but popular with modern
chefs. Improves with storage. Good
eaten with skins on and tossed in
salad dressings
Home growing: Good

BelRus
Maincrop – late
Origin: USA, 1978
Availability: Canada, USA (north-eastern
states and North Florida)
Suitability for cooking: Baking,
Chipping, Mashing
Description: Uniform, long smooth
potatoes with dark thick russeted skin

and creamy coloured flesh. Exceptional
cooking qualities, excellent in gratins and
when steamed; the heavy russeting gives
a thick and crunchy skin when baked

BF15
Second Early
Origin: France, 1947
Availability: France (seldom found
outside France)
Suitability for cooking: Boiling,
Salad
Description: Long, slightly bent,
with smooth yellow skin and
yellow flesh, firm and waxy
with very good flavour.
Derivative of Belle de Fontenay
but slightly earlier
Home growing: Available

Bintje
Maincrop – early
Origin: Netherlands, 1910
Availability: Australia, Brazil, Canada,
Denmark, Finland, Italy, Netherlands,
New Zealand, Sweden, Thailand,

United Kingdom
Suitability for cooking: Baking, Boiling,
Chipping, Processing, Roasting, Salad
Description: Long, oval, with pale yellow
skin and starchy flesh and a really
distinctive flavour. Used largely for chips
and processing
Home growing: Available

Above: BelRus
Main picture: Clockwise from right,
BF15, Bishop, Bintje

Bishop (the)
Maincrop – late
Origin: United Kingdom, 1912
Availability: United Kingdom
Suitability for cooking: Boiling,
Roasting, Salad
Description: Long, oval potatoes, with
white skins and yellow nutty-flavoured
flesh. Recently popular variety
Home growing: Available

British Queen(s)
Second Early
Origin: Scotland, 1894
Availability: United Kingdom
Suitability for cooking: Baking, Boiling,

Roasting, Processing, Salad
Description: Kidney-shaped, with smooth
white skin and very white flesh which is
dry, floury and has a very good taste.
Best cooked with skins on to retain
excellent flavour. Very popular at the turn
of the century and having a revival

CalWhite
Maincrop
Origin: USA, 1997
Availability: Canada, USA (California, Idaho)
Suitability for cooking: Baking, Chipping,
Processing
Description: Oblong shape with buff-
white smooth skin and white flesh

Cara White and Red
Maincrop – late
Origin: Irish Republic, 1976
Availability: Cyprus, Egypt, Irish
Republic, Israel, United Kingdom
Suitability for cooking: Baking, Boiling,
Chipping and all other methods,
especially wedges.
Description: Round or oval, white skin
with pink eyes, cream flesh, mild flavour
and moist, waxy texture. There is a pink-
skinned variety which has creamy flesh
Home growing: Good, but not in very
wet soil

Carlingford
First Early
Origin: Northern Ireland, 1982
Availability: Australia, United Kingdom
Suitability for cooking: Baking,
Boiling, Chipping
Description: Round or oval with white
skin and flesh, eyes shallow to medium,
firm and waxy cooked texture and
distinctive flavour. An excellent new or
baby potato. Best not overcooked, very
good steamed, microwaved and baked
in wedges. Relatively new potato but
growing in popularity
Home growing: Available

Above left: British Queen
Above right: Carlingford
Below: Cara White

Centennial Russet
Maincrop
Origin: USA, 1977
Availability: USA (California, Colorado, Idaho, Oregon, Texas, Washington)
Suitability for cooking: Baking, Boiling, Mashing
Description: Oblong to oval with thick, dark, netted skin, shallow eyes and white floury flesh

Champion
Maincrop – late
Origin: United Kingdom, 1876
Availability: No longer commercially grown, only found in collections
Suitability for cooking: Excellent all-round variety
Description: Round potato with white skin and yellow flesh on the inside. It has an excellent flavour. It was hugely successful for very many years until much of the stock was affected by blight, but remained Ireland's favourite until the 1930s

Charlotte *Noirmoutier*
Maincrop
Origin: France, 1981
Availability: France, Germany, Italy, Switzerland, United Kingdom
Suitability for cooking: Baking, Boiling, Salad
Description: Pear or long oval shape with pale yellow skin, yellow flesh, firm waxy texture and a hint of chestnut flavour. Excellent steamed and in salads. Especially popular in France
Home growing: Good

Catriona and Blue Catriona
Second Early
Origin: Scotland, 1920; Blue Catriona, United Kingdom, 1979
Availability: United Kingdom (mainly for gardeners, in few shops)
Suitability for cooking: Baking, Boiling and all other methods
Description: Large kidney-shaped potato with skin that has beautiful purple splashes around the eyes, pale yellow flesh and a very good flavour.
Home growing: Available

Above: Centennial Russet
Left: Catriona

Chieftain

Maincrop
Origin: USA, 1966
Availability: Canada, USA
Suitability for cooking: Baking, Boiling
Description: Oblong to round with a fairly
smooth, bright red skin and white flesh.
Good for most methods of cooking
except chipping

Chipeta

Maincrop – late
Origin: USA, 1993
Availability: Canada, USA
(Colorado, Idaho)
Suitability for cooking: Baking, Boiling,
Chipping, Processing
Description: Round with white skin and
patches of russeting, creamy white flesh.
Mainly developed for chipping

Claret

Maincrop – early
Origin: Scotland, 1996
Availability: Scotland
Suitability for cooking: Good all-round
Description: Smooth rosy red skin, with a
round to oval shape and cream, firm flesh
Home growing: Good

Top: Claret, Chieftain
Above: Cleopatra, Colmo

Cleopatra

First Early
Origin: Netherlands, 1980
Availability: Algeria, Hungary
Suitability for cooking: Boiling
Description: Oval with pink/red blemished
skin and light yellow, dense flesh

Colmo

First Early
Origin: Netherlands, 1973
Availability: Netherlands,
United Kingdom
Suitability for cooking: Boiling and good
for all other methods
Description: Medium-round, or oval-
shaped potato, with white skin and light
yellow firm flesh on the inside. Good for
making mashed potatoes

Congo

Maincrop – late
Origin: Congo
Availability: Australia, United Kingdom (for curiosity and fun for gardeners, not in shops)
Suitability for cooking: Boiling, Mashing, Salad
Description: Striking small, thin and knobbly shape, with very dark, purple-black shiny skin and beetroot black flesh. The flavour is surprisingly bland and the texture stodgy. It is dry when cooked but still retains its colour, making it impressive in salads and as a garnish. Peel after cooking and either boil briefly, steam or microwave. Makes good mashed potatoes or gnocchi
Home growing: Available mainly as a curiosity. Since they are small and dark, you might need to harvest them on a bright day

Above right: Désirée
Below: Congo

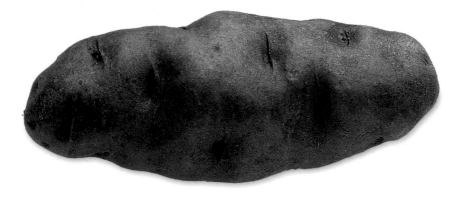

Delcora

Maincrop – early
Origin: Netherlands, 1988
Availability: Netherlands, New Zealand
Suitability for cooking: Boiling, Chipping, Mashing
Description: Long oval potato with pink/red skin and light yellow flesh which is not floury and has good flavour

Désirée

Maincrop
Origin: Netherlands, 1962
Availability: Algeria, America, Argentina, Australia, Cameroon, Chile, Iran, Irish Republic, Malawi, Morocco, Netherlands, New Zealand, Portugal, Sri Lanka, Pakistan, Tunisia, Turkey, United Kingdom
Suitability for cooking: Baking, Boiling, Chipping, Mashing, Roasting, Salad and all other methods
Description: Oval shape with shallow eyes and smooth red skin, pale creamy yellow flesh, firm texture and good taste. Said to be the world's most popular red-skinned potato. It is often sold direct from the farm and markets in large quantities as well as loose or pre-packed. Good roasted or cooked as wedges or slices; holds its shape
Home growing: Good

Diamant

Maincrop – early
Origin: Netherlands, 1982
Availability: Cameroon, Canada, Egypt, New Zealand, Pakistan
Suitability for cooking: Baking, Boiling
Description: Long oval shape, rough white skin with light yellow, firm, waxy flesh and nutty, sharp aftertaste. Popular in the 1930s

Below: Duke of York
Bottom: Clockwise from top left,
Diamant, Ditta, Dr McIntosh

Ditta
Second Early
Origin: Austria, 1950
Availability: Austria, Netherlands,
United Kingdom
Suitability for cooking: Boiling, Roasting
Description: Long, oval potato with
rough, brownish skin, pale yellow flesh
and firm waxy texture. When cooked
it has a very buttery taste, and an almost
melt-in-the-mouth flavour

Dr McIntosh
Maincrop – early
Origin: United Kingdom, 1944
Availability: New Zealand, United
Kingdom (rarely found today)
Suitability for cooking: Baking, Boiling,
quite good all-round
Description: Oval potato with quite a long
shape to it with white skin and light,
creamy flesh

Draga
Second Early
Origin: Netherlands, 1970
Availability: Iran, New Zealand
Suitability for cooking: Boiling, Mashing,
Salad, Good all-round variety
Description: Round, white/yellow skin,
creamy flesh, full-flavoured with waxy
texture. Keeps well

Duke of York *Eersteling*
First Early
Origin: Scotland, 1891
Availability: Netherlands, France,
United Kingdom
Suitability for cooking: Boiling and most
other methods
Description: Long, oval, with pale
whitish-yellow skin, light yellow flesh, firm
cooked texture and rich, sweet flavour.
Best eaten young
Home growing Very popular

Duke of York Red *Rode Eersteling*
First Early
Origin: Netherlands, 1842
Availability: Netherlands, United Kingdom (but quite rare)
Suitability for cooking: Boiling, Salad
Description: Long, oval, very red potato with light yellow tasty flesh. Loses its colour when cooked
Home growing: Available

Dunbar Standard
Maincrop – late
Origin: Scotland, 1936
Availability: United Kingdom, Ireland

Suitability for cooking: Good all-round
Description: Long, oval white-skinned potato with white flesh. Its full flavour and firmness suit most forms of cooking.
Home growing: Available. Does well in heavy soil

Dundrod
First Early
Origin: Northern Ireland, 1987
Availability: Canada, Netherlands, Northern Ireland, Sweden, United Kingdom
Suitability for cooking: Boiling, Chipping, Mashing
Description: Oval to round shaped potatoes with light yellow skin and creamy white flesh on the inside. Moderately waxy, so rarely falls apart. A very popular choice of potato for making chips in fish and chip shops

Edgcote Purple
Maincrop – early
Origin: United Kingdom, 1916
Availability: Collections only
Description: Long, oval potatoes with blue skin and light yellow flesh. Although it was an excellent cooker it never became popular and is no longer commercially available

Edzell Blue
Second Early
Origin: Scotland, pre-1915
Availability: Scotland (very little now grown)
Suitability for cooking: Boiling, Mashing
Description: Round, blue-skinned with bright white flesh, floury and tasty. Boil with care as it falls apart easily. Very good steamed and in microwave recipes
Home growing: Available

Eigenheimer
Maincrop – second early
Origin: Netherlands, 1893
Availability: Netherlands, Zaire (rarely seen elsewhere)
Suitability for cooking: Chipping
Description: Oval, white skin and yellow flesh, great for frying and chips, a favourite of Dutch gardeners

Top left: Duke of York Red
Top right: Edzell Blue
Left: Dunbar Standard

Estima

Second Early
Origin: Netherlands, 1973
Availability: Algeria Northern Europe
Suitability for cooking: Baking, Boiling,
Chipping, Roasting and most
other methods
Description: Uniform oval shape with
shallow eyes, light yellow skin and flesh,
firm moist texture and mild flavour.
Most widely grown second early and has
an exceptionally long season. Makes a
particularly good baking potato early in
the year – very popular at the moment.
One of the first to destroy the myth that
yellow potatoes could not be popular
Home growing: Good

Elvira

Origin: Unknown
Availability: Italy
Suitability for cooking: Boiling, Chipping
Description: Medium oval potato with
shallow eyes, yellow skin and creamy
yellow flesh

Epicure

First Early
Origin: United Kingdom, 1897
Availability: Canada, United Kingdom
Suitability for cooking: Baking, Boiling
Description: Round, white skin and
creamy white flesh, firm texture, but with
deep eyes and a distinctive flavour.
The traditional Ayrshire potato and still
grown extensively in Scottish gardens
Home growing: A popular and easy to
grow variety

Top left: Estima
Above right. Elvira
Right: Epicure

Fianna
Maincrop – early
Origin: Netherlands, 1987
Availability: Netherlands, New Zealand, United Kingdom

Suitability for cooking: Baking, Chipping, Mashing, Processing, Roasting
Description: Smooth white skin and firm flesh, with pleasant, floury texture
Home growing: Available

Forty Fold
Maincrop – early
Origin: United Kingdom, 1893; Russet, United Kingdom, 1919
Availability: United Kingdom (very limited)
Suitability for cooking: Quite good all-round variety
Description: Irregular tubers with deep eyes, white or vivid purple skin splashed with white or russet, creamy flesh, and good flavour. The potato was a popular Victorian speciality which is currently being revived
Home growing: Available

Above: Forty fold, white and russet
Left: Fianna

Francine
Maincrop
Origin: France, 1993
Availability: France, Germany, United Kingdom
Suitability for cooking: Boiling, Salad
Description: Red skin, white/cream flesh, soft yet waxy texture and an earthy taste. Great for gratins and for steaming

Frisia
Maincrop – early
Origin: Netherlands
Availability: Bulgaria, Canada, Europe, New Zealand
Suitability for cooking: Baking, Boiling, Roasting, Salad
Description: Oval, creamy yellow-skinned potato with white flesh and a moist, slightly waxy texture

Gemchip

Maincrop – late
Origin: USA, 1989
Availability: Canada, USA (Colorado, Idaho, Oregon, Washington)
Suitability for cooking: Baking, Boiling, Chipping, Processing
Description: Short and round with smooth, light tan skin and white flesh with the occasional scaly patch

Golden Wonder

Maincrop – late
Origin: United Kingdom, 1906
Availability: United Kingdom
Suitability for cooking: Boiling, Processing, Roasting
Description: Large oval potato with light yellow flesh and russet/brown skin, very floury when cooked and tasty. Creates some of the best crisps and the flavour improves with long storage.
Home growing: Good for home growing, popular in Scotland

Goldrush

Maincrop
Origin: North Dakota, 1992
Availability: Canada, USA
Suitability for cooking: Baking, Boiling, Roasting, quite good all-round
Description: A new russet type, oblong potato with light brown netted skin and very white flesh and good flavour.

Granola

Second Early – early main
Origin: West Germany, 1975
Availability: Australia, Germany, India, Indonesia, Nepal, Netherlands, Pakistan, Switzerland, Turkey, Vietnam
Suitability for cooking: Baking, Boiling, Chipping
Description: Oval with brilliant yellow skin and creamy yellow flesh

Home Guard

First Early
Origin: Scotland, 1942
Availability: United Kingdom (mainly in Cornwall and Pembrokeshire)
Suitability for cooking: Boiling, Chipping, Roasting and most other methods
Description: Round to oval, white skin and creamy white flesh, quite floury dry texture and good, almost bitter flavour. A World War II favourite, one of the first new potatoes to arrive on the market and at its best eaten early
Home growing: Good

Ilam Hardie

All year
Origin: Unknown
Availability: South Africa, New Zealand
Suitability for cooking: Baking, Boiling, Chipping, Mashing, Roasting, Salad, and most other methods
Description: Yellow skinned with white flesh, floury and well flavoured

International Kidney *Jersey Royal*

Maincrop – early
Origin: United Kingdom, 1879
Availability: Australia, Europe, United Kingdom
Suitability for cooking: Boiling, Salad
Description: Long ovals with very flaky, white/yellow skin and creamy white flesh, waxy with delicious buttery flavour. The International Kidney, developed in England in the 1870s and is slightly smaller than the original Jersey Royal. many countries have tried to grow the Jersey Royal, but only in Jersey's rich soil does this prized potato grow so well and it is now exported to many corners of the world.
Home growing: Available

Left: Francine
Above: Gemchip

Irish Cobbler *America*
First Early
Origin: USA, 1876
Availability: Canada, South Korea, USA
Suitability for cooking: Boiling, Chipping, Mashing and most other methods.
Description: Round white, medium to large potato, smooth creamy white skin and flesh. Was widely grown in the United Kingdom at the turn of the century probably because it matures earlier than others but has not been grown much since World War I – except in the USA. It is difficult to grow and bruises easily
Home growing: Available

Itasca
Maincrop
Origin: Minnesota, 1994
Availability: Canada, USA
Suitability for cooking: Baking, Boiling, Chipping, Mashing, Roasting
Description: Oblong to round shaped potato with smooth, pale skin and creamy white flesh

Jaerla
First Early
Origin: Netherlands, 1969
Availability: Algeria, Argentina, Greece, Netherlands, Turkey, Yugoslavia
Suitability for cooking: Baking, Boiling

and most other methods
Description: Long, oval light skinned with light yellow flesh and firm texture

Kanona
Maincrop
Origin: USA, 1989
Availability: Canada, USA
Suitability for cooking: Baking, Boiling, Chipping, Processing
Description: Large round potatoes with a white slightly netted skin and white flesh

Karlena
Origin: E. Germany, 1993
Availability: Egypt, France, Germany, Hungary, Israel, Scandinavia, United Kingdom (still very limited)
Suitability for cooking: Baking, Chipping, Mashing, Roasting
Description: A medium size round yellow skinned potato with golden yellow flesh and warm distinctive flavour but very floury. It is excellent as a very early season boiling potato; main season it is good steamed in skins, roasts and chips very well, but boil with care to avoid disintegration

Katahdin
Maincrop – late
Origin: USA, 1932
Availability: Canada, New Zealand, USA
Suitability for cooking: Baking, Boiling, Salad, and most other methods
Description: Round to oblong shape, with buff, smooth, thin skin and white, waxy, moist flesh. Most popular in Maine until recently

Above: Irish Cobbler
Below: Katahdin

Kennebec
Maincrop
Origin: USA, 1948
Availability: Argentina, Australia, Canada, Italy, New Zealand, Portugal, South Korea, Taiwan, Uruguay, USA
Suitability for cooking: Baking, Boiling, Chipping, Mashing, Roasting, Processing and most other methods
Description: Largish oval to round shaped potato, with smooth, buff, white skin and white flesh. Widely grown in many parts of the world now as it is adaptable and consistent. Was mainly used for chip processing but less so now although still a good all-round potato. A favourite variety for gardeners in North America

Kepplestone Kidney
Second Early – early main
Origin: United Kingdom, 1919
Availability: Not commercially available
Suitability for cooking: Boiling
Description: Blue skinned, classically shaped potatoes with yellow flesh and rich buttery taste
Home growing: Good

Kerr's Pink
Maincrop – late
Origin: Scotland, 1917
Availability: Irish Republic, Netherlands, United Kingdom
Suitability for cooking: Baking, Boiling, Chipping, Mashing, Roasting
Description: Round, pink skin, creamy white flesh, quite deep eyes, mealy, floury cooked texture
Home growing: Available

Above: From left to right, Kennebec, Kepplestone Kidney, Karlena
Below: Kerr's Pink

King Edward and Red
Maincrop
Origin: United Kingdom, 1902
(red 1916)
Availability: Australia, Canary Isles, New Zealand, Portugal, Spain, United Kingdom
Suitability for cooking: Baking, Chipping, Mashing, Roasting and most other methods
Description: Oval to kidney shape. White skin with pink colouration, cream to pale yellow flesh, floury texture. For much of the twentieth century it was the most popular potato in Britain and has seen a fall and rise in popularity since
Home growing: Available

Kipfler
Maincrop
Origin: Austria, 1955
Availability: Australia (rarely available)
Suitability for cooking: Baking, Boiling, Chipping, Roasting, Salad and most other methods
Description: Yellow flesh and skin, small to medium size, elongated, often called finger potato. They have a waxy texture when cooked and a buttery, nutty taste. Not ideal for chipping but microwaves well and excellent in salads

Krantz
Maincrop
Origin: USA, 1985
Availability: Canada, USA
Suitability for cooking: Baking, Boiling, Chipping, Processing
Description: Oblong with brown russet skin and white flesh

Linzer Delikatess
Second Early
Origin: Austria, 1976
Availability: Austria, United Kingdom (very rare)
Suitability for cooking: Boiling, Salad
Description: Small, oval- to pear-shaped potato with a pale yellow skin and yellow flesh. Firm and waxy texture. The flavour is similar to Ratte, but not so distinctive. Good cold and in most cooked dishes where you need firmness
Home growing: Available

Lumper
Maincrop – early
Origin: Ireland, 1806
Availability: Collections only
Description: Round, oval potato with white skin and flesh and very deep eyes giving it a lumpy shape. Lacking in flavour.Dating back to the Irish famine when it was a mainstay of the potato crop but was nearly wiped out. Its poor cooking qualities eventually led to the Lumper being consigned to the history books and seed collections only

Above: King Edward
Left: Lumper

Maori Chief *Peru*
Early
Origin: New Zealand
Availability: New Zealand
Suitability for cooking: Boiling, Roasting, Salad
Description: Purple/black skin, dark purple/black flesh, with a sweet new potato flavour. The very tender skin doesn't need peeling, tastes good steamed and is best eaten within ten days of harvesting. There is also a variety found in New Zealand, with a buttery yellow flesh, which has caused much debate as to which is the true original Maori Chief potato

Marfona
Second Early
Origin: Netherlands, 1975
Availability: Cyprus, Greece, Israel, Netherlands, Portugal, Turkey, United Kingdom
Suitability for cooking: Baking, Boiling, Chipping, Mashing
Description: Round oval with light beige to yellow skin and flesh, smooth waxy texture with slightly sharp taste
Home growing: Available

Maris Bard
First Early
Origin: United Kingdom, 1972
Availability: United Kingdom
Suitability for cooking: Boiling and most other methods
Description: White skin, white to cream flesh, soft yet waxy with an earthy taste. One of the most widely grown first earlies. Can disintegrate on cooking late in the season and lose its taste
Home growing: Available

Magnum Bonum
Maincrop – late
Origin: United Kingdom, 1876
Availability: Nepal, United Kingdom (collections only)
Suitability for cooking: Baking, Boiling, Mashing, Roasting
Description: Long, oval-shaped potato with white skin and dry, mealy white flesh. Has an excellent flavour. One of the early very successful potatoes which proved to be both a good grower, an excellent eater and withstood blight. The Victorians were delighted to find such a continually good cropper which eventually was used in producing other renowned potatoes, such as today's King Edward

Majestic
Maincrop – early
Origin: Scotland, 1911
Availability: Italy, United Kingdom (now only in Scotland for seed potato)
Suitability for cooking: Baking, Boiling, Mashing
Description: Large oval with white skin and soft white flesh, and a mild flavour. Was the most widely grown variety in Britain at one time but no longer suits the marketplace and is mainly grown for gardeners and prefers dry conditions
Home growing: Available

Top left: Marfona
Right: Maori Chief

Maris Peer
Second Early
Origin: United Kingdom, 1962
Availability: United Kingdom
Suitability for cooking: Boiling,
Chipping, Salad
Description: Round- to oval-shaped
potato with cream skin and flesh, eyes
shallow to medium, firm cooked texture.
Good when young to use as new potatoes
since they do not break up on cooking,
and the large later season ones bake well
either whole or in wedges
Home growing: Available

Maris Piper
Maincrop – early
Origin: United Kingdom, 1964
Availability: Portugal, United Kingdom
Suitability for cooking: Baking, Chipping,
Processing, Roasting
Description: Oval, cream skin and flesh
and pleasant floury texture and taste.
One of Britain's most popular potatoes,
especially in fish and chip shops but
breaks up easily if overcooked
Home growing: Good

Minerva
First Early
Origin: Netherlands, 1988
Availability: Netherlands
Suitability for cooking: Boiling, Chipping

Description: Oval-shaped potato with
white skin and creamy yellow flesh on
the inside. It is particularly good for
boiling since it retains a firm texture
when cooked

Mona Lisa
Second Early
Origin: Netherlands, 1982
Availability: France, Greece,
Netherlands, Portugal
Suitability for cooking: Baking, Boiling,
Chipping, Mashing, Roasting, Processing
Description: Long oval, sometimes
kidney-shaped with yellow skin and
flesh, waxy but becomes floury when
cooked. Has a good nutty flavour. Grows
quite large for a new potato but is
surprisingly versatile in cooking. Not
grown a great deal commercially yet
Home growing: Available

Mondial
Maincrop – early
Origin: Netherlands, 1987
Availability: Greece, Israel, Netherlands,
New Zealand
Suitability for cooking: Baking, Chipping,
Mashing, Roasting
Description: Long oval with yellow skin
and flesh and a slightly mealy texture
Home growing: Good in most conditions

Above: Maris Piper
*Left: Clockwise from top, Mondial, Mona
Lisa, Morene*

Monona
Maincrop – early
Origin: USA, 1964
Availability: Canada, USA (north central and north-eastern states)
Suitability for cooking: Baking, Boiling, Chipping
Description: Round or oval, with buff-white skin and white flesh. Mainly goes for chip processing

Morene
Maincrop – early
Origin: Netherlands, 1983
Availability: Netherlands, United Kingdom
Suitability for cooking: Baking, Boiling, Chipping, Processing
Description: Large, long oval potatoes with white skin and creamy coloured mealy flesh. During cooking the flesh has a tendency to break up so do not over-boil
Home growing: Available

Nadine
Second Early
Origin: Scotland, 1987
Availability: Australia, Canary Isles, New Zealand, Spain, United Kingdom
Suitability for cooking: Baking, Boiling, Mashing, Salad
Description: Creamy yellow skin and white flesh, firm, waxy texture but slightly disappointing taste. Sometimes available as small new potatoes with soft young skins which scrub easily. The larger ones are good baked and in wedges
Home growing: Available

Navan
Maincrop – late
Origin: Irish Republic, 1987
Availability: Irish Republic, United Kingdom

Suitability for cooking: Baking, Chipping, Roasting
Description: Oval, with white-buff skin, creamy flesh and pleasant flavour. Has a firm, waxy texture
Home growing: Available

Top: Nadine
Above: Monona

Below: Nicola

Nicola

Maincrop – all year
Origin: West Germany, 1973
Availability: Australia, Austria,
Cypus, Egypt, France, Germany,
Israel, Morocco, New Zealand,
Portugal, Switzerland, Tunisia,
United Kingdom
Suitability for cooking: Baking,
Boiling, Chipping, Mashing,
Roasting, Salad, and most other
cooking methods
Description: Oval to long oval, with
smooth yellow skin and deep yellow
flesh. The texture is waxy with an
excellent buttery taste. Originally grown
in Mediterranean countries but now the
salad-style potato has become so popular
that it is being grown much more widely.
Ideal for all-round use as well as being
particularly good in salads – also good

steamed, sautéed and sliced for
dishes taking longer to cook
Home growing: Good

Nooksak

Maincrop – late
Origin: USA, 1973
Availability: Canada, New Zealand,
USA
Suitability for cooking:
Baking, Boiling, Processing
Description: Oblong,
slightly flat potatoes with
heavily russeted skin and
very white flesh.
Excellent keeping potato,
good for baking

Norchip

Second Early
Origin: North Dakota, 1968
Availability: Canada, USA

(North Carolina, Dakota)
Suitability for cooking: Baking,
Boiling, Chipping
Description: Round to oblong shape with
smooth white skin and white flesh.
Excellent chipping qualities

NorDonna

Maincrop
Origin: North Dakota, 1995
Availability: Canada, USA
Suitability for cooking: Baking, Boiling,
Roasting, Salad
Description: Oval- to round-shaped
potatoes with dark red skin, white flesh
and a good flavour. Good for microwave
cooking, in soups and served cold

Above: Norchip

Norland

Early
Origin: North Dakota, 1957
Availability: Canada, USA,
United Kingdom
Suitability for cooking: Baking, Boiling,
Mashing, Salad
Description: Oblong, slightly flat with
medium-red skin and creamy flesh.
Also popular and available in Europe is
the Red Norland with a rich red skin and
pale flesh
Home growing: Available

Norwis

Maincrop
Origin: USA, 1965
Availability: USA
Suitability for cooking: Baking, Boiling,
Chipping, Processing
Description: Large ovals, slightly flat with
smooth, light tan to white skin and pale,
creamy, yellow flesh

Above: Norwis

Onaway
Early
Origin: USA, 1956
Availability: Canada, USA (north-eastern states and Michigan)
Suitability for cooking: Baking, Boiling
Description: Short and round with smooth, creamy white skin and flesh

Patrones
Maincrop – early
Origin: Netherlands, 1959
Availability: Australia, Indonesia, Malawi, Pakistan, Vietnam
Suitability for cooking: Baking, Boiling, Roasting, Salad
Description: Small, oval- to pear-shaped with light golden-yellow skin and flesh and a firm waxy texture. These potatoes are great for steaming, gratins and for rösti

Penta
Second Early
Origin: Netherlands, 1983
Availability: Canada, Netherlands
Suitability for cooking: Baking, Boiling, Mashing, Roasting
Description: Round, with quite deep pink/red eyes, creamy white skin and rich, creamy flesh. A fairly new Maincrop potato which has a tendency to disintegrate on boiling. Good for steaming and microwave dishes

Top: Penta
Left: Onaway

Pentland Hawk

Maincrop – early
Origin: Scotland, 1966
Availability: United Kingdom
Suitability for cooking: Baking, Boiling,
Chipping, Processing, Roasting
Description: Oval, white skin and creamy
flesh, with a good flavour.
Very popular in Scotland as it cooks well.
It is an excellent keeper, but has a slight
tendency to discolour after cooking. At its
best late in the season
Home growing: Available

Pentland Javelin

First Early
Origin: Scotland, 1968
Availability: United Kingdom
Suitability for cooking: Boiling, Salad
Description: Medium-sized oval, white
skin, white flesh, soft waxy texture. It is
a good new potato but also bakes and
roasts well later in the season
Home growing: Good

Pentland Marble

First Early
Origin: Scotland, 1970
Availability: United Kingdom
Suitability for cooking: Boiling, Salad
Description: Round to oval, white-
skinned with light yellow waxy flesh.
Good small, early, waxy salad potato,
unlike most of the other Pentlands
and only recently reintroduced into
the market
Home growing: Available

Pentland Crown

Maincrop
Origin: Scotland, 1959
Availability: United Kingdom (Scotland,
but rarely seen in shops), Malawi
Suitability for cooking: Baking,
Boiling, Roasting
Description: Oval to round with white
skin and creamy white flesh. The first of
the Pentland varieties to become
popular in the Seventies, especially in
eastern England but out of favour now
as it doesn't have the cooking
qualities required
Home growing: Available

Pentland Dell

Maincrop – early
Origin: Scotland, 1961
Availability: New Zealand, South Africa,
United Kingdom
Suitability for cooking: Baking, Chipping,
Processing, Roasting
Description: Medium-sized, oval potato
with white skin, creamy white flesh,
and a firm fairly dry texture.
It has a tendency to disintegrate during
boiling but can bake well
Home growing: Available

Pentland Squire

Maincrop – early
Origin: Scotland, 1970
Availability: United Kingdom
Suitability for cooking: Baking, Mashing,
Processing, Roasting
Description: Oval, white skin and creamy
white flesh, very floury texture and
good flavour. Very good baker and
popular with fish and chip shops
Home growing: Good

*Above: Clockwise from top, the
Pentland collection, Hawk, Javelin, Dell,
Marble, Crown, Squire*

Picasso
Maincrop – early
Origin: Netherlands, 1992
Availability: Balearic Islands, CIS,
Cyprus, Egypt, Netherlands, Spain,
Portugal, United Kingdom
Suitability for cooking: Boiling, Salad
Description: Small, oval-round potato
with quite deep red eyes, pale skin, with
white waxy flesh
Home growing: Available

Pike
Maincrop
Origin: Pennsylvania, 1996
Availability: Canada/USA
Suitability for cooking: Baking, Boiling,
Chipping, Processing
Description: Medium, spherical potatoes
with quite deep eyes, buff-coloured,
slightly netted skin and creamy flesh.
Has a tendency to discolour after it has
been cooked

Pimpernel
Maincrop – early
Origin: Netherlands, 1953
Availability: Chile, Malawi, Norway, South
Africa, Zaire

Suitability for cooking:
Good all-round
Description: An
oval shaped potato
with pink to red skin
and yellowish-
coloured flesh on
the inside

Pink Eye *Southern Gold,*
Sweet Gold or Pink Gourmet
Early
Origin: United Kingdom, 1862
Availability: Australia
Suitability for cooking: Boiling, Mashing,
Salad and most other methods
Description: A small, smooth, creamy-
skinned potato, with purple/blue blush,
and creamy yellow flesh, floury texture
and a nutty taste. Although it originated
in Kent, it is now only grown in Australia
and is commonly available as a new
potato variety

Pink Fir Apple
Maincrop – late
Origin: France, 1850
Availability: Australia, France,
United Kingdom

Suitability for cooking:
Baking, Boiling, Roasting, Salad
Description: Long, knobbly, misshapen
potatoes with a pink blush on white skins
and creamy yellow flesh. Firm and waxy
with a delicious, nutty flavour. Best
cooked in skins. Having a revival now but
they have always been popular with
gardeners as they are good keepers. The
shape makes them impossible to peel
until cooked, but they are best cold in
salads and tossed in warm dressings, or
served as new potatoes
Home growing: Good for home growing,
although tubers form clusters of roots
under stem and can be prone to blight

Above: Picasso
Left: Pink Fir Apple

Pompadour
Maincrop – early
Origin: Netherlands, 1976
Availability: France
Suitability for cooking: Boiling, Salad
Description: Long, oval and regular in shape with light yellow skin and flesh. Also good steamed and served on their own for a starter

Premiere
First Early
Origin: Netherlands, 1979
Availability: Bulgaria, Canada, Netherlands, United Kingdom
Suitability for cooking: Baking, Boiling, Chipping, Roasting
Description: Large, oval potatoes with light yellow skin, firm yellow flesh and good flavour. Not as waxy as many early potatoes
Home growing: Available

Primura
First Early
Origin: Netherlands, 1963
Availability: Denmark, Italy, Netherlands
Suitability for cooking: Boiling, Chipping
Description: Oval to round, medium size, yellow skin, light yellow flesh, shallow eyes and firm texture

Ratte (La) *Cornichon or Asparges or Princess*
Maincrop – early
Origin: France, 1872
Availability: Australia, Denmark, Germany, France (has only recently begun to be grown outside France), United Kingdom
Suitability for cooking: Boiling, Salad
Description: Long, tubular, almost banana-shaped, not as knobbly as Pink Fir. Has brown/yellow skin and creamy flesh, which is firm and waxy with a delicious nutty flavour. Very good for eating cold, exceptionally popular in France and growing in popularity in other parts of the world
Home growing: Good

Above: From top to bottom, Ratte, Record

Record
Maincrop – early
Origin: Netherlands, 1932
Availability: Greece, Holland, Yugoslavia, United Kingdom (grown in Britain for processing market)
Suitability for cooking: Baking, Chipping, Mashing, Roasting, Processing
Description: White skin with pinkish tinges, light yellow to yellow flesh, mealy texture and great flavour. Versatile potato often sold by the sack in farm shops
Home growing: Available

Above: From left to right, Primura, Premiere

Red Pontiac *Dakota Chief*
Maincrop – early
Origin: USA, 1983
Availability: Algeria, Australia, Canada, Philippines, Uruguay, USA (south-eastern states), Venezuela
Suitability for cooking: Baking, Boiling, Mashing,
Roasting, Salads
Description: Round to oval potatoes with dark red, sometimes netted skin, quite deep eyes and white waxy flesh. A red-skinned variety with worldwide popularity. Good for use in microwave cooking
Home growing: Available

Red Rascal
Maincrop
Origin: Unknown
Availability: New Zealand
Suitability for cooking: Baking, Mashing, Roasting
Description: Red-skinned and yellow-fleshed, slightly floury with good flavour

Red Rooster
Maincrop – early
Origin: Irish Republic, 1993
Availability: Irish Republic
Suitability for cooking: Baking, Boiling, Chipping, Processing, Roasting, Salad
Description: Flattish, oval potato with bright red skin and firm buttery, yellow, mild-tasting flesh. Fairly new potato not yet widely available outside Ireland
Home growing: Available

Red LaSoda
Maincrop – late
Origin: USA, 1953
Availability: Algeria, Australia, Canada, Uruguay, USA (south-eastern states), Venezuela

Suitability for cooking: Baking, Boiling, Roasting
Description: Round to oval with smooth, deep-red skin, quite deep eyes and creamy white flesh. Ideal for most cooked and baked dishes

Right: Red LaSoda
Above: Red Rooster
Left: Red Pontiac

Above: From left, Romano, Rocket, Roseval

Red Ruby
Maincrop
Origin: USA, 1994
Availability: Canada, USA
Suitability for cooking: Baking, Boiling
Description: Oblong in shape with dark red skin which has patches of russeting and bright white flesh. An attractive winter potato

Remarka
Maincrop
Origin: Netherlands, 1992
Availability: Netherlands, Portugal, Spain, United Kingdom
Suitability for cooking: Baking, Boiling, Chipping, Roasting
Description: Large oval potato with creamy white skin, pale yellow flesh and good flavour. Makes a particularly good baking potato
Home growing: Available for home growing and ideal for organic gardening as it is a very disease-resistant variety

Rocket
First Early
Origin: United Kingdom, 1987
Availability: New Zealand, United Kingdom
Suitability for cooking: Baking, Boiling, Chipping, Mashing, Roasting, Salad
Description: Uniformly round, white-skinned, white flesh, firm, waxy and well flavoured. This is one of the earliest potatoes
Home growing: Available

Romano
Maincrop – early
Origin: Netherlands, 1978
Availability: Balearic Islands, Cameroon, CIS, Hungary, Netherlands, Portugal, Spain, United Kingdom
Suitability for cooking: Baking, Boiling, Mashing, Roasting and most other methods
Description: Round to oval, red skin with creamy flesh, soft dry texture, with a pleasant, mild nutty taste. Lovely colour which tends to pale during cooking to a soft rusty beige
Home growing: Available

Roseval
Second Early – early main
Origin: France, 1950
Availability: Australia, France, Israel, New Zealand, United Kingdom
Suitability for cooking: Boiling, Salad
Description: Oval shape with dark red, almost purple skin with golden yellow flesh. Waxy texture with a really good buttery flavour. A very distinctive-looking potato which has a great flavour and is very popular in microwave cookery
Home growing: Good

Above: Remarka

Rosine

Maincrop – early
Origin: Brittany, 1972
Availability: France
Suitability for cooking: Boiling, Salad
Description: Great in steamed dishes and gratins, also in salads

Rouge (La)

Maincrop – late
Origin: USA, 1962
Availability: Canada, USA (south-eastern and eastern states)
Suitability for cooking: Boiling, Roasting
Description: Medium size, irregular flattened round/oval with smooth bright red skin, quite deep eyes and creamy white flesh. Brilliant colour which fades in storage, but an attractive winter potato. Very popular in Florida

Royal Kidney

Second Early
Origin: United Kingdom, 1899
Availability: United Kingdom (but now grown in Majorca for United Kingdom market)
Suitability for cooking: Salad
Description: Kidney-shaped, smooth white skin with pale yellow flesh and waxy texture. Good eaten cold so works particularly well in salads

Rua

Maincrop – early
Origin: New Zealand, 1960
Availability: New Zealand
Suitability for cooking: Baking, Boiling, Chipping, Mashing, Roasting, Salad and most other methods

Description: Round-shaped potato with creamy white skin and white flesh on the inside. It falls midway between being waxy and floury in texture when cooked. This potato has a really good flavour and is good for use in many dishes

Russet Burbank *Idaho Russet or Netted Gem*

Maincrop – late
Origin: USA, 1875
Availability: Australia, Canada, New Zealand, United Kingdom (for commercial use only), USA (north-west, central and mid-eastern states)
Suitability for cooking: Baking, Chipping, Mashing, Processing, Roasting
Description: Oval to long in shape, russeted skin with pale yellow to white flesh, floury and full of flavour, and turning a bright colour when cooked. The potato which made Idaho famous for potatoes and therefore is often referred to as an Idaho potato. Hugely popular in America for some time and more recently found in McDonald's fries. Most widespread potato grown in Canada

Above left: Russet Burbank
Below: Royal Kidney

Russet Norking
Maincrop
Origin: USA, 1977
Availability: Canada, USA
Suitability for cooking: Baking, Boiling, Chipping
Description: Oblong-shaped potato with medium-heavy russet skin and creamy white flesh

Russet Norkotah
Second Early
Origin: North Dakota, 1987
Availability: Canada, USA
Suitability for cooking: Baking, Chipping
Description: Oval long, darkly russeted potatoes with white flesh

Russet Nugget
Maincrop – late
Origin: Colorado, 1989
Availability: Canada, USA
Suitability for cooking: Baking, Boiling, Chipping, Processing, Roasting
Description: Oblong, slightly flat potatoes with evenly russeted skin and creamy white flesh

Russet Ranger
Maincrop – late
Origin: USA, 1991
Availability: Canada, USA (Colorado, Idaho, Oregon, Washington)
Suitability for cooking: Baking, Boiling, Chipping, Processing
Description: Long, russet or tannish-skinned potatoes, with bright white flesh

Samba
Maincrop – early
Origin: France, 1989
Availability: France, Portugal, Spain
Suitability for cooking: Baking, Boiling, Mashing and most other methods
Description: Regular, oval shape, white skin with yellow flesh and floury texture when cooked

Russet Century
Maincrop – late
Origin: USA, 1995
Availability: USA
Suitability for cooking: Baking, Boiling, Mashing, Roasting
Description: Long, cylindrical and slightly flat potatoes with pale, buff-coloured, slightly russeted skin and creamy flesh

Russet Frontier
Second Early
Origin: USA, 1990
Availability: Canada, USA
Suitability for cooking: Baking, Boiling, Chipping
Description: Long, oval potatoes with light, slightly russeted skins and creamy white flesh

Russet Lemhi
Maincrop – late
Origin: USA, 1981
Availability: USA
Suitability for cooking: Baking, Chipping and most other methods
Description: Large oblong with a tannish-brown netted skin and white eyes

Above: From top, Russet Frontier, Russet Burbank

Sangre

Maincrop
Origin: Colorado, 1982
Availability: Canada, USA
(western states)
Suitability for cooking: Baking, Boiling
Description: Oval shape with smooth
dark red skin, slightly netted, and
creamy flesh

Sante

Maincrop – early
Origin: Netherlands, 1983
Availability: Bulgaria, Canada,
Netherlands, United Kingdom
Suitability for cooking: Baking, Boiling,
Chipping, Roasting
Description: Oval or round with white
or light yellow skin and flesh and dry
firm texture. These have become the
most successful organic potato and are
often sold young as new potatoes too
Home growing: Available

Saxon

Second Early
Origin: United Kingdom, 1992
Availability: United Kingdom (still rare)
Suitability for cooking: Baking,
Boiling, Chipping
Description: This variety has white skin
and flesh, a firm moist texture and
excellent flavour. New general purpose
potato which is still finding its niche and
is very popular in the pre-packed
potato market
Home growing: Available

Sebago

Maincrop – late
Origin: USA, 1938
Availability: Australia, Canada, Malaysia,
New Zealand, South Africa, USA
(Northern states), Venezuela
Suitability for cooking: Baking, Boiling,
Chipping, Mashing, Roasting, Salad
Description: Round to oval shape, with
very white skin and white flesh.
Especially good for both boiling
and mashing. Most widely grown
potato in Australia

*Above: From left to right, Sante, Saxon
(bottom), Sebago*

Above: Sangre

Above: Sebago

Sharpe's Express
First – Second Early
Origin: United Kingdom, 1900
Availability: Not for commercial markets though occasionally available in Scotland
Suitability for cooking: Quite good all-round
Description: Oval to pear shaped, with white skin and creamy flesh. Needs careful cooking, especially when boiling
Home growing: Occasionally available for home growing

Shepody
Maincrop – early
Origin: New Brunswick, Canada, 1980
Availability: Canada, New Zealand, USA (Northern states)
Suitability for cooking: Baking, Boiling, Chipping, Mashing
Description: Long, oval shape, with white, slightly netted skin, light creamy yellow flesh and dry starchy texture. Developed for the chip processing market in America and seldom found in supermarkets

Shetland Black *Black Kidney*
Second Early
Origin: United Kingdom, 1923
Availability: United Kingdom (very limited)
Suitability for cooking: Boiling, Mashing
Description: Inky blue/black skin with yellow flesh and unique purple ring inside. Very fluffy and floury with an exceptionally sweet, buttery flavour. An attractive potato which, if handled carefully, can be great in salads or served simply with butter. Also good mashed, but the colour goes slightly grey/blue
Home growing: Available

Top: Shepody
Left: From top to bottom, Skerry Blue, Swedish Black, Shetland Black

Shula

Maincrop – early
Origin: United Kingdom, 1986
Availability: Scotland, but still rare
Suitability for cooking: Boiling, Mashing, Roasting, quite good all round
Description: Oval shape, partly pink skin, with light creamy flesh
Home growing: Occasionally available

Sieglinde

Second Early
Origin: West Germany, 1935
Availability: Cyprus, Germany
Suitability for cooking: Boiling, Roasting
Description: Long, oval

Top: Spunta
Above: Snowden

shape, with white skin and yellow flesh. Beware of overcooking as they tend to break up easily

Skerry Blue

Maincrop – late
Origin: United Kingdom, c.1846
Availability: United Kingdom (not commercially available)
Suitability for cooking: Boiling
Description: Rich violet skin with deep purple and white mottled or creamy flesh. Has a superb flavour
Home growing:
Available

Snowden

Maincrop – all year
Origin: USA, 1990
Availability: Canada, USA
Suitability for cooking: Baking, Boiling, Chipping, Processing
Description: Round, slightly flat potato with mildly netted, light tan skin and creamy flesh. Primarily used in Canada for the chip processing market

Spunta

Second Early
Origin: Netherlands, 1968
Availability: Argentina, Australia, Cyprus, Greece, Indonesia, Italy, Malaysia, Mauritius, Netherlands, New Zealand, Portugal, Thailand, Tunisia, United Kingdom, Vietnam
Suitability for cooking: Baking, Boiling, Chipping, Mashing, Roasting, Salad and most other methods
Description: Medium-large, long potato, often kidney- or pear-shaped, with light yellow skin and golden flesh
Home growing: Occasionally available

Stroma

Second Early
Origin: Scotland, 1989
Availability: New Zealand, United Kingdom (still rare)
Suitability for cooking: Baking, Boiling, Mashing, Roasting
Description: Attractive long, oval potato with pink/red skin, yellow/pink flesh, floury texture and good flavour
Home growing: Available

Superior

Second Early
Origin: USA, 1962
Availability: Canada, South Korea, USA (North Carolina)
Suitability for cooking: Chipping and most other methods
Description: Round to oblong, irregular shape with buff skin, occasionally slightly russeted or netted, and white flesh. Best early in the season

Swedish Black

Origin: Unknown
Availability: Collections only
Suitability for cooking: Baking, Boiling, Mashing
Description: Bluish-purple skinned medium to large potato with very deep eyes giving irregular shape. Blue flesh is very mealy on cooking

Sweet Potato

Maincrop
Origin: South America
Availability: Widely grown in southern United States and Pacific Islands, Japan, Soviet Union
Suitability for cooking: Baking, Boiling, Mashing, Processing, Roasting and most other methods
Description: Two varieties, white skinned and red-brown skinned, both with yellow flesh and quite a waxy texture. The redder are sweeter and firmer. The sweet potato is unrelated to the white potato or to the yam. However it has all the same characteristics: the edible part is the tuber which can vary in skin and flesh colour and can be treated just like the potato. It is a staple food in the West Indies, Africa and Asia and has seen a rise in popularity in Western cuisine

Above: Superior

Toolangi Delight

Origin: Australia
Availability: Australia (still new, so rarely available yet)
Suitability for cooking: Baking, Boiling, Chipping, Mashing, Roasting, Salad and good all-round variety
Description: A truly distinctive purple skin and pure smooth white flesh which is dry when cooked. It is one of the few potatoes bred in Australia where it is often used to make gnocchi

Above: Sweet Potato

Up to Date
Maincrop – late
Origin: Scotland, 1894
Availability: Burma, Cyprus, Malawi,
Mauritius, Nepal, South Africa,
United Kingdom
Suitability for cooking: Quite good all-
round variety
Description: Flattish oval shape, white
skin and flesh with a good flavour.
First potato to be grown in Cyprus for
export and still mainly grown for small
international markets. It was the main
variety available at the turn of the century
in the United Kingdom

Valor
Maincrop – early
Origin: Scotland, 1993
Availability: Canary Isles, Israel,
United Kingdom
Suitability for cooking: Baking, Boiling
Description: Oval potato with white skin
and creamy white flesh. A new potato not
yet widely available in the shops
Home growing Available

Tosca
Maincrop – late
Origin: United Kingdom, 1987
Availability: United Kingdom (still rare)
Suitability for cooking: Good
all-round variety
Description: Oval-shaped potato with
pink to red skin and light yellow pleasant
tasting flesh

Ulster Prince
First Early
Origin: United Kingdom, 1947
Availability: Irish Republic, United
Kingdom (very small quantities)
Suitability for cooking: Baking, Boiling,
Chipping, Roasting
Description: Large, kidney-shaped potato
with white skin and white flesh. This
potato is best eaten early in the season
when the flavour is delicious
Home growing: Available

Ulster Sceptre
First Early
Origin: Northern Ireland, 1963
Availability: Northern Ireland

Suitability for cooking: Boiling, Roasting,
Salad and most other methods
Description: Smaller ovals, with yellow-
white skin and creamy waxy firm flesh.
Sometimes blackening can occur after
cooking which has seen t gradually
being edged out of the market place

Top left: Tosca
Left: Ulster Prince (top), Ulster Sceptre
Above: Up to Date

White Rose *American Giant, Wisconsin Pride, California Long White*
First Early
Origin: USA, 1893
Availability: Canada, USA (California, Oregon, Washington)
Suitability for cooking: Baking, Boiling, Mashing
Description: Large, very long and flat with smooth white skin and quite deep eyes, and bright white flesh. Not as popular as it used to be

Wilja
Second Early
Origin: Netherlands, 1967
Availability: Netherlands, Pakistan
Suitability for cooking: Boiling, Chipping, Mashing, Roasting
Description: Long, oval shape with pale yellow skin and flesh, quite firm, with a slightly dry texture. Second most widely grown of the second-early potatoes. Often available in maincrop season
Home growing: Available

Vanessa
First Early
Origin: Netherlands, 1973
Availability: Netherlands, United Kingdom
Suitability for cooking: Boiling, Roasting, Salad
Description: Long oval with pink to red skin and light yellow flesh
Home growing: Available

Viking
Maincrop
Origin: North Dakota, USA, 1963
Availability: Canada, USA
Suitability for cooking: Baking, Boiling, Mashing and most other methods
Description: Ranging from large oblong to round with smooth, pale red skin and very white flesh

Vitelotte *Truffe de Chine*
Origin: Unknown
Availability: France, United Kingdom (very rare)
Suitability for cooking: Boiling, Salad
Description: Long, thin and smallish purple/black finger potatoes with dark greyish blue flesh. Firm waxy texture with a mild nutty taste. The colour does not fade on cooking. The name Truffe de Chine is not often used in France since there is also a Chinese Truffle (Truffe de Chine) found which causes confusion

Top right: Wilja
Above: Vitelotte
Right: White Rose

Winston
First Early
Origin: Scotland, 1992
Availability: New Zealand,
United Kingdom
Suitability for cooking: Baking, Chipping,
Roasting, Salad
Description: A uniform, oval-shaped
potato with almost no eyes, creamy white
skin and very firm texture. These
potatoes make particularly good early
season bakers
Home growing: Available

Right: Winston
Below: Yukon Gold

Yukon Gold
Second Early – Maincrop
Origin: Ontario, Canada, 1980
Availability: Canada, USA
(California, Michigan)
Suitability for cooking: Baking,
Boiling, Chipping
Description: Large, oval to round potato
with buff-coloured skin, yellow flesh, pink
eyes and a slightly mealy texture. An
excellent baking potato with a delicious
flavour, which is very popular in the
international speciality market. This was
the first successful North American
yellow-fleshed potato
Home growing: Available

The Recipes

Soups

Nothing beats a steaming hot bowl of soup, whether it's thick and creamy or light with a delicate broth. When potatoes are used as a base or as a finishing touch they add a special touch to the dish as well as a delicious texture. The flavour combinations are simply endless, from an Italian Minestrone Genoa to a spicy Chorizo Soup or a classic Leek and Potato Soup.

CHILLED LEEK AND POTATO SOUP

THIS CREAMY-SMOOTH COLD VERSION OF THE CLASSIC VICHYSSOISE IS SERVED WITH THE REFRESHING TANG OF YOGURT AS A TOPPING.

SERVES FOUR

INGREDIENTS

25g/1oz/2 tbsp butter
15ml/1 tbsp vegetable oil
1 small onion, chopped
3 leeks, sliced
2 medium floury potatoes, diced
600ml/1 pint/2½ cups
  vegetable stock
300ml/½ pint/1¼ cups milk
45ml/3 tbsp single cream
a little extra milk (optional)
salt and ground black pepper
60ml/4 tbsp natural yogurt and
  fried chopped leeks, to serve

1 Heat the butter and oil in a large pan and add the onion, leeks and potatoes. Cover and cook for 15 minutes, stirring occasionally. Bring to the boil, reduce the heat and simmer for 10 minutes.

2 Stir in the stock and milk and cover again.

3 Ladle the vegetables and liquid into a blender or a food processor in batches and purée until smooth. Return to the pan, stir in the cream and season.

4 Leave the soup to cool, and then chill for 3–4 hours. You may need to add a little extra milk to thin down the soup, as it will thicken slightly as it cools.

5 Ladle the soup into soup bowls and serve topped with a spoonful of natural yogurt and a sprinkling of leeks.

LEEK, POTATO AND ROCKET SOUP

ROCKET ADDS ITS DISTINCTIVE, PEPPERY TASTE TO THIS WONDERFULLY SATISFYING SOUP.
SERVE IT HOT, GARNISHED WITH A GENEROUS SPRINKLING OF TASTY CIABATTA CROÛTONS.

SERVES FOUR TO SIX

INGREDIENTS
    50g/2oz/4 tbsp butter
    1 onion, chopped
    3 leeks, chopped
    2 medium floury potatoes, diced
    900ml/1½ pints/3¾ cups light
      chicken stock or water
    2 large handfuls rocket, roughly
      chopped
    150ml/¼ pint/⅔ cup double cream
    salt and ground black pepper
    garlic-flavoured ciabatta croûtons,
      to serve

1 Melt the butter in a large heavy-based pan then add the onion, leeks and potatoes and stir until the vegetables are coated in butter. Heat the ingredients until sizzling then reduce the heat to low.

2 Cover and sweat the vegetables for 15 minutes. Pour in the stock or water and bring to the boil then reduce the heat, cover again and simmer for 20 minutes until the vegetables are tender.

3 Press the soup through a sieve or pass through a food mill and return to the rinsed-out pan. (When puréeing the soup, don't use a blender or food processor, as these will give the soup a gluey texture.) Add the chopped rocket to the pan and cook the soup gently, uncovered, for 5 minutes.

4 Stir in the cream, then season to taste and reheat gently. Ladle the soup into warmed soup bowls and serve with a scattering of garlic-flavoured ciabatta croûtons in each.

LEEK AND POTATO SOUP

THESE TWO VEGETABLES MAKE A REALLY TASTY AND SUBSTANTIAL, SIMPLE SOUP, AND ARE READILY AVAILABLE THROUGHOUT THE YEAR, MAKING THEM IDEAL FOR ANY SEASON.

SERVES FOUR

INGREDIENTS
  50g/2oz/4 tbsp butter
  2 leeks, chopped
  1 small onion, finely chopped
  350g/12oz floury potatoes, chopped
  900ml/1½ pints/3¾ cups chicken or
    vegetable stock
  salt and ground black pepper
  crusty bread, to serve

1 Heat 25g/1oz/2 tbsp of the butter in a large heavy-based saucepan, add the chopped leeks and onion and cook gently, stirring occasionally so that they do not stick to the bottom of the pan, for about 7 minutes until softened but not browned.

2 Add the potatoes to the pan and cook, stirring occasionally, for 2–3 minutes. Add the stock and bring to the boil then reduce the heat, cover and simmer gently for 30–35 minutes until the vegetables are very tender.

3 Season to taste, remove the pan from the heat and stir in the remaining butter in small pieces. Serve hot with slices of thick crusty bread.

COOK'S TIP
If you prefer your soup to have a smoother consistency, simply press the mixture through a sieve or pass through a food mill once it is cooked. Don't use a food processor as it can give the potatoes a gluey texture.

CLAM, MUSHROOM AND POTATO CHOWDER

THE DELICATE, SWEET SHELLFISH TASTE OF CLAMS AND THE SOFT EARTHINESS OF WILD MUSHROOMS COMBINE WITH POTATOES TO MAKE THIS A GREAT MEAL ON ITS OWN — FIT FOR ANY OCCASION.

SERVES FOUR

INGREDIENTS
  48 clams, scrubbed
  50g/2oz/4 tbsp unsalted butter
  1 large onion, chopped
  1 celery stick, sliced
  1 carrot, sliced
  225g/8oz assorted wild mushrooms,
    such as chanterelles, saffron milk-
    caps, chicken of the woods or
    St George's mushrooms, sliced
  225g/8oz floury potatoes,
    thickly sliced
  1.2 litres/2 pints/5 cups light
    chicken or vegetable stock, boiling
  1 thyme sprig
  4 parsley stalks
  salt and ground black pepper
  thyme sprigs, to garnish

1 Place the clams in a large saucepan, discarding any that are open. Put 1cm/½in of water in the pan, cover, bring to the boil and steam over a medium heat for 6–8 minutes until the clams open (discard any clams that do not open).

2 Drain the clams over a bowl, remove the shells from each one and chop. Strain the cooking juices into the bowl, add the chopped clams and set aside.

3 Add the butter, onion, celery and carrot to the pan and cook gently until softened but not coloured. Add the mushrooms and cook for 3–4 minutes until their juices begin to appear. Add the potatoes, the clams and their juices, the stock, thyme and parsley stalks.

4 Bring to the boil then reduce the heat, cover and simmer for 25 minutes. Season to taste, ladle into soup bowls, and garnish with thyme.

SWEETCORN AND POTATO CHOWDER

THIS CREAMY YET CHUNKY SOUP IS RICH WITH THE SWEET TASTE OF CORN. IT'S EXCELLENT SERVED WITH THICK CRUSTY BREAD AND TOPPED WITH SOME MELTED CHEDDAR CHEESE.

SERVES FOUR

INGREDIENTS

1 onion, chopped
1 garlic clove, crushed
1 medium baking potato, chopped
2 celery sticks, sliced
1 small green pepper, seeded, halved
  and sliced
30ml/2 tbsp sunflower oil
25g/1oz/2 tbsp butter
600ml/1 pint/2½ cups stock or water
300ml/½ pint/1¼ cups milk
200g/7oz can flageolet beans
300g/11oz can sweetcorn kernels
good pinch dried sage
salt and ground black pepper
Cheddar cheese, grated, to serve

1 Put the onion, garlic, potato, celery and green pepper into a large heavy-based saucepan with the oil and butter.

2 Heat the ingredients in a large saucepan until sizzling then reduce the heat to low. Cover and cook gently for about 10 minutes, shaking the pan occasionally.

3 Pour in the stock or water, season with salt and pepper to taste and bring to the boil. Reduce the heat, cover again and simmer gently for about 15 minutes until the vegetables are tender.

4 Add the milk, beans and sweetcorn – including their liquids – and the sage. Simmer, uncovered, for 5 minutes. Check the seasoning and serve hot, sprinkled with grated cheese.

GALICIAN BROTH

IN THIS HEARTY MAIN MEAL SOUP THE POTATOES COOK IN THE GAMMON STOCK, ABSORBING ITS RICH FLAVOUR AND GIVING IT A SALTY TASTE, SO BE CAREFUL NOT TO OVER SEASON IT.

SERVES FOUR

INGREDIENTS
450g/1lb gammon, in one piece
2 bay leaves
2 onions, sliced
10ml/2 tsp paprika
675g/1½lb baking potatoes, cut into
   large chunks
225g/8oz spring greens
425g/15oz can haricot or cannellini
   beans, drained
salt and ground black pepper

COOK'S TIP
Peel the potatoes if you prefer, but the flavour is best with the skin left on.

1 Soak the gammon overnight in cold water in the fridge. Drain and put in a large saucepan with the bay leaves and onions. Pour over 1.5 litres/2½ pints/6¼ cups fresh cold water.

2 Bring to the boil then reduce the heat and simmer very gently for about 1½ hours until the meat is tender. Keep an eye on the pan to make sure it doesn't boil over.

3 Remove the meat from the cooking liquid and leave to cool slightly. Discard the skin and any excess fat and cut the meat into small chunks. Return to the pan with the paprika and potatoes. Return to the boil, then reduce the heat, cover and simmer for 20 minutes until the potatoes are tender.

4 Meanwhile cut away the cores from the greens. Roll up the leaves and cut into thin shreds. Add to the pan with the beans and simmer, uncovered, for about 10 minutes. Remove the bay leaves. Season with salt and pepper to taste and serve hot.

VARIATION
Bacon knuckles can be used instead of the gammon. The bones will give the stock a delicious flavour. Freeze any stock you don't use.

CREAMED SPINACH AND POTATO SOUP

THIS IS A DELICIOUS LOW-FAT CREAMY SOUP. THIS RECIPE USES SPINACH BUT OTHER VEGETABLES WOULD WORK JUST AS WELL, SUCH AS CABBAGE OR SWISS CHARD.

SERVES FOUR

INGREDIENTS
1 large onion, finely chopped
1 garlic clove, crushed
900g/2lb floury potatoes, diced
2 celery sticks, chopped
1.2 litres/2 pints/5 cups
  vegetable stock
250g/9oz fresh spinach leaves
200g/7oz/scant 1 cup low-fat
  cream cheese
300ml/½ pint/1¼ cups milk
dash of dry sherry
salt and ground black pepper
chopped fresh parsley, to garnish
crusty bread, to serve

1 Place the onion, garlic, potatoes, celery and stock in a large saucepan. Simmer for 20 minutes.

2 Season the soup and add the spinach, cook for a further 10 minutes. Remove from the heat and cool slightly.

3 Process the soup in batches in a food processor or food mill and return to the saucepan.

4 Stir in the cream cheese and milk, simmer and check for seasoning. Add a dash of sherry and serve crusty bread and chopped fresh parsley.

POTATO AND GARLIC BROTH

ALTHOUGH THERE IS PLENTY OF GARLIC IN THIS SOUP, THE END RESULT IS NOT OVERPOWERING. SERVE PIPING HOT WITH BREAD, AS THE PERFECT WINTER WARMER.

SERVES FOUR

INGREDIENTS
2 small or 1 large whole head of
  garlic (about 20 cloves)
4 medium potatoes, diced
1.75 litres/3 pints/7½ cups
  vegetable stock
salt and ground black pepper
flat leaf parsley, to garnish

VARIATION
Make the soup more substantial by placing in each bowl a slice of French bread which has been toasted and topped with melted cheese. Pour the soup over so that the bread soaks it up.

1 Preheat the oven to 190°C/375°F/ Gas 5. Place the unpeeled garlic bulbs or bulb in a small roasting tin and bake for 30 minutes until they are soft in the centre.

2 Meanwhile, par-boil the potatoes in a large saucepan of lightly salted boiling water for 10 minutes.

3 Simmer the stock for 5 minutes. Drain the potatoes and add to the stock.

4 Squeeze the garlic pulp into the soup, reserving a few cloves to garnish, stir and season to taste. Simmer for 15 minutes and serve garnished with whole cloves and parsley.

SMOKED HADDOCK AND POTATO SOUP

*"Cullen Skink" is a classic Scottish dish using one of the country's tastiest fish.
The result is a thick, creamy soup with a rich, smoky fish flavour.*

SERVES SIX

INGREDIENTS
  350g/12oz smoked haddock fillet
  1 onion, chopped
  bouquet garni
  900ml/1½ pints/3¾ cups water
  500g/1¼lb floury potatoes, quartered
  600ml/1 pint/2½ cups milk
  40g/1½oz/3 tbsp butter
  salt and ground black pepper
  snipped chives, to garnish
  crusty bread, to serve

1 Put the haddock, onion, bouquet garni and water into a large heavy-based saucepan and bring to the boil. Skim the scum from the surface, then cover, reduce the heat and poach gently for 10–15 minutes until the haddock flakes easily.

2 Lift the haddock from the pan and cool slightly, then remove the skin and bones. Flake the flesh and put to one side. Return the skin and bones to the pan and simmer, for 30 minutes.

3 Strain the fish stock and return to the pan, then add the potatoes and simmer for about 25 minutes. Remove the potatoes from the pan. Add the milk to the pan and bring to the boil.

4 Mash the potatoes with the butter, then whisk into the soup. Add the flaked fish to the pan and heat through. Season. Ladle into soup bowls, sprinkle with chives and serve with crusty bread.

NORTH AFRICAN SPICED SOUP

CLASSICALLY KNOWN AS HARIRA, THIS SOUP IS OFTEN SERVED IN THE EVENING DURING RAMADAN, THE MUSLIM RELIGIOUS FESTIVAL WHEN FOLLOWERS FAST DURING THE DAYTIME FOR A MONTH.

SERVES SIX

INGREDIENTS

1 large onion, chopped
1.2 litres/2 pints/5 cups
  vegetable stock
5ml/1 tsp ground cinnamon
5ml/1 tsp turmeric
15ml/1 tbsp grated ginger
pinch cayenne pepper
2 carrots, diced
2 celery sticks, diced
400g/14oz can chopped tomatoes
450g/1lb floury potatoes, diced
5 strands saffron
400g/14oz can chick-peas, drained
30ml/2 tbsp chopped fresh coriander
15ml/1 tbsp lemon juice
salt and ground black pepper
fried wedges of lemon, to serve

1 Place the onion in a large pot with 300ml /½ pint/1¼ cups of the vegetable stock. Simmer gently for about 10 minutes.

2 Meanwhile, mix together the cinnamon, turmeric, ginger, cayenne pepper and 30ml/2 tbsp of stock to form a paste. Stir into the onion mixture with the carrots, celery and remaining stock.

3 Bring the mixture to a boil, reduce the heat, then cover and gently simmer for 5 minutes.

4 Add the tomatoes and potatoes and simmer gently, covered, for 20 minutes. Add the saffron, chick-peas, coriander and lemon juice. Season to taste and when piping hot serve with fried wedges of lemon.

KALE, CHORIZO AND POTATO SOUP

THIS HEARTY WINTER SOUP HAS A SPICY KICK TO IT, WHICH COMES FROM THE CHORIZO SAUSAGE. THE SOUP BECOMES MORE POTENT IF CHILLED OVERNIGHT AND IT IS WORTH BUYING THE BEST POSSIBLE CHORIZO SAUSAGE TO IMPROVE THE FLAVOUR.

SERVES SIX TO EIGHT

INGREDIENTS
  225g/8oz kale, stems removed
  225g/8oz chorizo sausage
  675g/1½lb red potatoes
  1.75 litres/3 pints/7½ cups
    vegetable stock
  5ml/1 tsp ground black pepper
  pinch cayenne pepper (optional)
  12 slices French bread, grilled
  salt and ground black pepper

1 Place the kale in a food processor and process for a few seconds to chop it finely.

2 Prick the sausages and place in a pan with enough water to cover. Simmer for 15 minutes. Drain and cut into thin slices.

3 Boil the potatoes for about 15 minutes or until tender. Drain, and place in a bowl, then mash adding a little of the cooking liquid to form a thick paste.

4 Bring the vegetable stock to the boil and add the kale. Add the chorizo and simmer for 5 minutes. Add the paste gradually, simmer for 20 minutes. Season with black pepper and cayenne.

5 Place bread slices in each bowl, and pour the soup over. Serve sprinkled with pepper.

CREAM OF CAULIFLOWER SOUP

THIS SOUP IS LIGHT IN FLAVOUR YET SATISFYING ENOUGH FOR A LUNCHTIME SNACK.
YOU CAN TRY GREEN CAULIFLOWER FOR A COLOURFUL CHANGE.

SERVES SIX

INGREDIENTS
30ml/2 tbsp olive oil
2 large onions, finely diced
1 garlic clove, crushed
3 large floury potatoes, finely diced
3 celery sticks, finely diced
1.75 litres/3 pints/7½ cups
  vegetable stock
2 carrots, finely diced
1 medium cauliflower, chopped
15ml/1 tbsp chopped fresh dill
15ml/1 tbsp lemon juice
5ml/1 tsp mustard powder
1.5ml/¼ tsp caraway seeds
300ml/½ pint/1¼ cups single cream
salt and ground black pepper
shredded spring onions, to garnish

3 Add the cauliflower, fresh dill, lemon juice, mustard powder and caraway seeds and simmer for 20 minutes.

4 Process the soup in a blender or food processor until smooth, return to the saucepan and stir in the cream. Season to taste and serve garnished with shredded spring onions.

1 Heat the oil in a large saucepan, add the onions and garlic and fry them for a few minutes until they soften. Add the potatoes, celery and stock and simmer for 10 minutes.

2 Add the carrots and simmer for a further 10 minutes.

CORN AND SWEET POTATO SOUP

THE COMBINATION OF SWEETCORN AND SWEET POTATO GIVES THIS SOUP A REAL DEPTH OF FLAVOUR AS WELL AS MAKING IT LOOK VERY COLOURFUL.

SERVES SIX

INGREDIENTS
  15ml/1 tbsp olive oil
  1 onion, finely chopped
  2 garlic cloves, crushed
  1 small red chilli, seeded and
    finely chopped
  1.75 litres/3 pints/7½ cups
    vegetable stock
  10ml/2 tsp ground cumin
  1 medium sweet potato, diced
  ½ red pepper, finely chopped
  450g/1lb sweetcorn kernels
  salt and ground black pepper
  lime wedges, to serve

1 Heat the oil and fry the onion for 5 minutes until softened. Add the garlic and chilli and fry for a further 2 minutes.

2 In the same pan, add 300ml/½ pint/ 1¼ cups of the stock, and simmer for 10 minutes.

3 Mix the cumin with a little stock to form a paste and then stir into the soup. Add the diced sweet potato, stir and simmer for 10 minutes. Season and stir again.

4 Add the pepper, sweetcorn and remaining stock and simmer for 10 minutes. Process half of the soup until smooth and then stir into the chunky soup. Season and serve with lime wedges for squeezing over.

MINESTRONE GENOA

THE VARIATIONS ON THIS SOUP ARE ENDLESS. THIS PASTA-FREE VERSION IS PACKED WITH HEAPS OF VEGETABLES TO MAKE A SUBSTANTIAL, HEARTY LUNCH WITH CRUSTY BREAD.

SERVES SIX

INGREDIENTS
  1.75 litres/3 pints/7½ cups
    vegetable stock
  1 large onion, chopped
  3 celery sticks, chopped
  2 carrots, finely diced
  2 large floury potatoes, finely diced
  ½ head of cabbage, very finely diced
  225g/8oz runner beans, sliced
    diagonally
  2 x 400g/14oz cans cannellini
    beans, drained
  60ml/4 tbsp ready-made pesto sauce
  salt and ground black pepper
  crusty bread, to serve
  freshly grated Parmesan cheese,
    to serve

1 Pour the stock into a large saucepan. Add the onion, celery and carrots. Simmer for 10 minutes.

2 Add the potatoes, cabbage, and beans and simmer for 10–12 minutes or until the potatoes are tender.

3 Stir in the cannellini beans and pesto, and bring the mixture to the boil. Season to taste and serve hot with crusty bread and plenty of freshly grated Parmesan cheese.

CATALAN POTATO BROAD BEAN SOUP

BROAD BEANS ARE ALSO KNOWN AS FAVA BEANS. WHILE THEY ARE IN SEASON FRESH BEANS ARE PERFECT, BUT TINNED OR FROZEN WILL MAKE AN IDEAL SUBSTITUTE.

SERVES SIX

INGREDIENTS
30ml/2 tbsp olive oil
2 onions, chopped
3 large floury potatoes, diced
450g/1lb fresh broad beans
1.75 litres/3 pints/7½ cups
   vegetable stock
1 bunch coriander, finely chopped
150ml/¼ pint/⅔ cup single cream
salt and ground black pepper
coriander leaves, to garnish

COOK'S TIP
Broad beans sometimes have a tough outer skin, particularly if they are large. To remove this, first cook the beans briefly, peel off the skin, and add the tender centre part to the soup.

1 Heat the oil in a large saucepan and fry the onions, stirring occasionally, for about 5 minutes until softened but not brown.

2 Add the potatoes, beans (reserving a few for garnishing) and stock to the mixture in the saucepan and bring to the boil, then simmer for 5 minutes.

3 Stir in the coriander and simmer for a further 10 minutes.

4 Process in batches in a blender or food processor, then return the soup to the pan.

5 Stir in the cream (reserving a little for garnishing), season, and bring to a simmer. Serve garnished with more coriander leaves, beans and cream.

SPANISH POTATO AND GARLIC SOUP

SERVED IN EARTHENWARE DISHES, THIS CLASSIC SPANISH SOUP SHOULD BE SAVOURED.

SERVES SIX

INGREDIENTS
30ml/2 tbsp olive oil
1 large onion, finely sliced
4 garlic cloves, crushed
1 large potato, halved and cut into
   thin slices
5ml/1 tsp paprika
400g/14oz can chopped
   tomatoes, drained
5ml/1 tsp thyme leaves
900ml/1½ pints/3¾ cups
   vegetable stock
5ml/1 tsp cornflour
salt and ground black pepper
chopped thyme leaves, to garnish

1 Heat the oil in a large saucepan, fry the onions, garlic, potato and paprika for 5 minutes, until the onions have softened, but not browned.

2 Add the tomatoes, thyme and stock and simmer for 15–20 minutes until the potatoes have cooked through.

3 Mix the cornflour with a little water to form a paste and stir into the soup, then simmer for 5 minutes until thickened.

4 Using a wooden spoon break the potatoes up slightly. Season to taste. Serve garnished with the chopped thyme leaves.

Starters and Snacks

POTATOES ARE RARELY ENJOYED AS A
SNACK OR STARTER BUT THEY DESERVE
TO BE. FOR A SIMPLE, TASTY SNACK
SERVE BAKED POTATO SKINS WITH A
SPICY CAJUN DIP. OR FOR A SMART
DINNER PARTY STARTER DISH, TRY
TWICE BAKED GRUYÈRE AND POTATO
SOUFFLÉ OR THE FRENCH CLASSIC,
COQUILLE ST JACQUES
WITH ITS
DECORATIVE
POTATO-PIPED
BORDER.

COQUILLES ST JACQUES

A CLASSIC FRENCH STARTER, THAT CALLS FOR THE BEST QUALITY SCALLOPS POSSIBLE TO ENSURE A TRULY WONDERFUL RESULT. YOU WILL NEED FOUR SCALLOP SHELLS TO SERVE THESE.

SERVES FOUR

INGREDIENTS

　450g/1lb potatoes, chopped
　50g/2oz/4 tbsp butter
　4 large or 8 small scallops
　120ml/4fl oz/½ cup fish stock
For the sauce
　25g/1oz/2 tbsp butter
　25g/1oz/¼ cup plain flour
　300ml/½ pint/1¼ cups milk
　30ml/2 tbsp single cream
　115g/4oz/1 cup mature Cheddar
　　cheese, grated
　salt and ground black pepper
　dill sprigs, to garnish
　grilled lemon wedges, to serve

1 Preheat oven to 200°C/400°F/Gas 6. Place the chopped potatoes in a large saucepan, cover with water and boil for 15 minutes or until tender. Drain and mash with the butter.

2 Spoon the mixture into a piping bag fitted with a star nozzle. Pipe the potatoes around the outside of a cleaned scallop shell. Repeat the process, making four in total.

3 Simmer the scallops in a little fish stock for 3 minutes or until just firm. Drain and slice the scallops finely. Set them aside.

4 To make the sauce, melt the butter in a small saucepan, add the flour and cook over a low heat for a couple of minutes, gradually add the milk and cream, stirring continuously and cook until thickened.

5 Stir in the cheese and cook until melted. Season to taste. Spoon a little sauce in the base of each shell. Divide the scallops between the shells and then pour the remaining sauce over the scallops.

6 Bake the scallops for 10 minutes or until golden. Garnish with dill. Serve with grilled lemon wedges.

TWICE BAKED GRUYÈRE <u>AND</u> POTATO SOUFFLÉ

A GREAT STARTER DISH, THIS RECIPE CAN BE PREPARED IN ADVANCE IF YOU ARE ENTERTAINING AND GIVEN ITS SECOND BAKING JUST BEFORE YOU SERVE IT UP.

SERVES FOUR

INGREDIENTS

225g/8oz floury potatoes
2 eggs, separated
175g/6oz/1½ cups Gruyère, grated
50g/2oz/½ cup self-raising flour
50g/2oz spinach leaves
butter for greasing
salt and ground black pepper
salad leaves, to serve

VARIATION

For a different flavouring try replacing the Gruyère with a crumbled blue cheese, such as Stilton or Shropshire Blue, which have a stronger taste to them.

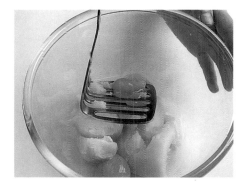

1 Preheat the oven to 200°C/400°F/ Gas 6. Cock the potatoes in lightly salted boiling water for 20 minutes until very tender. Drain and mash with the 2 egg yolks.

2 Stir in half of the Gruyère cheese and all of the flour. Season to taste with salt and pepper.

3 Finely chop the spinach and fold into the potato mixture.

4 Whip the egg whites until they form soft peaks. Fold a little of the egg white into the mixture to loosen it slightly. Using a large spoon, fold the remaining egg white into the mixture.

5 Grease 4 large ramekin dishes. Pour the mixture in and place on a baking sheet and bake for 20 minutes. Remove from the oven and allow to cool.

6 Turn the soufflés out on to a baking sheet and scatter with the remaining cheese. Bake again for 5 minutes and serve with salad leaves.

New Potatoes with Mock Caviar and Cream Cheese

A perfect one-bite snack for a party that makes the most of tender new potatoes with their waxy texture. Danish mock caviar is another name for lumpfish roe.

MAKES THIRTY

INGREDIENTS
    30 small new potatoes
    200g/7oz/scant 1 cup full-fat
      cream cheese
    15ml/1 tbsp chopped fresh parsley
    1 jar Danish black mock caviar
      (lumpfish roe)
    1 jar salmon roe
    salt and ground black pepper
    dill sprigs, to garnish

VARIATION
If you can't get hold of any mock caviar, then top the new potatoes with thin slices of smoked salmon.

1 Cook the potatoes in a large saucepan of boiling water for 20 minutes or until tender. Drain through a colander and then trim off both ends of each potato.

2 Sit the potatoes on the cut end. Beat the cream cheese and parsley together and season. Spoon the mixture on to the potatoes and top with a little mock caviar and salmon roe. Garnish with dill.

Potato Blinis

This crisp, light pancake originates from Russia, where it is served with the best caviar, or use the topping from the recipe above, if you prefer.

SERVES SIX

INGREDIENTS
    115g/4oz maincrop potatoes, boiled
      and mashed
    15ml/1 tbsp easy-blend dried yeast
    175g/6oz/1½ cups plain flour
    oil for greasing
    90ml/6 tbsp soured cream
    6 slices smoked salmon
    salt and ground black pepper
    lemon slices, to garnish

COOK'S TIP
These small pancakes can easily be prepared in advance and stored in the refrigerator until ready for use. Simply warm them up in a low oven.

1 In a large bowl, mix together the potatoes, yeast, flour and 300ml/½ pint/1¼ cups hand-hot water.

2 Leave to rise in a warm place for 30 minutes until the mixture has doubled in size.

3 Heat a non-stick frying pan and add a little oil. Drop spoonfuls of the mixture on to the preheated pan. Cook the blinis for 2 minutes until lightly golden on the underside, toss with a spatula and cook on the second side. Season to taste before serving.

4 Serve with a little soured cream and a small slice of smoked salmon folded on top. Garnish with black pepper and a small slice of lemon.

POTATO SKEWERS <u>WITH</u> MUSTARD DIP

POTATOES COOKED ON THE BARBECUE HAVE A GREAT FLAVOUR AND CRISP SKIN. TRY THESE DELICIOUS KEBABS SERVED WITH A THICK, GARLIC-RICH DIP.

SERVES FOUR

INGREDIENTS
For the dip
    4 garlic cloves, crushed
    2 egg yolks
    30ml/2 tbsp lemon juice
    300ml/½ pint/1¼ cups extra virgin
      olive oil
    10ml/2 tsp whole-grain mustard
    salt and ground black pepper
For the skewers
    1kg/2¼lb small new potatoes
    200g/7oz shallots, halved
    30ml/2 tbsp olive oil
    15ml/1 tbsp sea salt

1 Prepare the barbecue for cooking the skewers before you begin. To make the dip, place the garlic, egg yolks and lemon juice in a blender or a food processor fitted with the metal blade and process for a few seconds until the mixture is smooth.

2 Keep the blender motor running and add the oil very gradually, pouring it in a thin stream, until the mixture forms a thick, glossy cream. Add the mustard and stir the ingredients together, then season with salt and pepper. Chill until ready to use.

COOK'S TIP
Early or "new" potatoes, and salad potatoes have a firmness necessary to stay on the skewer. Don't be tempted to use other types of small potato, they will probably split or fall off the skewers during cooking.

3 Par-boil the potatoes in their skins in boiling water for 5 minutes. Drain well and then thread them on to metal skewers alternating with the shallots.

4 Brush the skewers with oil and sprinkle with salt. Cook over a barbeque for 10–12 minutes, turning occasionally, Serve with the dip.

POTATO SKINS WITH CAJUN DIP

DIVINELY CRISP AND NAUGHTY, THESE POTATO SKINS ARE GREAT ON THEIR OWN OR SERVED WITH THIS PIQUANT DIP AS A GARNISH OR TO THE SIDE.

SERVES TWO

INGREDIENTS
2 large baking potatoes
vegetable oil, for deep frying
For the dip
120ml/4fl oz/½ cup natural yogurt
1 garlic clove, crushed
5ml/1 tsp tomato purée
2.5ml/½ tsp green chilli purée or
  ½ small green chilli, chopped
1.5ml/¼ tsp celery salt
salt and ground black pepper

COOK'S TIP
If you prefer, you can microwave the potatoes to save time. This will take about 10 minutes.

1 Preheat the oven to 180°C/350°F/Gas 4. Bake the potatoes for 45–50 minutes until tender. Cut them in half and scoop out the flesh, leaving a thin layer on the skins. Keep the flesh for another meal.

2 To make the dip, mix together all the ingredients and chill.

3 Heat a 1cm/½in layer of oil in a large saucepan or deep-fat fryer. Cut each potato half in half again, then fry them until crisp and golden on both sides. Drain on kitchen paper, sprinkle with salt and black pepper and serve with a bowl of dip or a dollop of dip in each skin.

DEEP-FRIED NEW POTATOES
WITH SAFFRON AÏOLI

*SERVE THESE CRISPY LITTLE GOLDEN POTATOES DIPPED INTO A WICKEDLY GARLICKY MAYONNAISE —
THEN WATCH THEM DISAPPEAR IN A MATTER OF MINUTES!*

SERVES FOUR

INGREDIENTS
1 egg yolk
2.5ml/½ tsp Dijon mustard
300ml/½ pint/1¼ cups extra virgin
  olive oil
15–30ml/1–2 tbsp lemon juice
1 garlic clove, crushed
2.5ml/½ tsp saffron strands
20 baby, new or salad potatoes
vegetable oil, for deep frying
salt and ground black pepper

1 For the aïoli, put the egg yolk in a bowl with the mustard and a pinch of salt. Mix. Beat in the olive oil very slowly, drop by drop, then in a thin stream. Add the lemon juice.

2 Season the aïoli with salt and pepper then add the crushed garlic and beat the mixture thoroughly to combine.

3 Place the saffron in a small bowl and add 10ml/2 tsp hot water. Press the saffron with the back of a teaspoon, to extract the colour and flavour, and leave to infuse for 5 minutes. Beat the saffron and the liquid into the aïoli.

4 Cook the potatoes in their skins in boiling salted water for 5 minutes, then turn off the heat. Cover the pan and leave for 15 minutes. Drain the potatoes, then dry them thoroughly in a tea towel.

5 Heat a 1cm/½in layer of vegetable oil in a deep pan. When the oil is very hot, add the potatoes and fry quickly, turning, until crisp and golden. Drain on kitchen paper and serve hot with the saffron aïoli.

MINI BAKED POTATOES <u>WITH</u> BLUE CHEESE

PERFECT AS FINGER FOOD FOR A PARTY, ESPECIALLY AS YOU CAN PREPARE THEM IN ADVANCE.

MAKES TWENTY

INGREDIENTS

   20 small new or salad potatoes
   60ml/4 tbsp vegetable oil
   coarse salt
   120ml/4fl oz/½ cup soured cream
   25g/1oz blue cheese, crumbled
   30ml/2 tbsp chopped fresh chives,
    for sprinkling

COOK'S TIP

This dish works just as well as a light snack; if you don't want to be bothered with lots of fiddly small potatoes, simply bake an ordinary baking potato.

1 Preheat the oven to 180°C/350°F/ Gas 4. Wash and dry the potatoes. Pour the oil into a bowl. Add the potatoes and toss to coat well with oil.

2 Dip the potatoes in the coarse salt to coat lightly. Spread out the potatoes on a baking sheet. Bake for 45–50 minutes until tender.

3 In a small bowl, combine the soured cream and blue cheese.

4 Cut a cross in the top of each potato. Press gently with your fingers to open the potatoes.

5 Top each potato with a dollop of the cheese mixture. It will melt down into the potato nicely. Sprinkle with chives on a serving dish and serve hot or at room temperature.

SWEET POTATO CRISPS

YOU CAN USE THESE PINK POTATOES TO MAKE SWEET OR SAVOURY CRISPS, AND THEY HAVE A LOVELY COLOUR AND A UNIQUE, ALMOST FRUITY FLAVOUR.

SERVES FOUR

INGREDIENTS
  2 medium sweet potatoes
  vegetable oil, for deep-frying
  salt

VARIATIONS
For a sweet version, sprinkle with cinnamon and caster sugar, and toss well, before cooling. You can prepare yams in just the same way.

COOK'S TIP
These sweet potato crisps are delicious served warm, but if you don't manage to finish them they are equally good as a cold snack. Serve with a dip, either sweet or savoury.

1 Peel the sweet potatoes under cold running water, cut into 3mm/⅛in thick slices with a sharp knife or vegetable slicer and place in a bowl of salted cold water.

2 Heat a 1cm/½in layer of oil in a large saucepan or deep-fat fryer. While the oil is heating, remove the slices from the water and pat dry on kitchen paper.

3 Fry a few slices at a time until crisp, then drain on kitchen paper. Sprinkle with salt and serve warm.

INDIAN POTATO PANCAKES

ALTHOUGH CALLED A PANCAKE, THESE CRISPY SPICED CAKES ARE MORE LIKE A BHAJI. THEY MAKE AN IDEAL STARTER FOR A MEAL WITH A CURRY AS THE MAIN DISH.

MAKES TEN

INGREDIENTS
  300g/11oz potatoes, grated
  25ml/1½ tsp garam masala or curry
    powder
  4 spring onions, finely chopped
  1 large egg white, lightly beaten
  30ml/2 tbsp vegetable oil
  salt and ground black pepper
  chutney and relishes, to serve

COOK'S TIP
Don't grate the potatoes too soon before use as the flesh will quickly turn brown.

1 Using your hands, squeeze the excess liquid from the grated potatoes and pat dry.

2 Place the dry, grated potatoes in a separate bowl and add the spices, spring onions, egg white and seasoning, stir to combine.

3 Heat a non-stick frying pan over a medium heat and add the oil.

4 Drop tablespoonfuls of the potato on to the pan and flatten out with the back of a spoon (you will need to cook the pancakes in two batches).

5 Cook for a few minutes and then flip the pancakes over. Cook for a further 3 minutes.

6 Drain on kitchen paper and serve with chutney and relishes.

POTATO PIZZA

THIS "PIZZA" MADE OF MASHED POTATOES, WITH A ROBUSTLY FLAVOURED FILLING OF ANCHOVIES, CAPERS AND TOMATOES, IS A SPECIALITY OF PUGLIA IN NORTHERN ITALY.

SERVES FOUR

INGREDIENTS
    1kg/2¼lb floury potatoes
    120ml/4fl oz/½ cup extra virgin
        olive oil
    2 garlic cloves, finely chopped
    350g/12oz tomatoes, chopped
    3 anchovy fillets, chopped
    30ml/2 tbsp capers, rinsed
    salt and ground black pepper

1 Cook the potatoes in their skins in boiling water until tender. Drain well and leave to cool slightly. When they are cool enough to handle, peel and mash or pass through a food mill. Beat in 45ml/3 tbsp of the oil and season to taste. Set aside.

2 Heat another 45ml/3 tbsp of the oil in a medium saucepan. Add the garlic and the chopped tomatoes and cook over a medium heat for 12–15 minutes stirring a little to cook evenly, until the tomatoes soften and begin to dry out. Meanwhile preheat the oven to 200°C/400°F/Gas 6.

3 Oil a round shallow baking dish. Spread half the mashed potatoes into the dish in an even layer. Cover with the tomatoes, and dot with the chopped anchovies and the capers.

4 Spread over the rest of the potatoes in an even layer. Brush the top with the remaining oil and bake for 20–25 minutes until the top is golden brown. Sprinkle with black pepper and serve hot.

VARIATION
For a vegetarian version of this dish, simply omit the anchovies. A few pitted and chopped olives may be added to the filling instead. Add them in step 3, on top of the tomatoes.

SPICED SWEET POTATO TURNOVERS

THE SUBTLE SWEETNESS OF THESE WONDERFUL PINK "POTATOES" MAKES A GREAT TURNOVER FILLING WHEN FLAVOURED WITH A SELECTION OF LIGHT SPICES.

SERVES FOUR

INGREDIENTS
For the filling
   1 sweet potato, about 225g/8oz
   30ml/2 tbsp vegetable oil
   2 shallots, finely chopped
   10ml/2 tsp coriander seeds, crushed
   5ml/1 tsp ground cumin
   5ml/1 tsp garam masala
   115g/4oz/1 cup frozen petit pois,
    thawed
   15ml/1 tbsp chopped fresh mint
   salt and ground black pepper
   mint sprigs, to garnish
For the pastry
   15ml/1 tbsp olive oil
   1 small egg
   150ml/¼ pint/⅔ cup natural yogurt
   115g/4oz/8 tbsp butter, melted
   275g/10oz/2½ cups plain flour
   1.5ml/¼ tsp bicarbonate of soda
   10ml/2 tsp paprika
   5ml/1 tsp salt
   beaten egg, to glaze

1 Cook the sweet potato in boiling salted water for 15–20 minutes, until tender. Drain well and leave to cool. When cool enough to handle, peel the potato and cut into 1cm/½in cubes.

2 Heat the oil in a frying pan, add the shallots and cook until softened. Add the sweet potato and fry until it browns at the edges. Add the spices and fry, stirring, for a few seconds. Remove the pan from the heat and add the peas, mint and seasoning to taste. Leave to cool.

3 Preheat the oven to 200°C/400°F/ Gas 6. Grease a baking sheet. To make the pastry, whisk together the oil and egg, stir in the yogurt, then add the melted butter. Sift the flour, bicarbonate of soda, paprika and salt into a bowl, then stir into the yogurt mixture to form a soft dough. Turn out the dough, and knead gently. Roll it out, then stamp it cut into rounds.

4 Spoon about 10ml/2 tsp of the filling on to one side of each round, then fold over and seal the edges.

5 Re-roll the trimmings and stamp out more rounds until the filling is used up.

6 Arrange the turnovers on the prepared baking sheet and brush the tops with beaten egg. Bake in the oven for about 20 minutes until crisp and golden brown. Serve hot, garnished with mint sprigs.

MIDDLE EASTERN LAMB AND POTATO CAKES

AN UNUSUAL VARIATION, THESE MINCED LAMB TRIANGLES ARE EASY TO SERVE HOT FOR A BUFFET, OR THEY CAN BE EATEN COLD AS A SNACK OR FOR PICNICS.

MAKES TWELVE TO FIFTEEN

INGREDIENTS
  450g/1lb new or small, firm potatoes
  3 eggs
  1 onion, grated
  30ml/2 tbsp chopped fresh parsley
  450g/1lb finely minced lean lamb
  115g/4oz/2 cups breadcrumbs
  vegetable oil, for frying
  salt and ground black pepper
  mint leaves, to garnish
  pitta bread and herby green salad,
    to serve

1 Cook the potatoes in a large pan of boiling salted water for 20 minutes until tender, then drain and leave to cool. Beat the eggs in a large bowl. Add the onion, parsley and seasoning and beat together.

2 When the potatoes are cold, grate them coarsely and stir into the egg mixture together with the minced lamb. Knead for 3–4 minutes until all the ingredients are thoroughly blended.

3 Take a handful of the lamb mixture and roll it into a ball. Repeat this process until all is used. Roll the balls in the breadcrumbs and then mould them into triangular shapes, about 13cm/5in long. Coat them in the breadcrumbs again on both sides.

4 Heat a 1cm/½in layer of oil in a frying pan over a medium heat. When the oil is hot, fry the potato cakes for 8–12 minutes until golden brown on both sides, turning occasionally. Drain on kitchen paper. Serve hot, garnished with mint and accompanied by pitta bread and salad.

IDAHO POTATO SLICES

THIS DISH IS MADE FROM A LAYERED RING OF POTATOES, CHEESE AND HERBS. COOKING THE INGREDIENTS TOGETHER GIVES THEM A VERY RICH FLAVOUR.

3 Scatter some of the onion rings over the potatoes and top with a little of the cheese. Scatter over some thyme and then continue to layer the ingredients, finishing with cheese and seasoning.

4 Press the potato layers right down. (The mixture may seem quite high at this point but it will cook down.)

SERVES FOUR

INGREDIENTS
3 large potatoes
butter, for greasing
1 small onion, finely sliced into rings
200g/7oz/1¾ cups red Leicester or
  mature Cheddar cheese, grated
fresh thyme sprigs
150ml/¼ pint/⅔ cup single cream
salt and ground black pepper
salad leaves, to serve

1 Preheat the oven to 200°C/400°F/ Gas 6. Peel the potatoes and cook in boiling water for 10 minutes until they are just starting to soften. Remove from the water and pat dry.

2 Finely slice the potatoes, using the straight edge of a grater or a mandoline. Grease the base and sides of an 18cm/ 7in cake tin with butter and lay some of the potatoes on the base to cover it completely. Season.

5 Pour the cream over and cook in the oven for 35–45 minutes. Remove from the oven and cool. Invert on to a plate and cut into wedges. Serve with a few salad leaves.

VARIATION
If you want to make this snack more substantial, top the wedges with slices of grilled bacon, or grilled red peppers.

POLPETTES

YUMMY LITTLE FRIED MOUTHFULS OF POTATO AND TANGY-SHARP GREEK FETA CHEESE, FLAVOURED WITH DILL AND LEMON JUICE. SERVE AS A STARTER OR PARTY BITE.

SERVES FOUR

INGREDIENTS
  500g/1¼lb floury potatoes
  115g/4oz/1 cup feta cheese
  4 spring onions, chopped
  45ml/3 tbsp chopped fresh dill
  1 egg, beaten
  15ml/1 tbsp lemon juice
  salt and ground black pepper
  plain flour, for dredging
  45ml/3 tbsp olive oil
  dill sprigs, to garnish
  shredded spring onions, to garnish
  lemon wedges, to serve

1 Cook the potatoes in their skins in boiling lightly salted water until soft. Drain and leave to cool slightly, then chop them in half and peel while still warm.

2 Place in a bowl and mash. Crumble the feta cheese into the potatoes and add the spring onions, dill, egg and lemon juice and season with salt and pepper. (The cheese is salty, so taste before you add salt.) Stir well.

3 Cover and chill until firm. Divide the mixture into walnut-size balls, then flatten them slightly. Dredge with flour, shaking off the excess.

4 Heat the oil in a frying pan and fry the polpettes in batches until golden brown on both sides. Drain on kitchen paper and serve hot, garnished with spring onions, dill and lemon wedges.

SAVOURY POTATO CAKES

GOLDEN AND CRISP, BUT SOFT WHEN YOU BITE INTO THEM, THESE POTATO CAKES ARE WONDERFUL FOR BREAKFAST OR SUPPER, WITH OR WITHOUT ANYTHING ELSE.

SERVES FOUR

INGREDIENTS
450g/1lb waxy potatoes
1 small onion, grated
4 slices streaky bacon, finely chopped
30ml/2 tbsp self-raising flour
2 eggs, beaten
vegetable oil, for deep-frying
salt and ground black pepper
parsley, to garnish

VARIATION
For a vegetarian alternative, omit the bacon and replace it with red pepper.

1 Coarsely grate the potatoes, rinse, drain and pat dry on kitchen paper, then mix with the onion, half the bacon, flour, eggs and seasoning.

2 Heat a 1cm/½in layer of oil in a frying pan until really hot, then add about 15ml/1 tbsp of the potato mixture and quickly spread the mixture out with the back of the spoon taking care that it does not break up.

3 Add a few more spoonfuls of the mixture in the same way, leaving space between each one so they do not stick together, and fry them for 4–5 minutes until golden on the undersides.

4 Turn the cakes over and fry the other side. Drain on kitchen paper, transfer to an ovenproof dish and keep warm in a low oven while frying the remainder. Fry the remaining bacon and parsley and serve sprinkled over the hot cakes.

Salads

Warm or chilled potatoes add a new dimension to salads. Add flavour and colour to chunky cut potatoes with freshly cooked beetroot or sliced radishes. Or try sweet potato, baked until soft in the centre and then combined with a coriander and lime dressing, a perfect combination of refreshing and aromatic flavours.

TANGY POTATO SALAD

IF YOU LIKE A GOOD KICK OF MUSTARD, YOU'LL LOVE THIS COMBINATION. IT'S ALSO WELL FLAVOURED WITH TARRAGON, USED IN THE DRESSING AND AS A GARNISH.

SERVES EIGHT

INGREDIENTS

1.55kg/3lb small new or salad
  potatoes
30ml/2 tbsp white wine vinegar
15ml/1 tbsp Dijon mustard
45ml/3 tbsp vegetable or olive oil
75g/3oz/6 tbsp chopped red onion
125ml/4fl oz/½ cup mayonnaise
30ml/2 tbsp chopped fresh tarragon,
  or 7.5ml/1½ tsp dried tarragon
1 celery stick, thinly sliced
salt and ground black pepper
celery leaves, to garnish
tarragon leaves, to garnish

VARIATIONS
When available, use small red or even
blue potatoes to give a nice colour to
the salad.

1 Cook the potatoes in their skins in boiling salted water for about 15–20 minutes until tender. Drain well.

2 Mix together the vinegar and mustard, then slowly whisk in the oil.

3 When the potatoes are cool enough to handle, slice them into a large bowl.

4 Add the onion to the potatoes and pour the dressing over them. Season, then toss gently to combine. Leave to stand for at least 30 minutes.

5 Mix together the mayonnaise and tarragon. Gently stir into the potatoes, along with the celery. Serve garnished with celery leaves and tarragon.

TOULOUSE POTATO SALAD

*WELL-FLAVOURED SAUSAGES AND FIRM CHUNKY POTATOES MAKE A REALLY GREAT LUNCH,
SIMPLY DRESSED WITH A QUICK AND EASY VINAIGRETTE.*

3 Peel the potatoes if you like or leave in their skins, and cut into 5mm/¼in slices. Place them in a large bowl and sprinkle with the wine and shallots.

4 To make the vinaigrette, mix together the mustard and vinegar in a small bowl, then very slowly whisk in the oil. Season and pour over the potatoes.

SERVES FOUR

INGREDIENTS
  450g/1lb small waxy or
    salad potatoes
  30–45ml/2–3 tbsp dry white wine
  2 shallots, finely chopped
  15ml/1 tbsp chopped fresh parsley
  15ml/1 tbsp chopped fresh tarragon
  175g/6oz cooked garlic or
    Toulouse sausage
  chopped fresh parsley, to garnish
For the vinaigrette
  10ml/2 tsp Dijon mustard
  15ml/1 tbsp tarragon vinegar or
    white wine vinegar
  75ml/5 tbsp extra virgin olive oil
  salt and ground black pepper

1 Cook the potatoes in their skins in a large saucepan of boiling salted water for 10–12 minutes until tender.

2 Drain the potatoes, rinse under cold running water, then drain them again.

5 Add the chopped herbs to the potatoes and toss until well mixed.

6 Slice the sausage and toss with the potatoes. Season to taste and serve at room temperature with a parsley garnish.

THE SIMPLEST POTATO SALAD

THE SECRET OF THIS POTATO SALAD IS TO MIX THE POTATOES WITH THE DRESSING WHILE THEY ARE STILL HOT SO THAT THEY ABSORB IT. THIS IS PERFECT WITH GRILLED PORK, LAMB CHOPS OR ROAST CHICKEN OR FOR VEGETARIANS SERVE WITH A SELECTION OF ROASTED VEGETABLES.

SERVES FOUR TO SIX

INGREDIENTS
  675g/1½lb small new or
    salad potatoes
  4 spring onions
  45ml/3 tbsp olive oil
  15ml/1 tbsp white wine vinegar
  175ml/6fl oz/¾ cup good
    mayonnaise, preferably home-made
  45ml/3 tbsp snipped chives
  salt and ground black pepper

1 Cook the potatoes in their skins in a large saucepan of boiling salted water until tender.

2 Meanwhile, finely chop the white parts of the spring onions along with a little of the green parts; they look more attractive cut on the diagonal. Put to one side.

3 Whisk together the oil and vinegar. Drain the potatoes well and place them in a large bowl, then immediately toss lightly with the vinegar mixture and spring onions. Put the bowl to one side to cool.

4 Stir the mayonnaise and chives into the potatoes, season well and chill thoroughly until ready to serve. Adjust the seasoning before serving.

POTATO AND RADISH SALAD

RADISHES ADD A SPLASH OF CRUNCH AND PEPPERY FLAVOUR TO THIS HONEY-SCENTED SALAD. SO MANY POTATO SALADS ARE DRESSED IN A THICK SAUCE. THIS ONE HOWEVER, IS QUITE LIGHT AND COLOURFUL WITH A TASTY YET DELICATE DRESSING.

SERVES FOUR TO SIX

INGREDIENTS
  450g/1lb new or salad potatoes
  45ml/3 tbsp olive oil
  15ml/1 tbsp walnut or hazelnut oil
    (optional)
  30ml/2 tbsp wine vinegar
  10ml/2 tsp coarse-grain mustard
  5ml/1 tsp honey
  about 6–8 radishes, thinly sliced
  30ml/2 tbsp snipped chives
  salt and ground black pepper

VARIATIONS
Sliced celery, diced red onion and/or chopped walnuts would make good alternatives to the radishes if you can't get hold of any.

COOK'S TIP
For best effect, serve on a platter lined with frilly lettuce leaves.

1 Cook the potatoes in their skins in a large saucepan of boiling salted water until just tender. Drain the potatoes through a colander and leave to cool slightly. When cool enough to handle, cut the potatoes in half, but leave any small ones whole. Return the potatoes to a large bowl.

2 To make the dressing, place the oils, vinegar, mustard, honey and seasoning in a bowl. Mix them together until thoroughly combined.

3 Toss the dressing into the potatoes in the bowl while they are still cooling and leave to stand for an hour or so to allow the flavours to penetrate.

4 Finally mix in the sliced radishes and snipped chives and chill in the fridge until ready to serve.

5 When ready to serve, toss the salad mixture together again, as some of the dressing may have settled on the bottom and adjust the seasoning.

HOT HOT CAJUN POTATO SALAD

IN CAJUN COUNTRY WHERE TABASCO ORIGINATES, HOT MEANS REALLY HOT, SO YOU CAN GO TO TOWN WITH THIS SALAD IF YOU THINK YOU CAN TAKE IT!

SERVES SIX TO EIGHT

INGREDIENTS
    8 waxy potatoes
    1 green pepper, seeded and diced
    1 large gherkin, chopped
    4 spring onions, shredded
    3 hard-boiled eggs, shelled
     and chopped
    250ml/8fl oz/1 cup mayonnaise
    15ml/1 tbsp Dijon mustard
    salt and ground black pepper
    Tabasco sauce, to taste
    pinch or two of cayenne
    sliced gherkin, to garnish
    mayonnaise, to serve

1 Cook the potatoes in their skins in boiling salted water until tender. Drain and leave to cool. When they are cool enough to handle, peel them and cut into coarse chunks.

2 Place the potatoes in a large bowl and add the green pepper, gherkin, spring onions and hard-boiled eggs. Toss gently to combine.

3 In a separate bowl, mix the mayonnaise with the mustard and season with salt, black pepper and Tabasco sauce to taste.

4 Toss the dressing into the potato mixture and sprinkle with a pinch or two of cayenne. Serve with mayonnaise and a garnish of sliced gherkin.

CARIBBEAN POTATO SALAD

COLOURFUL VEGETABLES IN A CREAMY SMOOTH DRESSING MAKE THIS PIQUANT SALAD IDEAL TO SERVE ON ITS OWN OR WITH GRILLED OR COLD MEATS.

SERVES SIX

INGREDIENTS

900g/2lb small waxy or
  salad potatoes
2 red peppers, seeded and diced
2 celery sticks, finely chopped
1 shallot, finely chopped
2 or 3 spring onions, finely chopped
1 mild fresh green chilli, seeded and
  finely chopped
1 garlic clove, crushed
10ml/2 tsp finely snipped chives
10ml/2 tsp finely chopped basil
15ml/1 tbsp finely chopped parsley
15ml/1 tbsp single cream
30ml/2 tbsp salad cream
15ml/1 tbsp mayonnaise
5ml/1 tsp Dijon mustard
7.5ml/½ tbsp sugar
snipped chives, to garnish
chopped red chilli, to garnish

1 Cook the potatoes in a large saucepan of boiling water until tender but still firm. Drain and leave to one side. When cool enough to handle, cut into 2.5cm/1in cubes and place in a large salad bowl.

2 Add all the vegetables to the potatoes in the salad bowl, together with the chilli, garlic and all the chopped herbs.

3 Mix together the cream, salad cream, mayonnaise, mustard and sugar in a small bowl. Stir well until the mixture is thoroughly combined and forms a smooth dressing.

4 Pour the dressing over the potato mixture and stir gently to coat evenly. Serve garnished with the snipped chives, and chopped red chilli.

WARM POTATO SALAD WITH HERB DRESSING

TOSS THE POTATOES IN THE DRESSING AS SOON AS POSSIBLE, SO THE FLAVOURS ARE FULLY ABSORBED.
USE THE BEST OLIVE OIL FOR AN AUTHENTIC MEDITERRANEAN TASTE.

SERVES SIX

INGREDIENTS
  1kg/2¼lb waxy or salad potatoes
  90ml/6 tbsp extra virgin olive oil
  juice of 1 lemon
  1 garlic clove, very finely chopped
  30ml/2 tbsp chopped fresh herbs
    such as parsley, basil or thyme
  salt and ground black pepper
  basil leaves, to garnish

1 Cook the potatoes in their skins in boiling salted water, or steam them until tender.

2 Meanwhile make the dressing. Mix together the olive oil, lemon juice, garlic, herbs and season the mixture thoroughly.

3 Drain the potatoes and leave to cool slightly. When they are cool enough to handle, peel them. Cut the potatoes into chunks and place in a large bowl.

4 Pour the dressing over the potatoes while they are still warm and mix well. Serve at once, garnished with basil leaves and black pepper.

WARM HAZELNUT AND PISTACHIO SALAD

TWO KINDS OF CRUNCHY NUTS TURN ORDINARY POTATO SALAD INTO A REALLY SPECIAL
ACCOMPANIMENT. IT WOULD BE LOVELY WITH COLD SLICED ROAST BEEF, TONGUE OR HAM, BUT YOU
CAN SERVE IT ON ITS OWN AS A HEALTHY SNACK.

SERVES FOUR

INGREDIENTS
  900g/2lb small new or salad potatoes
  30ml/2 tbsp hazelnut or walnut oil
  60ml/4 tbsp sunflower oil
  juice of 1 lemon
  25g/1oz/¼ cup hazelnuts
  15 pistachio nuts
  salt and ground black pepper
  flat leaf parsley sprig, to garnish

VARIATION
Use chopped walnuts in place of the hazelnuts. Buy the broken pieces of nut, which are less expensive than walnut halves, but chop them smaller before adding to the salad.

1 Cook the potatoes in their skins in boiling salted water for about 10–15 minutes until tender.

2 Drain the potatoes well and leave to cool slightly.

3 Meanwhile mix together the hazelnut or walnut oil with the sunflower oil and lemon juice. Season well.

4 Using a sharp knife, roughly chop the nuts.

5 Put the cooled potatoes into a large bowl and pour the dressing over. Toss to combine.

6 Sprinkle the salad with the chopped nuts. Serve immediately, garnished with flat leaf parsley.

CURRIED POTATO SALAD
WITH MANGO DRESSING

THIS SWEET AND SPICY SALAD IS A WONDERFUL ACCOMPANIMENT TO ROASTED MEATS.

SERVES FOUR TO SIX

INGREDIENTS
 15ml/1 tbsp olive oil
 1 onion, sliced into rings
 1 garlic clove, crushed
 5ml/1 tsp ground cumin
 5ml/1 tsp ground coriander
 1 mango, peeled, stoned and diced
 30ml/2 tbsp demerara sugar
 30ml/2 tbsp lime juice
 900g/2lb new potatoes, cut in half
  and boiled
 15ml/1 tbsp sesame seeds
 salt and ground black pepper
 deep fried coriander leaves,
  to garnish

1 Heat the oil in a frying pan and fry the onion and garlic over a low heat for 10 minutes until they start to brown.

2 Stir in the cumin and coriander and fry for a few seconds. Stir in the mango and sugar and fry for 5 minutes, until soft. Remove the pan from the heat and squeeze in the lime juice. Season.

3 Place the potatoes in a large bowl and spoon the mango dressing over. Sprinkle with sesame seeds and serve whilst the dressing is still warm. Garnish with the coriander leaves.

POTATO SALAD WITH CAPERS
AND BLACK OLIVES

A DISH FROM SOUTHERN ITALY, THE COMBINATION OF OLIVES, CAPERS AND ANCHOVIES IS PERFECT.

SERVES FOUR TO SIX

INGREDIENTS
 900g/2lb large white potatoes
 50ml/2fl oz/¼ cup white wine vinegar
 75ml/5 tbsp olive oil
 30ml/2 tbsp chopped flat leaf parsley
 30ml/2 tbsp capers, finely chopped
 50g/2oz/½ cup pitted black olives,
  chopped in half
 3 garlic cloves, finely chopped
 50g/2oz marinated anchovies
  (unsalted)
 salt and ground black pepper

VARIATION
If you want to serve this dish to vegetarians, simply omit the anchovies, it tastes delicious even without them.

1 Boil the potatoes in their skins in a large pan for 20 minutes or until just tender. Remove from the pan using a slotted spoon and place them in a separate bowl.

2 When the potatoes are cool enough to handle, peel off the skins.

3 Cut the peeled potatoes into even chunks and place in a large, flat earthenware dish.

4 Mix together the vinegar and oil, season to taste and add the parsley, capers, olives and garlic. Toss carefully to combine and then pour over the potato chunks,

5 Lay the anchovies on top of the salad. Cover with a cloth and leave the salad to settle for 30 minutes or so before serving to allow the flavours to penetrate.

BAKED SWEET POTATO SALAD

THIS SALAD HAS A TRULY TROPICAL TASTE AND IS IDEAL SERVED WITH ASIAN OR CARIBBEAN DISHES.

SERVES FOUR TO SIX

INGREDIENTS
  1kg/2¼lb sweet potatoes
For the dressing
  45ml/3 tbsp chopped fresh coriander
  juice of 1 lime
  150ml/¼ pint/⅔ cup natural yogurt
For the salad
  1 red pepper, seeded and
   finely diced
  3 celery sticks, finely diced
  ¼ red skinned onion, finely chopped
  1 red chilli, finely chopped
  salt and ground black pepper
  coriander leaves, to garnish

1 Preheat the oven to 200°C/400°F/ Gas 6. Wash and pierce the potatoes all over and bake in the oven for 40 minutes or until tender.

2 Meanwhile, mix the dressing ingredients together in a bowl and season to taste. Chill while you prepare the remaining ingredients.

3 In a large bowl mix the red pepper, celery, onion and chilli together.

4 Remove the potatoes from the oven and when cool enough to handle, peel them. Cut the potatoes into cubes and add them to the bowl. Drizzle the dressing over and toss carefully. Season again to taste and serve, garnished with fresh coriander.

MARINATED BEEF <u>AND</u> POTATO SALAD

THIS DISH NEEDS TO MARINATE OVERNIGHT, BUT ONCE YOU HAVE DONE THAT IT IS VERY QUICK TO ASSEMBLE AND MAKES A SUBSTANTIAL MAIN MEAL.

SERVES SIX

INGREDIENTS
   900g/2lb sirloin steak
   3 large white potatoes
   ½ red pepper, seeded and diced
   ½ green pepper, seeded and diced
   1 small red skinned onion,
    finely chopped
   2 garlic cloves, crushed
   4 spring onions, diagonally sliced
   1 small cos lettuce, leaves torn
   salt and ground black pepper
   olive oil, to serve
   Parmesan cheese shavings, to serve
For the marinade
   120ml/4fl oz/½ cup olive oil
   120ml/4fl oz/½ cup red wine vinegar
   90ml/6 tbsp soy sauce

1 Place the beef in a large, non-metallic container. Mix together the marinade ingredients. Season with pepper and pour over the meat.

2 Cover and leave to marinate for several hours, or overnight.

3 To prepare the salad, drain the marinade from the meat and pat the joint dry. Preheat the frying pan, cut the meat carefully into thin slices and fry for a few minutes until just cooked on each side, but still slightly pink. Set aside to cool.

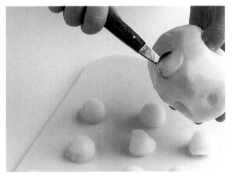

4 Using a melon baller, scoop out rounds from each potato. Boil in lightly salted water for 5 minutes or until just tender.

5 Drain and transfer to a bowl, and add the remaining ingredients. Transfer to a plate with the beef. Drizzle with a little extra olive oil and serve with Parmesan.

New Potato and Quail's Egg Salad

Freshly cooked eggs and tender potatoes mix perfectly with the flavour of celery salt and the peppery tasting rocket leaves.

SERVES SIX

INGREDIENTS
900g/2lb new potatoes
50g/2oz/4 tbsp butter
15ml/1 tbsp snipped chives
a pinch of celery salt
a pinch of paprika
12 quail's eggs
a few rocket leaves
salt and ground black pepper
snipped chives, to garnish

COOK'S TIP
You can buy bags of rocket, on its own, or mixed with other leaves, in many supermarkets. It is also easy to grow from seed and makes a worthwhile addition to a herb patch.

1 Boil the potatoes in a large saucepan of salted water for 20 minutes or until tender. Meanwhile, beat the butter and chives together with the celery salt and the paprika.

2 Whilst the potatoes are cooking, boil the eggs for 3 minutes, drain and plunge into cold water. Peel the eggs under running water.

3 Arrange the rocket leaves on plates and divide the eggs between. Drain the potatoes and add the seasoned butter. Toss well to melt the butter and spoon the potatoes on to the plates. Garnish the salad with a few more chives.

Beetroot and Potato Salad

A brightly coloured salad with a lovely texture. The sweetness of the beetroot contrasts perfectly with the tangy dressing.

SERVES FOUR

INGREDIENTS
4 medium beetroot
4 potatoes, peeled and diced
1 red-skinned onion, finely chopped
150ml/¼ pint/⅔ cup low-fat yogurt
10ml/2 tsp cider vinegar
2 small sweet and sour cucumbers, finely chopped
10ml/2 tsp creamed horseradish
salt and ground black pepper
parsley sprigs, to garnish

COOK'S TIP
To save yourself time and energy, buy ready cooked and peeled beetroot. They are readily available in most supermarkets.

1 Boil the beetroot in a large saucepan, in plenty of water for 40 minutes or until tender.

2 Meanwhile, boil the potatoes in a separate saucepan for 20 minutes until just tender.

3 When the beetroot are cooked, rinse and pull the skins off, chop into rough pieces and place in a bowl. Drain the potatoes and add to the bowl with the onions. Mix the yogurt, vinegar, cucumbers and horseradish. Reserve a little for a garnish and pour the remainder over the salad. Toss and serve with parsley sprigs and dressing.

ITALIAN SALAD

A COMBINATION OF ANTIPASTO INGREDIENTS AND POTATOES MAKES THIS A VERY SUBSTANTIAL DISH.

SERVES SIX

INGREDIENTS
  1 aubergine, sliced
  75ml/5 tbsp olive oil
  2 garlic cloves, cut into slivers
  4 sun-dried tomatoes in oil, halved
  2 red peppers, halved, seeded and
    cut into large chunks
  2 large baking potatoes, cut
    into wedges
  10ml/2 tsp mixed dried Italian herbs
  30–45ml/2–3 tbsp balsamic vinegar
  salt and ground black pepper

1 Preheat the oven to 200°C/400°F/ Gas 6. Place the aubergines in a medium roasting tin with the olive oil, garlic and sun-dried tomatoes. Lay the pepper chunks over the aubergines.

2 Lay the potato wedges on top of the other ingredients in the roasting tin. Scatter the herbs over and season with salt and black pepper. Cover the tin with foil and bake in the oven for 45 minutes.

3 Remove from the oven and turn the vegetables over. Then return to the oven and cook uncovered for 30 minutes. Remove the vegetables with a slotted spoon. Add the vinegar and seasoning to the pan, whisk and pour over the vegetables. Garnish with salt and black pepper.

PINK FIR APPLE POTATO SALAD

A RICH MUSTARD SAUCE GIVES THE POTATOES ADDED FLAVOUR AND COLOUR.

SERVES FOUR TO SIX

INGREDIENTS
5 eggs
30–45ml/2–3 tbsp Dijon mustard
200g/7oz jar mayonnaise
3 celery sticks, finely chopped
115g/4oz bacon lardons
900g/2lb Pink Fir Apple potatoes
30ml/2 tbsp chopped flat leaf parsley
salt and ground black pepper

1 Place the eggs carefully into a saucepan of water and bring to the boil. Simmer for 5–8 minutes, drain and plunge the eggs straight into a bowl containing cold water.

2 Peel the eggs and mash three of them in a large bowl with a fork. Stir in the mustard, mayonnaise, celery and seasoning. Thin down with a little water if you wish. Set aside.

3 Dry fry the bacon until crisp and toss half of it into the mayonnaise mixture. Reserve the remainder.

4 Boil the potatoes for 20 minutes until tender. Drain and leave to cool. Toss into the mayonnaise mixture and spoon into a serving platter. Slice the remaining eggs and scatter over the salad with the reserved bacon pieces. Scatter the parsley over the top and serve.

Side Dishes

Classic potato side dishes have long been essential partners to numerous main courses. For a change, try something a little different to serve alongside a simple roast, such as Boulangère Potatoes or colourful Candied Sweet Potatoes. And add a garlic twist to a steaming plate of mash – perfect on its own or to go with a main course.

MARQUIS POTATOES

A VARIATION ON THE DUCHESSE MIXTURE, FINISHED WITH A DELICIOUSLY TANGY TOMATO MIXTURE SET IN THE CENTRE OF THE POTATO NEST.

SERVES SIX

INGREDIENTS
   900g/2 lb floury potatoes
   450g/1lb ripe tomatoes
   15ml/1tbsp olive oil
   2 shallots, finely chopped
   25g/1oz/2 tbsp butter
   3 egg yolks
   60ml/4 tbsp milk
   chopped fresh parsley, to garnish
   sea salt and ground black pepper

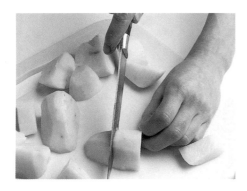

1 Peel and cut the potatoes into small chunks, boil in lightly salted water for 20 minutes or until very tender. Meanwhile, blanch the tomatoes in boiling water and then plunge into a bowl of cold water. Peel the skins and then scoop the seeds out. Chop the tomato flesh.

4 Grease a baking sheet. Spoon the potato into a piping bag fitted with a medium star nozzle. Pipe six oval nests onto the baking sheet. Beat the remaining egg with a little water and carefully brush over the potato. Grill for 5 minutes or until golden.

5 Spoon the tomato mixture inside the nests and top with a little parsley. Serve them immediately.

2 Heat the olive oil in a large frying pan and fry the shallots for 2 minutes stirring continuously. Add the chopped tomatoes to the pan and fry for a further 10 minutes until the moisture has evaporated. Set aside.

3 Drain the potatoes through a colander and return to the pan and allow the steam to dry off. Cool slightly and mash well with the butter and 2 of the egg yolks and the milk. Season with salt and ground black pepper.

BERRICHONNE POTATOES

A POTATO DISH WITH A DIFFERENCE. THE TOP OF THE POTATOES WILL BE CRISPY WITH A SOFTLY
COOKED BASE IN THE STOCK, ONIONS AND BACON.

SERVES FOUR

INGREDIENTS
  900g/2 lb maincrop potatoes
  25g/1oz/2 tbsp butter
  1 onion, finely chopped
  115g/4oz unsmoked streaky bacon,
    rinds removed
  350ml/12fl oz /1½ cups
    vegetable stock
  chopped parsley, to garnish
  sea salt and ground black pepper

1 Preheat the oven to 200°C/400°F/
Gas 6 Peel the potatoes and trim them
into barrel shapes. Leave the potatoes
to stand in a bowl of cold water.

2 Melt the butter in a frying pan. Add
the onions, stir and cover with a lid.
Cook for 2–3 minutes, until they are soft
but not brown.

3 Chop the bacon and add to the
onions, cover and cook for 2 minutes.

4 Spoon the onion mixture into the
base of a 1.5 litres /2½ pints/6¼ cups
rectangular shallow ovenproof dish. Lay
the potatoes over the onion mixture and
pour the stock over, making sure that it
comes halfway up the sides of them.
Season and cook for 1 hour. Garnish
with chopped parsley.

BIARRITZ POTATOES

A COMBINATION OF CLASSIC MASHED POTATOES WITH FINELY DICED HAM AND PEPPERS MIXED IN.
THIS DISH IS GREAT SERVED WITH ROASTED CHICKEN.

SERVES FOUR

INGREDIENTS
  900g/2lb floury potatoes
  50g/2oz/4 tbsp butter
  90ml/6 tbsp milk
  50g/2oz cooked ham, finely diced
  1 red pepper, deseeded and
  finely diced
  15ml/1tbsp chopped fresh parsley
  sea salt and ground black pepper

1   Peel and cut the potatoes into chunks. Boil in lightly salted water for 20 minutes or until very tender.

2   Drain and return the potatoes to the pan and allow the steam to dry off over a low heat.

3   Either mash or pass the potatoes through a potato ricer. Add the butter and milk and stir in the cooked ham, peppers and parsley. Season and serve.

LYONNAISE POTATOES

TWO SIMPLE INGREDIENTS ARE PREPARED SEPARATELY AND THEN TOSSED TOGETHER TO CREATE THE
PERFECT COMBINATION. THESE POTATOES GO VERY WELL WITH A SIMPLE MEAT DISH, SUCH AS STEAK
OR PORK CHOPS. SERVE WITH A BOWL OF FRENCH BEANS, TOSSED IN BUTTER.

SERVES SIX

INGREDIENTS
  900g/2lb floury potatoes
  vegetable oil for shallow frying
  25g/1oz/2 tbsp butter
  15ml/1 tbsp olive oil
  2 medium onions, sliced into rings
  sea salt
  15ml/1 tbsp chopped fresh parsley

VARIATION
For a more substantial version of this dish, ham or bacon can be added. Use about 50g/2oz chopped roast ham or bacon and fry with the onions until cooked through.

1   Scrub the potatoes clean and cook in a large saucepan with plenty of boiling water for 10 minutes.

2   Drain the potatoes through a colander and leave to cool slightly. When the potatoes are cool enough to handle, peel and finely slice them.

3   Heat the vegetable oil and shallow fry the potatoes in two batches for about 10 minutes until crisp, turning occasionally.

4   Meanwhile, melt the butter with the oil in a frying pan and fry the onions for 10 minutes until golden. Drain on kitchen paper.

5   Remove the potatoes with a slotted spoon and drain on kitchen paper. Toss with sea salt and carefully mix with the onions. Sprinkle with the parsley.

BYRON POTATOES

A MEAL IN ITSELF, THIS DISH IS BASED ON BAKED POTATOES WITH A RICH CREAMY CHEESE FILLING.

SERVES SIX

INGREDIENTS
    3 baking potatoes
    115g/4oz/1 cup mature Cheddar
      cheese, grated
    90ml/6 tbsp single cream
    sea salt and ground black pepper

COOK'S TIP
You can speed up this recipe by starting
the potatoes off in the microwave. Prick
the scrubbed potatoes well and place in
a covered microwave dish. Cook on high
until starting to soften – test after two
minutes, then every minute. Place in the
oven to crisp the skins and finish
cooking for about 45 minutes.

1 Preheat the oven to 200°C/400°F/
Gas 6. Scrub the potatoes and pat dry.
Prick each one with a fork and cook
directly on the middle shelf for 1 hour
20 minutes.

2 Remove the potatoes from the oven
and halve. Place the halves on a baking
sheet and make shallow dips in the
centre of each potato, raising the potato
up at the edges.

3 Mix the cheese and cream together
and divide between the potatoes.

4 Grill for 5 minutes until the cheese
has melted and started to bubble.
Serve hot, sprinkled with sea salt and
black pepper.

BOULANGÈRE POTATOES

*LAYERS OF POTATO AND ONIONS COOKED IN BUTTER AND STOCK. A DELICIOUS SAVOURY POTATO DISH
THAT MAKES A GREAT ACCOMPANIMENT TO BOTH MEAT AND FISH.*

SERVES SIX

INGREDIENTS
    butter for greasing
    450g/1lb maincrop potatoes, very
      finely sliced
    2 onions, finely sliced into rings
    2 garlic cloves, crushed
    50g/2oz/4 tbsp butter, diced
    300ml/½ pint/1¼ cups
      vegetable stock
    chopped parsley
    sea salt and ground black pepper

VARIATION
If you want to make this dish more
substantial, add some grated cheese,
sprinkled over the top just before you
bake it.

1 Preheat the oven to 180°C/350°F/
Gas 4. Grease the base and sides of a
1.5 litre/2½ pint/6¼ cup ovenproof dish.

2 Line the dish with some of the
sliced potatoes. Scatter some onions
and garlic on top. Layer up the
remaining potatoes and onions,
seasoning between each layer.

3 Push the vegetables down into the
dish and dot the top with the butter.
Pour the stock over and bake in the
oven for 1½ hours covering with foil
after 1 hour if the top starts to over
brown. Serve with parsley and plenty of
salt and pepper sprinkled over the top.

POTATO LATKES

LATKES ARE TRADITIONAL JEWISH POTATO PANCAKES, FRIED UNTIL GOLDEN AND CRISP AND SERVED WITH HOT SALT BEEF OR APPLE SAUCE AND SOURED CREAM.

SERVES FOUR

INGREDIENTS
    2 medium floury potatoes
    1 onion
    1 large egg, beaten
    30ml/2 tbsp medium-ground
      matzo meal
    vegetable oil, for frying
    salt and ground black pepper

1 Coarsely grate the potatoes and the onion. Put them in a large colander but don't rinse them. Press them down, squeezing out as much of the thick starchy liquid as possible. Transfer the potato mixture to a bowl.

2 Immediately stir in the beaten egg. Add the matzo meal, stirring gently to mix. Season with salt and plenty of pepper.

VARIATION
Try using equal quantities of potatoes and Jerusalem artichokes for a really distinct flavour.

3 Heat a 1cm/½in layer of oil in a heavy-based frying pan for a few minutes (test it by throwing in a small piece of bread – it should sizzle). Take a spoonful of the potato mixture and lower it carefully into the oil. Continue adding spoonfuls, leaving space between each one.

4 Flatten the pancakes slightly with the back of a spoon. Fry for a few minutes until the latkes are golden brown on the underside, carefully turn them over and continue frying until golden brown.

5 Drain the latkes on kitchen paper, then transfer to an ovenproof serving dish and keep warm in a low oven while frying the remainder. Serve hot.

SWISS SOUFFLÉ POTATOES

A FABULOUS COMBINATION OF RICH AND SATISFYING INGREDIENTS — CHEESE, EGGS, CREAM, BUTTER AND POTATOES. THIS IS PERFECT FOR COLD-WEATHER EATING.

SERVES FOUR

INGREDIENTS
4 floury baking potatoes
115g/4oz/1 cup Gruyère
  cheese, grated
115g/4oz/8 tbsp herb-flavoured butter
60ml/4 tbsp double cream
2 eggs, separated
salt and ground black pepper

1 Preheat the oven to 220°C/425°F/ Gas 7. Prick the potatoes all over with a fork. Bake for 1–1½ hours until tender. Remove them from the oven and reduce the temperature to 180°C/350°F/Gas 4.

2 Cut each potato in half and scoop out the flesh into a bowl. Return the potato shells to the oven to crisp them up while making the filling.

3 Mash the potato flesh using a fork, then add the Gruyère, herb-flavoured butter, cream, egg yolks and seasoning. Beat well until smooth.

4 Whisk the egg whites in a separate bowl until they hold stiff but not dry peaks, then carefully fold into the potato mixture.

5 Pile the mixture back into the potato shells and place on a baking sheet. Bake in the oven for 20–25 minutes until risen and golden brown.

6 Serve the potatoes hot, sprinkled with fresh, snipped chives, if wished, and a bowl of mayonnaise to the side.

YORKSHIRE POTATO PUFFS

MINI YORKSHIRE PUDDINGS WITH A SOFT CENTRE OF HERBY POTATO MASH WILL BE DELICIOUS WITH THE SUNDAY ROAST, OR SERVE THEM FOR A WEEKDAY SUPPER WITH THE FAMILY'S FAVOURITE SAUSAGES.

MAKES SIX

INGREDIENTS
275g/10oz floury potatoes
creamy milk and butter for mashing
5ml/1 tsp chopped fresh parsley
5ml/1 tsp chopped fresh tarragon
75g/3oz/⅔ cup plain flour
1 egg
120ml/4fl oz/½ cup milk
vegetable oil or sunflower fat,
    for baking
salt and ground black pepper

1 Cook the potatoes in a large saucepan of boiling water until tender, then mash with a little creamy milk and butter.

2 Stir in the chopped parsley and tarragon and season well to taste. Preheat the oven to 200°C/400°F/Gas 6.

3 Process the flour, egg, milk and a little salt in a food processor fitted with the metal blade or a blender to make a smooth batter.

4 Place about 2.5ml/½ tsp of oil or a small knob of sunflower fat in each of six ramekin dishes and place in the oven on a baking tray for 2–3 minutes until the oil or fat is very hot.

5 Working quickly, pour a small amount of batter (about 20ml/4 tsp) into each ramekin dish. Add a heaped tablespoon of the mashed potatoes and then pour an equal amount of the remaining batter in each dish. Bake for 15–20 minutes until the puddings are puffy and golden brown.

6 Using a palette knife, carefully ease the puddings out of the ramekin dishes and arrange on a large warm serving dish. Serve at once.

COOK'S TIP
Cook and mash the potatoes the day before to save time making a quick supper dish, or to prepare for a dinner party in advance.

GARLICKY ROASTIES

POTATOES ROASTED IN THEIR SKINS RETAIN A DEEP, EARTHY TASTE (AND, AS A BONUS, ABSORB LESS FAT TOO) WHILE THE GARLIC MELLOWS ON COOKING TO GIVE A PUNGENT BUT NOT OVERLY-STRONG TASTE TO SERVE ALONGSIDE OR SQUEEZED OVER AS A GARNISH.

SERVES FOUR

INGREDIENTS
1kg/2¼lb small floury potatoes
60–75ml/4–5 tbsp sunflower oil
10ml/2 tsp walnut oil
2 whole garlic bulbs, unpeeled
salt

COOK'S TIP
If anyone really does not want to try the garlic paste, you can save the cloves to squeeze into your next pot of soup or mashed potato.

1 Preheat the oven to 240°C/475°F/ Gas 9. Place the potatoes in a pan of cold water and bring to the boil. Drain.

2 Combine the oils in a roasting tin and place in the oven to get really hot. Add the potatoes and garlic and coat in oil.

3 Sprinkle with salt and roast for 10 minutes. Reduce the heat to 200°C/400°F/Gas 6. Continue roasting, basting occasionally, for 30–40 minutes.

4 Serve each portion with several cloves of garlic.

POTATOES, PEPPERS AND SHALLOTS ROASTED WITH ROSEMARY

THESE POTATOES SOAK UP BOTH THE TASTE AND WONDERFUL AROMAS OF THE SHALLOTS AND ROSEMARY — JUST WAIT TILL YOU OPEN THE OVEN DOOR.

<u>SERVES FOUR</u>

INGREDIENTS
   500g/1¼lb waxy potatoes
   12 shallots
   2 sweet yellow peppers
   olive oil
   2 rosemary sprigs
   salt and ground black pepper
   crushed peppercorns, to garnish

1 Preheat the oven to 200°C/400°F/ Gas 6. Par-boil the potatoes in their skins in boiling salted water for 5 minutes. Drain and when they are cool, peel them and halve lengthways.

COOK'S TIP
Liven up a simple dish of roast or grilled lamb or chicken with these delicious and easy potatoes.

2 Peel the shallots, allowing them to fall into their natural segments. Cut each sweet pepper lengthways into eight strips, discarding seeds and pith.

3 Oil a shallow ovenproof dish thoroughly with olive oil. Arrange the potatoes and peppers in alternating rows and stud with the shallots.

4 Cut the rosemary sprigs into 5cm/2in lengths and tuck among the vegetables. Season the vegetables generously with salt and pepper, add the olive oil and roast, uncovered, for 30–40 minutes until all the vegetables are tender. Turn the vegetables occasionally to cook and brown evenly. Serve hot or at room temperature, with crushed peppercorns.

GLAZED SWEET POTATOES WITH BACON

SMOKY BACON IS THE PERFECT ADDITION TO THESE MELT-IN-THE-MOUTH SUGAR-TOPPED POTATOES. THEY TASTE GREAT AS A CHANGE FROM ROAST POTATOES, WITH ROAST DUCK OR CHICKEN.

SERVES FOUR TO SIX

INGREDIENTS
butter, for greasing
900g/2lb sweet potatoes
115g/4oz/½ cup soft light
  brown sugar
30ml/2 tbsp lemon juice
45ml/3 tbsp butter
4 strips smoked lean bacon, cut
  into matchsticks
salt and ground black pepper
1 flat leaf parsley sprig, to garnish

1 Preheat the oven to 190°C/375°F/ Gas 5 and lightly butter a shallow ovenproof dish. Cut each unpeeled sweet potato crosswise into three and cook in boiling water, covered, for about 25 minutes until just tender.

2 Drain and leave to cool. When cool enough to handle, peel and slice thickly. Arrange in a single layer, overlapping the slices, in the prepared dish.

3 Sprinkle over the sugar and lemon juice and dot with butter.

4 Top with the bacon and season well. Bake uncovered for 35–40 minutes, basting once or twice.

5 The potatoes are ready once they are tender, test them with a knife to make sure. Remove from the oven once they are cooked.

6 Preheat the grill to a high heat. Sprinkle the potatoes with parsley. Place the pan under the grill for 2–3 minutes until the potatoes are browned and the bacon is crispy. Serve hot.

HERBY POTATO BAKE

WONDERFULLY CREAMY POTATOES WELL FLAVOURED WITH LOTS OF FRESH HERBS AND SPRINKLED WITH CHEESE TO MAKE A GOLDEN, CRUNCHY TOPPING.

SERVES FOUR

INGREDIENTS
    butter, for greasing
    675g/1½lb waxy potatoes
    25g/1oz/2 tbsp butter
    1 onion, finely chopped
    1 garlic clove, crushed
    2 eggs
    300ml/½ pint/1¼ cups crème fraîche
      or double cream
    115g/4oz/1 cup Gruyère, grated
    60ml/4 tbsp chopped mixed fresh
      herbs, such as chervil, thyme,
      chives and parsley
    freshly grated nutmeg
    salt and ground black pepper

1 Place a baking sheet in the oven and preheat to 190°C/375°F/Gas 5. Butter an ovenproof dish.

2 Peel the potatoes and cut them into matchsticks. Set aside while you make up the sauce mixture. Start by melting the butter in a pan and fry the onion and garlic until softened. Remove from the heat to cool slightly. In a large bowl, whisk together the eggs, crème fraîche or cream and about half of the grated Gruyère cheese.

3 Stir in the onion mixture, herbs, potatoes, salt, pepper and nutmeg. Spoon the mixture into the prepared dish and sprinkle over the remaining cheese. Bake on the hot baking sheet for 50 minutes to 1 hour until the top is golden brown. Serve immediately, straight from the dish, as this will ensure that the potatoes stay really hot.

OVEN CHIP ROASTIES

THIS EASY ALTERNATIVE TO FRIED CHIPS TASTES JUST AS GOOD AND IS MUCH EASIER TO COOK.

SERVES FOUR TO SIX

INGREDIENTS
    150ml/¼ pint/⅔ cup olive oil
    4 medium to large baking potatoes
    5ml/1 tsp mixed dried herbs
      (optional)
    sea salt flakes
    mayonnaise, to serve

VARIATION
Sweet potatoes also make fine oven chips. Prepare and roast in the same way as above, although you may find they do not take as long to cook.

COOK'S TIP
Oven chip roasties make great mid-week suppers served with fried eggs, mushrooms and tomatoes.

1 Preheat the oven to the highest temperature, generally 240°C/475°F/Gas 9. Lightly oil a large shallow roasting tin and place it in the oven to get really hot while you prepare the potatoes.

2 Cut the potatoes in half lengthwise, then into long thin wedges, or thicker ones if you prefer. Brush each side lightly with oil.

3 When the oven is really hot, remove the pan carefully and scatter the potato wedges over it, spreading them out in a single layer over the hot oil.

4 Sprinkle the potato wedges with the herbs and salt and roast for about 20 minutes, or longer if they are thicker, until they are golden brown, crisp and lightly puffy. Remove from the oven and serve with a dollop of mayonnaise.

GARLIC MASHED POTATOES

THESE CREAMY MASHED POTATOES ARE DELICIOUS WITH ALL KINDS OF ROAST OR SAUTÉED MEATS AS WELL AS VEGETARIAN MAIN DISHES AND ALTHOUGH IT SEEMS LIKE A LOT OF GARLIC, THE FLAVOUR TURNS SWEET AND SUBTLE WHEN COOKED IN THIS WAY.

SERVES SIX TO EIGHT

INGREDIENTS
   3 whole garlic bulbs, separated into
      cloves, unpeeled
   115g/4oz/8 tbsp unsalted butter
   1.5kg/3lb baking potatoes, quartered
   120–175ml/4–6fl oz/½–¾ cup milk
   salt and ground white pepper

COOK'S TIP
This recipe makes a very light, creamy purée. Use less milk to achieve a firmer purée, more for a softer purée. Be sure the milk is almost boiling or it will cool the potato mixture. Keep the purée warm in a bowl over simmering water.

1 Bring a small saucepan of water to the boil over a high heat. Add two thirds of the garlic cloves and boil for 2 minutes. Drain the pan and then peel the garlic cloves.

2 Place the remaining garlic cloves in a roasting tin and bake in a preheated oven at 200°C/400°F/Gas 6 for 30–40 minutes.

3 In a heavy-based frying pan, melt 50g/2oz/4 tbsp of the butter over a low heat. Add the blanched garlic cloves, then cover and cook gently for 20–25 minutes until very tender and just golden, shaking the pan and stirring occasionally. Do not allow the garlic to scorch or brown.

4 Remove the pan from the heat and cool. Spoon the garlic and melted butter into a blender or a food processor fitted with the metal blade and process until smooth. Tip into a bowl, press clear film on to the surface to prevent a skin forming and set aside.

5 Cook the potatoes in boiling salted water until tender, then drain and pass through a food mill or press through a sieve back into the saucepan. Return the pan to a medium heat and, using a wooden spoon, stir the potatoes for 1–2 minutes to dry out completely. Remove the pan from the heat.

6 Warm the milk over a medium-high heat until bubbles form around the edge. Gradually beat the milk, remaining butter and garlic purée into the potatoes. Season with salt, if needed, and white pepper, and serve hot, with the roasted garlic cloves.

CHAMP

SIMPLE BUT UNBELIEVABLY TASTY, THIS TRADITIONAL IRISH WAY WITH MASHED POTATOES MAKES AN EXCELLENT COMPANION FOR A HEARTY STEW OF LAMB OR BEEF.

SERVES FOUR

INGREDIENTS
900g/2lb floury potatoes
1 small bunch spring onions,
  finely chopped
150ml/¼ pint/⅔ cup milk
50g/2oz/4 tbsp butter
salt and ground black pepper

COOK'S TIP
If you make too much mashed potato, don't worry. It keeps well in the fridge and simply needs re-heating.

1 Cut the potatoes up into large chunks. Place in a large pan and cook in boiling water for 20 minutes until tender.

2 Meanwhile put the spring onions into a saucepan with the milk. Bring to the boil then reduce the heat and simmer until the spring onions are just tender.

3 Drain the potatoes well and leave to cool. When they are cool enough to handle, peel and return to the saucepan. Put the pan on the heat and, using a wooden spoon, stir for 1 minute until the moisture has evaporated. Remove the pan from the heat.

4 Mash the potatoes with the milk and spring onions and season. Serve hot with a pool of melted butter in each portion.

PERFECT CREAMED POTATOES

REAL CREAMED POTATOES ARE A SIMPLE LUXURY YOU WILL FIND IN ANY FASHIONABLE RESTAURANT TODAY BUT ARE SO EASY TO MAKE AT HOME AS WELL.

SERVES FOUR

INGREDIENTS
900g/2lb firm but not waxy
    potatoes, diced
45ml/3 tbsp extra virgin olive oil
about 150ml/¼ pint/⅔ cup hot milk
freshly grated nutmeg
a few fresh basil leaves or parsley
    sprigs, chopped
salt and ground black pepper
basil leaves, to garnish
fried bacon, to serve

COOK'S TIP
Choosing the right potato makes all the difference to creamed ones. A waxy variety won't be light and fluffy, and a potato which breaks down too quickly on boiling will become a slurry.

1 Cook the potatoes in boiling water until just tender but not too mushy. Drain very well. Press the potatoes through a special potato "ricer" (rather like a large garlic press) or mash them well with a potato masher. Do not use a food processor as it can give the potatoes a gluey consistency.

2 Beat in olive oil and enough hot milk to make a smooth, thick purée.

3 Flavour to taste with the nutmeg and seasoning, then stir in the chopped fresh herbs. Spoon into a warm serving dish and serve at once, garnished with basil leaves and fried bacon.

POTATOES WITH RED CHILLIES

IF YOU LIKE CHILLIES, YOU'LL LOVE THESE POTATOES! IF YOU'RE NOT A FAN OF FIERY FLAVOURS, THEN SIMPLY LEAVE OUT ALL THE CHILLI SEEDS AND USE THE FLESH BY ITSELF.

SERVES FOUR

INGREDIENTS
12–14 small new or salad
    potatoes, halved
30ml/2 tbsp vegetable oil
2.5ml/½ tsp crushed dried
    red chillies
2.5ml/½ tsp white cumin seeds
2.5ml/½ tsp fennel seeds
2.5ml/½ tsp crushed coriander seeds
5ml/1 tsp salt
1 onion, sliced
1–4 fresh red chillies, chopped
15ml/1 tbsp chopped fresh coriander
chopped fresh coriander, to garnish

COOK'S TIP
To prepare fresh chillies, slit down one side and scrape out the seeds, unless you want a really hot dish. Finely slice or chop the flesh. Wear rubber gloves if you have very sensitive skin.

1 Cook the potatoes in boiling salted water until tender but still firm. Remove from the heat and drain off the water. Set aside until needed.

2 In a deep frying pan, heat the oil over a medium-high heat, then reduce the heat to medium. Add the crushed chillies, cumin, fennel and coriander seeds and salt and fry, stirring, for 30–40 seconds.

3 Add the sliced onion and fry until golden brown. Then add the potatoes, red chillies and coriander and stir well.

4 Reduce the heat to very low, then cover and cook for 5–7 minutes. Serve the potatoes hot, garnished with more fresh coriander.

STRAW POTATO CAKE

THIS DISH GETS ITS NAME FROM ITS INTERESTING STRAW-LIKE TEXTURE.

SERVES FOUR

INGREDIENTS
450g/1lb firm baking potatoes
25ml/1½ tbsp butter, melted
15ml/1 tbsp vegetable oil
salt and ground black pepper

1 Peel and grate the potatoes, then toss with melted butter and season.

2 Heat the oil in a large heavy-based frying pan. Add the potato and press down to form an even layer that covers the base of the pan. Cook over a medium heat for 7–10 minutes until the base is well browned.

3 Loosen the cake if it has stuck to the bottom by shaking the pan or running a knife under it.

4 To turn the cake, invert a large baking tray over the frying pan and, holding it tightly against the pan, turn them both over together. Lift off the frying pan, return it to the heat and add a little more oil if it looks dry. Slide the potato cake back into the frying pan, browned side uppermost, and continue cooking until the underside is crisp and golden.

5 Serve the cake hot, cut into individual wedges.

COOK'S TIP
Another nice way to serve this dish is to make several small cakes instead of a large one. They will not take quite so long to cook, so follow the method as for the large cake, but adjust the cooking time accordingly.

SAUTÉED POTATOES

THESE ROSEMARY-SCENTED, CRISP GOLDEN POTATOES ARE A FAVOURITE IN FRENCH HOUSEHOLDS.

SERVES SIX

INGREDIENTS
1.5kg/3lb firm baking potatoes
60–90ml/4–6 tbsp oil, bacon
    dripping or clarified butter
2 rosemary sprigs, leaves chopped
salt and ground black pepper

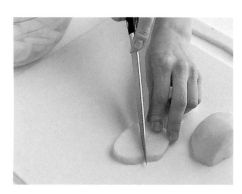

1 Peel and cut the potatoes into 2.5cm/1in slices.

2 Place the slices in a bowl of cold water and soak for 10 minutes. Drain, rinse and drain again, then pat dry.

3 In a large heavy-based frying pan, heat 60ml/4 tbsp of the oil, dripping or butter over a medium-high heat until very hot, but not smoking. Add the potatoes and cook for 2 minutes without stirring so that they seal completely and brown on one side.

4 Shake the pan and toss the potatoes to brown on another side and continue to stir and shake the pan until potatoes are evenly browned on all sides. Season with salt and pepper.

5 Add a little more oil, dripping or butter, reduce the heat to medium-low to low, and continue cooking the potatoes for 20–25 minutes until tender when pierced with a knife, stirring and shaking the pan frequently.

6 About 5 minutes before the end of cooking, sprinkle the potatoes with the chopped rosemary. Serve at once.

BUBBLE <u>AND</u> SQUEAK

WHETHER YOU HAVE LEFTOVERS, OR COOK THIS OLD-FASHIONED CLASSIC FROM FRESH, BE SURE TO GIVE IT A REALLY GOOD "SQUEAK" (FRY) IN THE PAN SO IT TURNS A RICH HONEY BROWN AS ALL THE FLAVOURS CARAMELIZE TOGETHER. IT IS KNOWN AS COLCANNON IN IRELAND, WHERE IT IS TURNED IN CHUNKS OR SECTIONS, PRODUCING A CREAMY BROWN AND WHITE CAKE.

SERVES FOUR

INGREDIENTS
60ml/4 tbsp dripping, bacon fat or
   vegetable oil
1 onion, finely chopped
450g/1lb floury potatoes, cooked
   and mashed
225g/8oz cooked cabbage or Brussels
   sprouts, finely chopped
salt and ground black pepper

1 Heat 30ml/2 tbsp of the dripping, fat or oil in a heavy-based frying pan. Add the onion and cook, stirring frequently, until softened but not browned.

2 In a large bowl, mix together the potatoes and cooked cabbage or sprouts and season with salt and plenty of pepper to taste.

3 Add the vegetables to the pan with the cooked onions, stir well, then press the vegetable mixture into a large, even cake.

4 Cook over a medium heat for about 15 minutes until the cake is browned underneath.

5 Invert a large plate over the pan, and, holding it tightly against the pan, turn them both over together. Lift off the frying pan, return it to the heat and add the remaining dripping, fat or oil. When hot, slide the cake back into the pan, browned side uppermost.

6 Cook over a medium heat for 10 minutes or until the underside is golden brown. Serve hot, in wedges.

COOK'S TIP
If you don't have leftover cooked cabbage or Brussels sprouts, shred raw cabbage and cook both in boiling salted water until tender. Drain, then chop.

ORANGE CANDIED SWEET POTATOES

A TRUE TASTE OF AMERICA, NO THANKSGIVING OR CHRISTMAS TABLE IS COMPLETE UNLESS SWEET POTATOES ARE ON THE MENU. SERVE WITH EXTRA ORANGE SEGMENTS TO MAKE IT REALLY SPECIAL.

SERVES EIGHT

INGREDIENTS
 900g/2 lb sweet potatoes
 250ml/8 fl oz/1 cup orange juice
 50ml/2fl oz/¼ cup maple syrup
 5ml/1 tsp freshly grated ginger
 7.5ml/1½ tsp ground cinnamon
 6.5ml/1¼ tsp ground cardamom
 7.5ml/1½ tsp salt
 ground black pepper
 ground cinnamon, to garnish
 orange segments, to serve

1 Preheat the oven to 130°C/350°F/ Gas 4. Peel and dice the potatoes and then boil in water for 5 minutes.

2 Meanwhile, stir the remaining ingredients together. Spread out onto a non-stick shallow baking tin.

3 Drain the potatoes and scatter over the tray, cook for 1 hour, stirring the potatoes every 15 minutes until the potatoes are tender and they are well coated. Serve as a accompaniment to a main dish, with orange segments and ground cinnamon.

HASH BROWNS

*CRISPY GOLDEN WEDGES OF POTATOES, "HASHED" UP WITH A LITTLE ONION, ARE A FAVOURITE
AMERICAN BREAKFAST DISH, BUT TASTE DELICIOUS ANYTIME.*

SERVES 4

INGREDIENTS
60ml/4 tbsp sunflower or olive oil
450g/1lb cooked potatoes, diced
  or grated
1 small onion, chopped
salt and ground black pepper
chives, to garnish
tomato sauce, to serve

VARIATION
Turn this side dish into a main meal by
adding other ingredients to the potatoes
in the pan, such as cooked diced meat,
sliced sausages or even corned beef
for a northern English corned beef
hash supper.

1 Heat the oil in a large heavy-based
frying pan until very hot. Add the
potatoes in a single layer. Scatter the
onion on top and season well.

2 Cook on a medium heat, pressing
down on the potatoes with a spoon or
spatula to squash them together.

3 When the potatoes are nicely
browned underneath, turn them over in
sections with a spatula and fry until the
other side is golden brown and lightly
crispy, pressing them down again.

4 Serve hot with a garnish of chives
and tomato sauce alongside.

SPANISH CHILLI POTATOES

*THE NAME OF THIS SPANISH TAPAS DISH, "PATATAS BRAVAS", MEANS FIERCELY HOT POTATOES,
BUT LUCKILY TAPAS ARE USUALLY ONLY EATEN IN SMALL QUANTITIES!*

SERVES FOUR

INGREDIENTS
900g/2lb small new or salad potatoes
60ml/4 tbsp olive oil
1 onion, finely chopped
2 garlic cloves, crushed
15ml/1 tbsp tomato paste
200g/7oz can chopped tomatoes
15ml/1 tbsp red wine vinegar
2–3 small dried red chillies, seeded
  and finely chopped, or 5–10ml/
  1–2 tsp hot chilli powder
5ml/1 tsp paprika
salt and ground black pepper
1 flat leaf parsley sprig, to garnish
chopped fresh red chillies, to garnish

COOK'S TIP
If you don't like your potatoes to be too
fierce simply reduce the amount of
chilli to taste.

1 Cook the potatoes in their skins in
boiling water for 10–12 minutes until
just tender. Drain well and leave to cool,
then cut in half and reserve.

2 Heat the oil in a large pan and add
the onion and garlic. Fry them gently for
5–6 minutes until just softened. Stir in
the tomato paste, tomatoes, vinegar,
chillies or chilli powder and paprika and
simmer for about 5 minutes.

3 Stir the potatoes into the sauce
mixture until well coated. Cover and
simmer gently for 8–10 minutes until
the potatoes are tender.

4 Season the potatoes well and
transfer to a warmed serving dish.
Serve at once, garnished with a sprig
of flat leaf parsley. To make the dish
even hotter, add a garnish of chopped
fresh red chillies.

ALOO SAAG

TRADITIONAL INDIAN SPICES — MUSTARD SEED, GINGER AND CHILLI — GIVE A REALLY GOOD KICK TO POTATOES AND SPINACH IN THIS DELICIOUS AND AUTHENTIC CURRY.

SERVES FOUR

INGREDIENTS
    450g/1lb spinach
    30ml/2 tbsp vegetable oil
    5ml/1 tsp black mustard seeds
    1 onion, thinly sliced
    2 garlic cloves, crushed
    2.5cm/1in piece root ginger,
      finely chopped
    675g/1½lb firm potatoes, cut into
      2.5cm/1in chunks
    5ml/1 tsp chilli powder
    5ml/1 tsp salt
    120ml/4fl oz/½ cup water

COOK'S TIPS
To make certain that the spinach is dry, put it in a clean tea towel, roll up tightly and squeeze gently to remove any excess liquid. Choose a firm waxy variety of potato or a salad potato so the pieces do not break up during cooking.

1 Blanch the spinach in boiling water for 3–4 minutes.

2 Drain the spinach thoroughly and leave to cool. When it is cool enough to handle, use your hands to squeeze out any remaining liquid.

3 Heat the oil in a large saucepan and fry the mustard seeds for 2 minutes, stirring, until they begin to splutter.

4 Add the onion, garlic and ginger and fry for 5 minutes, stirring.

5 Stir in the potatoes, chilli powder, salt and water and cook for 8 minutes, stirring occasionally.

6 Finally, add the spinach to the pan. Cover and simmer for 10–15 minutes until the spinach is cooked and the potatoes are tender. Serve hot.

POTATOES IN A YOGURT SAUCE

TINY POTATOES WITH SKINS ON ARE DELICIOUS IN THIS FAIRLY SPICY YET TANGY YOGURT SAUCE.
SERVE WITH ANY MEAT OR FISH DISH OR JUST WITH HOT CHAPATIS.

SERVES FOUR

INGREDIENTS

12 small new or salad
   potatoes, halved
275g/10oz/1¼ cups natural
   low-fat yogurt
300ml/½ pint/1¼ cups water
1.5ml/¼ tsp turmeric
5ml/1 tsp chilli powder
5ml/1 tsp ground coriander
2.5ml/½ tsp ground cumin
5ml/1 tsp salt
5ml/1 tsp soft brown sugar
30ml/2 tbsp vegetable oil
5ml/1 tsp white cumin seeds
15ml/1 tbsp chopped fresh coriander
2 fresh green chillies, sliced
1 coriander sprig, to garnish
   (optional)

1 Cook the potatoes in their skins in boiling salted water until just tender, then drain and set aside.

2 Mix together the yogurt, water, turmeric, chilli powder, ground coriander, ground cumin, salt and sugar in a bowl. Set aside.

3 Heat the oil in a medium saucepan over a medium-high heat and stir in the white cumin seeds.

4 Reduce the heat to medium, and stir in the prepared yogurt mixture. Cook the sauce, stirring continuously, for about 3 minutes.

5 Add the fresh coriander, green chillies and potatoes to the sauce. Mix well and cook for 5–7 minutes, stirring occasionally.

6 Transfer to a serving dish, garnish with the coriander sprig, if wished and serve hot.

COOK'S TIP

If new or salad potatoes are unavailable, use 450g/1lb ordinary potatoes instead, but not the floury type. Peel them and cut into large chunks, then cook as described above.

MASALA MASHED POTATOES

THESE WELL-SPICED POTATOES ARE DELICIOUS SERVED ALONGSIDE RICH MEATS SUCH AS DUCK, LAMB OR PORK THAT HAS BEEN SIMPLY GRILLED OR ROASTED.

SERVES FOUR

INGREDIENTS

   3 medium floury potatoes
   15ml/1 tbsp mixed chopped fresh
     mint and coriander
   5ml/1 tsp mango powder or chutney
   5ml/1 tsp salt
   5ml/1 tsp crushed black peppercorns
   1 fresh red chilli, finely chopped
   1 fresh green chilli, finely chopped
   50g/2oz/4 tbsp butter or
     margarine, softened

1 Cook the potatoes in a large pan of lightly salted boiling water until tender. Drain very well. Mash them well with a potato masher.

2 Blend together the remaining ingredients in a small bowl.

3 Stir the mixture into the mashed potatoes reserving a little for a garnish and mix together with a fork.

4 Serve hot in a pile, with the remaining mixture on the top.

BOMBAY POTATOES

A CLASSIC GUJERATI (INDIAN VEGETARIAN) DISH OF POTATOES SLOWLY COOKED IN A RICHLY FLAVOURED CURRY SAUCE WITH FRESH CHILLIES FOR AN ADDED KICK.

SERVES FOUR TO SIX

INGREDIENTS

   450g/1lb new or small salad potatoes
   5ml/1 tsp turmeric
   60ml/4 tbsp vegetable oil
   2 dried red chillies
   6–8 curry leaves
   2 onions, finely chopped
   2 fresh green chillies, finely chopped
   50g/2oz coriander leaves,
     coarsely chopped
   1.5ml/¼ tsp asafoetida
   2.5ml/½ tsp each cumin, mustard,
     onion, fennel and nigella seeds
   lemon juice
   salt
   fresh fried curry leaves, to garnish

1 Chop the potatoes into small chunks and cook in boiling lightly salted water with ½ tsp of the turmeric until tender. Drain, then coarsely mash. Set aside.

2 Heat the oil in a large heavy-based pan and fry the red chillies and curry leaves until the chillies are nearly burnt. Add the onions, green chillies, coriander, remaining turmeric, asafoetida and spice seeds and cook until the onions are tender.

3 Fold in the potatoes and add a few drops of water. Cook on a low heat for about 10 minutes, mixing well to ensure the even distribution of the spices. Remove the dried chillies and curry leaves.

4 Serve the potatoes hot, with lemon juice squeezed or poured over, and garnish with the fresh fried curry leaves, if you wish.

Meat and Poultry Dishes

These meat and poultry dishes make the most of the potatoes in season throughout the year. Lamb shanks slowly cooked in spices are finished with halved new potatoes. Chicken in a light sauce is topped with herby dumplings made with mashed potatoes, and a rich beef dish is finished with a crispy grated potato crust.

TEX-MEX BAKED POTATOES WITH CHILLI

CLASSIC CHILLI MINCE TOPS CRISP, FLOURY-CENTRED BAKED POTATOES. EASY TO PREPARE AND GREAT FOR A SIMPLE, YET SUBSTANTIAL FAMILY SUPPER.

SERVES FOUR

INGREDIENTS

2 large baking potatoes
15ml/1 tbsp vegetable oil, plus more
  for brushing
1 garlic clove, crushed
1 small onion, chopped
½ red pepper, seeded and chopped
225g/8oz lean beef mince
½ small fresh red chilli, seeded
  and chopped
5ml/1 tsp ground cumin
pinch of cayenne pepper
200g/7oz can chopped tomatoes
30ml/2 tbsp tomato paste
2.5ml/½ tsp fresh oregano
2.5ml/½ tsp fresh marjoram
200g/7oz can red kidney beans,
  drained
15ml/1 tbsp chopped fresh coriander
salt and ground black pepper
chopped fresh marjoram, to garnish
lettuce leaves, to serve
60ml/4 tbsp soured cream, to serve

1 Preheat the oven to 220°C/425°F/ Gas 7. Brush or rub the potatoes with a little of the oil and then pierce them with skewers.

2 Place the potatoes on the top shelf of the oven and bake them for 30 minutes before beginning to cook the chilli.

3 Heat the oil in a large heavy pan and add the garlic, onion and pepper. Fry gently for 4–5 minutes until softened.

4 Add the beef and fry until browned, then stir in the chilli, cumin, cayenne pepper, tomatoes, tomato paste, 60ml/4 tbsp water and the herbs. Bring to a boil then reduce the heat, cover and simmer for about 25 minutes, stirring occasionally.

5 Stir in the kidney beans and cook, uncovered, for 5 minutes. Remove from the heat and stir in the chopped coriander. Season well and set aside.

6 Cut the baked potatoes in half and place them in serving bowls. Top with the chilli mixture and a dollop of soured cream. Garnish with chopped fresh marjoram and serve hot accompanied by a few lettuce leaves.

CORNED BEEF AND EGG HASH

THIS IS REAL NURSERY, OR COMFORT, FOOD AT ITS BEST! WHETHER YOU REMEMBER GRAN'S VERSION, OR PREFER THIS AMERICAN-STYLE HASH, IT TURNS CORNED BEEF INTO A SUPPER FIT FOR ANY GUEST.

SERVES FOUR

INGREDIENTS
  30ml/2 tbsp vegetable oil
  25g/1oz/2 tbsp butter
  1 onion, finely chopped
  1 green pepper, seeded and diced
  2 large firm boiled potatoes, diced
  350g/12oz can corned beef, cubed
  1.5ml/¼ tsp grated nutmeg
  1.5ml/¼ tsp paprika
  4 eggs
  salt and ground black pepper
  deep fried parsley, to garnish
  sweet chilli sauce or tomato sauce,
    to serve

COOK'S TIP
Put the can of corned beef into the fridge to chill for about half an hour before using – it will firm up and cut into cubes more easily.

1 Heat the oil and butter together in a large frying pan. Add the onion and fry for 5–6 minutes until softened.

2 In a bowl, mix together the green pepper, potatoes, corned beef, nutmeg and paprika and season well. Add to the pan and toss gently to distribute the cooked onion. Press down lightly and fry without stirring on a medium heat for about 3–4 minutes until a golden brown crust has formed on the underside.

3 Stir the mixture through to distribute the crust, then repeat the frying twice, until the mixture is well browned.

4 Make four wells in the hash and carefully crack an egg into each. Cover and cook gently for about 4–5 minutes until the egg whites are set.

5 Sprinkle with deep fried parsley and cut into quarters. Serve hot with sweet chilli sauce or tomato sauce.

WILD MUSHROOM AND BACON RÖSTI

DRIED CEPS OR PORCINI MUSHROOMS HAVE A WONDERFUL WOODY, EARTHY AROMA AND TASTE. WITH THE SALTY BACON LARDONS, THEY TURN POTATO RÖSTI INTO A MEMORABLE SUPPER.

SERVES FOUR

INGREDIENTS

675g/1½lb floury potatoes
10g/¼oz dried ceps or porcini
  mushrooms
225g/8oz very thick smoked bacon,
  cut into lardons or strips
2 thyme sprigs, chopped
30ml/2 tbsp chopped fresh parsley
30ml/2 tbsp vegetable oil
4 eggs, to serve
1 bunch watercress, to garnish
crushed peppercorns, to garnish

1 Cook the potatoes in a saucepan of boiling salted water for 5 minutes and not longer, as they need to remain firm enough to grate at the next stage.

2 Meanwhile cover the mushrooms with boiling water and leave to soften for 5–10 minutes. Drain and chop.

3 Fry the bacon gently in a non-stick pan until all the fat runs out. Remove the bacon using a slotted spoon and reserve the fat.

4 Drain the potatoes and leave to cool. When they are cool enough to handle, grate them coarsely, then thoroughly pat dry on kitchen paper to remove all moisture. Place them in a large bowl and add the mushrooms, thyme, parsley and bacon. Mix together well.

5 Heat the bacon fat with a little of the oil in the frying pan until really hot. Spoon in the rösti mixture in heaps and flatten. Fry in batches for about 6 minutes until crisp and golden on both sides, turning once. Drain on kitchen paper and keep warm in a low oven.

6 Heat the remaining oil in the hot pan and fry the eggs as you like them. Serve the rösti at once with the eggs, watercress and crushed peppercorns.

POTATO CHORIZO AND CHEESE TORTILLA

SLICED POTATOES AND CHILLI-HOT SAUSAGES MAKE A POTATO CAKE WITH A REAL KICK TO IT.

SERVES FOUR

INGREDIENTS

15ml/1 tbsp vegetable oil
½ onion, sliced
1 small green pepper, seeded and cut
  into rings
1 garlic clove, finely chopped
1 tomato, chopped
6 pitted black olives, chopped
275g/10oz cooked firm, waxy
  potatoes, sliced
225g/8oz sliced chorizo, in strips
1 fresh green chilli, seeded
  and chopped
50g/2oz/½ cup Cheddar
  cheese, grated
6 large eggs
45ml/3 tbsp milk
1.5ml/¼ tsp ground cumin
1.5ml/¼ tsp dried oregano
1.5ml/¼ tsp paprika
salt and ground black pepper
rocket leaves, to garnish

1 Preheat the oven to 190°C/375°F/ Gas 5. Line a 23cm/9in round cake tin with grease-proof paper.

2 Heat the oil in a large non-stick frying pan. Add the onion, green pepper and garlic and cook over a medium heat for 5–8 minutes until softened.

3 Spoon into the tin with the tomato, olives, potatoes, chorizo and chilli. Mix and sprinkle with cheese.

4 In a small bowl, whisk together the eggs and milk until frothy. Add the cumin, oregano, paprika and salt and pepper to taste. Whisk to blend.

5 Pour the egg mixture on to the vegetables, tilting the tin so that the egg mixture spreads evenly.

6 Bake for 30 minutes until set and lightly golden. Serve in wedges, hot or cold, with rocket leaves.

STEAK WITH STOUT AND POTATOES

THE IRISH WAY TO BRAISE BEEF IS IN STOUT OF COURSE AND TOPPED WITH THICKLY SLICED
POTATOES. BAKE IT IN A MODERATE OVEN FOR LONG, SLOW TENDERISING IF YOU PREFER.

SERVES FOUR

INGREDIENTS
  675g/1½lb stewing beef
  15ml/1 tbsp vegetable oil
  25g/1oz/2 tbsp butter
  225g/8oz tiny white onions
  175ml/6fl oz/¾ cup stout or dark beer
  300ml/½ pint/1¼ cups beef stock
  bouquet garni
  675g/1½lb firm, waxy potatoes, cut
    into thick slices
  225g/8oz/3 cups large mushrooms,
    sliced
  15ml/1 tbsp plain flour
  2.5ml/½ tsp mild mustard
  salt and ground black pepper
  chopped thyme sprigs, to garnish

3 Add the tiny white onions to the pan and cook for 3–4 minutes until lightly browned all over. Return the steak to the pan with the onions. Pour on the stout or beer and stock and season the whole mixture to taste.

5 Add the sliced mushrooms over the potatoes. Cover again and simmer for a further 30 minutes or so. Remove the steak and vegetables with a slotted spoon and arrange on a platter.

1 Trim any excess fat from the steak and cut into four pieces. Season both sides of the meat. Heat the oil and 10g/¼oz/1½ tsp of the butter in a large heavy-based pan.

4 Next add the bouquet garni to the pan and top with the potato slices distributing them evenly over the surface to cover the steak. Bring the ingredients to a boil then reduce the heat, cover with a tight-fitting lid and simmer gently for 1 hour.

VARIATION
For a dish that is lighter, but just as tasty, substitute four lamb leg steaks for the beef, and use dry cider instead of the stout or beer, and lamb or chicken stock instead of beef.

COOK'S TIP
To make onion peeling easier, first put the onions in a bowl and cover with boiling water. Allow them to soak for about 5 minutes and drain. The skins should now peel away easily.

6 Mix the remaining butter with the flour to make a roux. Whisk a little at a time into the cooking liquid in the pan. Stir in the mustard. Cook over a medium heat for 2–3 minutes, stirring all the while, until thickened.

7 Season the sauce and pour over the steak. Garnish with plenty of thyme sprigs and serve the dish at once.

2 Add the steak and brown on both sides, taking care not to burn the butter. Remove from the pan and set aside.

POTATO, BEEF, BEETROOT AND MUSHROOM GRATIN

THIS VARIATION OF AN UNUSUAL POLISH MIX OF FLAVOURS PRODUCES A VERY HEARTY MAIN MEAL. HORSERADISH AND MUSTARD ARE GREAT WITH BOTH THE BEEF AND THE BEETROOT, MOST OF WHICH IS HIDDEN UNDERNEATH MAKING A COLOURFUL SURPRISE WHEN YOU SERVE IT.

SERVES FOUR

INGREDIENTS

   30ml/2 tbsp vegetable oil
   1 small onion, chopped
   15ml/1 tbsp plain flour
   150ml/¼ pint/⅔ cup vegetable stock
   225g/8oz cooked beetroot, drained
    well and chopped
   15ml/1 tbsp creamed horseradish
   15ml/1 tbsp caraway seeds
   3 shallots, or 1 medium
    onion, chopped
   450g/1lb frying or grilling steak, cut
    into thin strips
   225g/8oz assorted wild or cultivated
    mushrooms, sliced
   10–15ml/2–3 tsp hot mustard
   60ml/4 tbsp soured cream
   45ml/3 tbsp chopped fresh parsley
For the potato border
   900g/2lb floury potatoes
   150ml/¼ pint/⅔ cup milk
   25g/1oz/2 tbsp butter or margarine
   15ml/1 tbsp chopped fresh dill
    (optional)
   salt and ground black pepper

2 Return to the heat and simmer until thickened, stirring all the while. Add the beetroot (reserve a few pieces for the topping, if you wish), horseradish and caraway seeds. Mix gently, then put to one side.

4 Spoon the potatoes into the prepared dish and push well up the sides, making a large hollow in the middle for the filling. Spoon the beetroot mixture into the well, evening it out with the back of a spoon and set aside.

3 To make the potato border, first cook the potatoes in a large saucepan with plenty of boiling salted water for 20 minutes until tender. Drain well through a colander and mash with the milk and butter or margarine. Add the chopped dill, if using, and season the mixture with salt and pepper to taste. Stir to combine the seasonings.

COOK'S TIP
If planning ahead, for instance for a dinner party, this entire dish can be made in advance and heated through when needed. Allow 50 minutes baking time from room temperature. Add the beetroot pieces to the topping near the end of the cooking time.

5 Heat the remaining oil in a large frying pan, add the shallots or onion and fry until softened but not coloured. Add the steak and stir-fry quickly until browned all over. Then add the mushrooms and fry quickly until most of their juices have cooked away. Remove the pan from the heat and gently stir in the mustard, soured cream, seasoning to taste and half the parsley until well blended.

6 Spoon the steak mixture over the beetroot mixture in the baking dish, sprinkling the reserved beetroot over the top, cover and bake for 30 minutes. Serve hot, sprinkled with the remaining parsley.

1 Preheat the oven to 190°C/375°F/ Gas 5. Lightly oil a baking or gratin dish. Heat 15ml/1 tbsp of the oil in a large saucepan, add the onion and fry until softened but not coloured. Stir in the flour, remove from the heat and gradually add the stock, stirring until well blended and smooth.

SLOW BAKED BEEF WITH A POTATO CRUST

THIS RECIPE MAKES THE BEST OF BRAISING BEEF BY MARINATING IT IN RED WINE AND TOPPING IT WITH A CHEESY GRATED POTATO CRUST THAT BAKES TO A GOLDEN, CRUNCHY CONSISTENCY. FOR A CHANGE, INSTEAD OF GRATING THE POTATOES, SLICE THEM THINLY AND LAYER OVER THE TOP OF THE BEEF WITH ONION RINGS AND CRUSHED GARLIC.

SERVES FOUR

INGREDIENTS
  675g/1½lb stewing beef, diced
  300ml/½ pint/1¼ cups red wine
  3 juniper berries, crushed
  slice of orange peel
  30ml/2 tbsp olive oil
  2 onions, cut into chunks
  2 carrots, cut into chunks
  1 garlic clove, crushed
  225g/8oz/3 cups button
    mushrooms
  150ml/¼ pint/⅔ cup beef stock
  30ml/2 tbsp cornflour
  salt and ground black pepper
For the crust
  450g/1lb potatoes, grated
  15ml/1 tbsp olive oil
  30ml/2 tbsp creamed horseradish
  50g/2oz/½ cup mature Cheddar
    cheese, grated
  salt and ground black pepper

VARIATION
Any hard mature cheese is suitable for cooking on the crust. Try Red Leicester to add some colour, or Munster, for a more pungent flavour.

1 Place the diced beef in a non-metallic bowl. Add the wine, berries, and orange peel and season with black pepper. Mix the ingredients together and then cover and leave to marinate for at least 4 hours or overnight if possible.

2 Preheat the oven to 160°C/325°F/ Gas 3. Drain the beef, reserving the marinade.

3 Heat the oil in a large flameproof casserole and fry the meat in batches for 5 minutes to seal. Add the onions, carrots and garlic and cook for 5 minutes. Stir in the mushrooms, red wine marinade and beef stock. Simmer.

4 Mix the cornflour with water to make a smooth paste. Stir into the pan. Season, cover and cook for 1½ hours.

5 Make the crust 30 minutes before the end of the cooking time for the beef. Start by blanching the grated potatoes in boiling water for 5 minutes. Drain well and then squeeze out all the extra liquid.

6 Stir in the remaining ingredients and then scatter evenly over the surface of the beef. Increase the oven temperature to 200°C/400°F/Gas 6 and cook the dish for a further 30 minutes so that the top is crispy and slightly browned.

COOK'S TIP
Use a large grater on the food processor for the potatoes. They will hold their shape better whilst being blanched than if you use a finer blade.

MOUSSAKA

THIS CLASSIC GREEK DISH WITH LAMB, POTATOES AND AUBERGINES IS LAYERED THROUGH WITH A RICH CHEESY TOPPING TO MAKE A SUBSTANTIAL MEAL.

SERVES SIX

INGREDIENTS
  30ml/2 tbsp olive oil
  30ml/2 tbsp chopped
    fresh oregano
  1 large onion, finely chopped
  675g/1½lb lean lamb, minced
  1 large aubergine, sliced
  2 x 400g/14oz cans
    chopped tomatoes
  45ml/3 tbsp tomato purée
  1 lamb stock cube, crumbled
  2 floury main crop
    potatoes, halved
  115g/4oz/1 cup Cheddar
    cheese, grated
  150ml/¼ pint/⅔ cup
    single cream
salt and ground black pepper
fresh bread, to serve

2 Stir in the lamb and cook for 10 minutes until browned. Meanwhile, grill the aubergine slices for 5 minutes until browned, turning once.

3 Stir the tomatoes and purée into the mince mixture, and crumble the stock cube over it, stir well, season with salt and pepper and simmer uncovered for a further 15 minutes.

5 Layer the aubergines, mince and potatoes in a 1.75 litre/3 pint/7½ cup oval ovenproof dish, finishing with a layer of potatoes.

6 Mix the cheese and cream together in a bowl and pour over the top of the other ingredients in the dish. Cook for 45–50 minutes until bubbling and golden on the top. Serve straight from the dish, while hot, with plenty of fresh, crusty bread.

COOK'S TIP
The larger the surface area of the dish, the quicker the Moussaka will cook in the oven.

1 Preheat the oven to 180°C/350°F/ Gas 4. Heat the olive oil in a large deep-sided frying pan. Fry the oregano and onions over a low heat, stirring frequently, for about 5 minutes or until the onions have softened.

VARIATION
If you want to add more vegetables to the dish, use slices of courgette, grilled in the same way as the aubergines, instead of the sliced potato in the layers, then top the dish with a layer of well-seasoned mashed potatoes before pouring over the sauce. To make the dish even richer, add a sprinkling of freshly grated Parmesan cheese with each layer of aubergine.

4 Meanwhile, cook the potatoes in lightly salted boiling water for 5–10 minutes until just tender. Drain, and when cool enough to handle, cut into thin slices.

IRISH STEW

SIMPLE AND DELICIOUS, THIS IS THE QUINTESSENTIAL IRISH MAIN COURSE. TRADITIONALLY MUTTON CHOPS ARE USED, BUT AS THEY ARE HARDER TO FIND THESE DAYS YOU CAN USE LAMB INSTEAD.

SERVES FOUR

INGREDIENTS
  1.5kg/2½lb boneless lamb chops
  15ml/1 tbsp vegetable oil
  3 large onions, quartered
  4 large carrots, thickly sliced
  900ml/1½ pints/3¾ cups water
  4 large firm potatoes, cut into chunks
  1 large thyme sprig
  15g/½oz/1 tbsp butter
  15ml/1 tbsp chopped fresh parsley
  salt and ground black pepper
  Savoy cabbage, to serve (optional)

COOK'S TIP
If you can't find boneless chops, use the same weight of middle neck of lamb. Ask the butcher to chop the meat into cutlets, which should then be trimmed of excess fat.

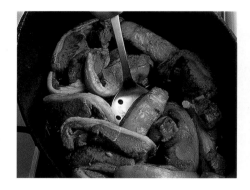

1 Trim any excess fat from the lamb. Heat the oil in a flameproof casserole, add the lamb and brown on both sides. Remove from the pan.

2 Add the onions and carrots to the casserole and cook for 5 minutes until the onions are browned. Return the lamb to the pan with the water. Season with salt and pepper. Bring to a boil then reduce the heat, cover and simmer for 1 hour.

3 Add the potatoes to the pan with the thyme, cover again, and simmer for a further hour.

4 Leave the stew to settle for a few minutes. Remove the fat from the liquid with a ladle, then pour off the liquid into a clean saucepan. Bring to a simmer and stir in the butter, then the parsley. Season well and pour back into the casserole. Serve with Savoy cabbage, boiled or steamed, if liked.

MIDDLE EASTERN ROAST LAMB AND POTATOES

WHEN THE EASTERN AROMA OF THE GARLIC AND SAFFRON COME WAFTING OUT OF THE OVEN, THIS DELICIOUSLY GARLICKY LAMB WON'T LAST VERY LONG!

SERVES SIX TO EIGHT

INGREDIENTS
  2.75kg/6lb leg of lamb
  4 garlic cloves, halved
  60ml/4 tbsp olive oil
  juice of 1 lemon
  2–3 saffron strands, soaked in
    15ml/1 tbsp boiling water
  5ml/1 tsp mixed dried herbs
  450g/1lb baking potatoes,
    thickly sliced
  2 large onions, thickly sliced
  salt and ground black pepper
  fresh thyme, to garnish

1 Make eight incisions in the lamb, press the garlic into the slits and place the lamb in a non-metallic dish.

2 Mix together the oil, lemon juice, saffron mixture and herbs. Rub over the lamb and marinate for 2 hours.

3 Preheat the oven to 180°C/350°F/ Gas 4. Layer the potatoes and onions in a large roasting tin. Lift the lamb out of the marinade and place the lamb on top of the potatoes and onions, fat side up and season.

4 Pour any remaining marinade over the lamb and roast for 2 hours, basting occasionally. Remove from the oven, cover with foil and rest for 10–15 minutes before carving. Garnish with thyme.

CHICKEN WITH POTATO DUMPLINGS

POACHED CHICKEN BREAST IN A CREAMY SAUCE TOPPED WITH LIGHT HERB AND POTATO DUMPLINGS MAKES A DELICATE YET HEARTY AND WARMING MEAL.

SERVES SIX

INGREDIENTS
  1 onion, chopped
  300ml/½ pint/1¼ cups
    vegetable stock
  120ml/4fl oz/½ cup white wine
  4 large chicken breasts
  300ml/½ pint/1¼ cups single cream
  15ml/1 tbsp chopped fresh tarragon
  salt and ground black pepper
For the dumplings
  225g/8oz main crop potatoes, boiled
    and mashed
  175g/6oz/1¼ cups suet
  115g/4oz/1 cup self-raising flour
  50ml/2fl oz/¼ cup water
  30ml/2 tbsp chopped mixed
    fresh herbs
  salt and ground black pepper

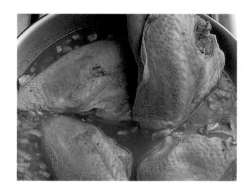

1 Place the onion, stock and wine in a deep-sided frying pan. Add the chicken and simmer for 20 minutes, covered.

2 Remove the chicken from the stock, cut into chunks and reserve. Strain the stock and discard the onion. Reduce the stock by one-third over a high heat. Stir in the cream and tarragon and simmer until just thickened. Stir in the chicken and season with salt and ground black pepper.

3 Spoon the mixture into a 900ml/ 1½ pint/3¾ cup ovenproof dish.

4 Preheat the oven to 190°C/375°F/ Gas 5. Mix together the dumpling ingredients and stir in the water to make a soft dough. Divide into six and shape into balls with floured hands. Place on top of the chicken mixture and bake uncovered for 30 minutes.

COOK'S TIP
Make sure that you do not reduce the sauce too much before it is cooked in the oven as the dumplings absorb quite a lot of the liquid.

SPINACH AND POTATO STUFFED CHICKEN BREASTS

THIS DISH CONSISTS OF LARGE CHICKEN BREASTS, FILLED WITH A HERBY SPINACH MIXTURE, THEN TOPPED WITH BUTTER AND BAKED UNTIL MOUTH-WATERINGLY TENDER.

2 Stir the spinach into the potato with the egg and coriander. Season with salt and pepper to taste.

3 Cut almost all the way through the chicken breasts and open out to form a pocket in each. Spoon the filling into the centre and fold the chicken back over again. Secure with cocktail sticks and place in a roasting tin.

4 Dot with butter and cover with foil. Bake for 25 minutes. Remove the foil and cook for a further 10 minutes until the chicken is golden.

5 Meanwhile, to make the sauce heat the tomatoes, garlic and stock in a saucepan. Boil rapidly for 10 minutes. Season and stir in the coriander. Remove the chicken from the oven and serve with the sauce and fried mushrooms.

SERVES SIX

INGREDIENTS
115g/4oz floury main crop
  potatoes, diced
115g/4oz spinach leaves,
  finely chopped
1 egg, beaten
30ml/2 tbsp chopped fresh coriander
4 large chicken breasts
50g/2oz/4 tbsp butter
For the sauce
400g/14oz can chopped tomatoes
1 garlic clove, crushed
150ml/¼ pint/⅔ cup hot chicken stock
30ml/2 tbsp chopped fresh coriander
salt and ground black pepper
fried mushrooms, to serve

1 Preheat the oven to 180°C/350°F/ Gas 4. Boil the potatoes in a large saucepan of boiling water for 15 minutes or until tender. Drain the potatoes, place them in a large bowl and roughly mash with a fork.

COOK'S TIP
Young spinach leaves have a sweeter flavour and are ideal for this dish.

STOVED CHICKEN

"STOVIES" WERE ORIGINALLY — NOT SURPRISINGLY — POTATOES SLOWLY COOKED ON THE STOVE WITH ONIONS AND DRIPPING OR BUTTER UNTIL FALLING TO PIECES. THIS VERSION INCLUDES A DELICIOUS LAYER OF BACON AND CHICKEN HIDDEN IN THE MIDDLE OF THE VEGETABLES.

SERVES FOUR

INGREDIENTS
butter, for greasing
1kg/2¼lb baking potatoes, cut into
   5mm/¼in slices
2 large onions, thinly sliced
15ml/1 tbsp chopped fresh thyme
25g/1oz/2 tbsp butter
15ml/1 tbsp vegetable oil
2 large bacon slices, chopped
4 large chicken joints, halved
600ml/1 pint/2½ cups chicken stock
1 bay leaf
salt and ground black pepper

COOK'S TIP
Instead of chicken joints, choose eight chicken thighs or chicken drumsticks.

1 Preheat the oven to 150°C/300°F/ Gas 2. Arrange a thick layer of half the potato slices in the bottom of a large lightly greased heavy-based casserole, then cover with half the onions. Sprinkle with half of the thyme, and season with salt and pepper to taste.

2 Heat the butter and oil in a large heavy-based frying pan, add the bacon and chicken, stirring frequently, and brown on all sides. Using a slotted spoon, transfer the chicken and bacon to the casserole. Reserve the fat in the pan.

3 Sprinkle the remaining thyme over the chicken, season with salt and pepper, then cover with the remaining onion slices, followed by a neat layer of overlapping potato slices. Season the dish well.

4 Pour the stock into the casserole, add the bay leaf and brush the potatoes with the reserved fat. Cover tightly and bake for about 2 hours until the chicken is very tender.

5 Preheat the grill. Take the cover off the casserole and place it under the grill until the slices of potato are beginning to turn golden brown and crisp. Remove the bay leaf and serve hot.

TURKEY CROQUETTES

A CRISP PATTY OF SMOKED TURKEY MIXED WITH MASHED POTATO AND SPRING ONIONS AND ROLLED IN BREADCRUMBS, SERVED WITH A TANGY TOMATO SAUCE.

3 Meanwhile, to make the sauce heat the oil in a frying pan and fry the onion for 5 minutes until softened. Add the tomatoes and purée, stir and simmer for 10 minutes. Stir in the parsley, season with salt and pepper and keep the sauce warm until needed.

SERVES FOUR

INGREDIENTS
450g/1lb main crop potatoes, diced
3 eggs
30ml/2 tbsp milk
175g/6oz smoked turkey rashers, finely chopped
2 spring onions, finely sliced
115g/4oz/2 cups fresh white breadcrumbs
vegetable oil, for deep fat frying
For the sauce
15ml/1 tbsp olive oil
1 onion, finely chopped
400g/14oz can tomatoes, drained
30ml/2 tbsp tomato purée
15ml/1 tbsp chopped fresh parsley
salt and ground black pepper

1 Boil the potatoes for 20 minutes or until tender. Drain and return the pan to a low heat to make sure all the excess water evaporates.

2 Mash the potatoes with 2 eggs and the milk. Season well with salt and pepper. Stir in the turkey and spring onions. Chill for 1 hour.

4 Remove the potato mixture from the fridge and divide into 8 pieces. Shape each piece into a sausage shape and dip in the remaining beaten egg and then the breadcrumbs.

5 Heat the vegetable oil in a saucepan or deep-fat fryer to 175°C/330°F and deep fry the croquettes for 5 minutes, or until golden and crisp. Serve with the sauce.

COOK'S TIP
Test the oil is at the correct temperature by dropping a cube of bread on to the surface. If it sinks, rises and sizzles in 10 seconds the oil is ready to use.

LAYERED CHICKEN AND MUSHROOM POTATO BAKE

A DELICIOUS AND MOIST COMBINATION OF CHICKEN, VEGETABLES AND GRAVY IN A SIMPLE, ONE-DISH MEAL TOPPED WITH CRUNCHY SLICES OF POTATO.

SERVES FOUR TO SIX

INGREDIENTS

15ml/1 tbsp olive oil
4 large chicken breasts, cut
  into chunks
1 leek, finely sliced into rings
50g/2oz/4 tbsp butter
25g/1oz/¼ cup plain flour
475ml/16fl oz/2 cups milk
5ml/1 tsp wholegrain mustard
1 carrot, very finely diced
225g/8oz/3 cups button mushrooms,
  finely sliced
900g/2lb main crop potatoes,
  finely sliced
salt and ground black pepper

1 Preheat the oven to 180°C/350°F/ Gas 4. Heat the oil in a large saucepan. Fry the chicken for 5 minutes until browned. Add the leek and fry for a further 5 minutes.

2 Add half the butter to the pan and allow it to melt. Then sprinkle the flour over and stir in the milk. Cook over a low heat until thickened, then stir in the mustard.

3 Add the carrots with the mushrooms. Season with salt and black pepper.

4 Lay enough potato slices to line the base of a 1.75 litre/3 pint/7½ cup ovenproof dish. Spoon one-third of the chicken mixture over. Cover with another layer of potatoes. Repeat layering, finishing with a layer of potatoes. Top with the remaining butter in knobs.

5 Bake for 1½ hours in the oven, covering with foil after 30 minutes' cooking time. Serve hot.

COOK'S TIP
The liquid from the mushrooms keeps the chicken moist and the potatoes help to mop up any excess juices.

ROASTED DUCKLING <u>ON A</u> BED <u>OF</u> HONEYED POTATOES

THE RICH FLAVOUR OF DUCK COMBINED WITH THESE SWEETENED POTATOES GLAZED WITH HONEY MAKES AN EXCELLENT TREAT FOR A DINNER PARTY OR SPECIAL OCCASION.

SERVES FOUR

INGREDIENTS

1 duckling, giblets removed
60ml/4 tbsp light soy sauce
150ml/¼ pint/⅔ cup fresh
   orange juice
3 large floury potatoes, cut
   into chunks
30ml/2 tbsp clear honey
15ml/1 tbsp sesame seeds
salt and ground black pepper

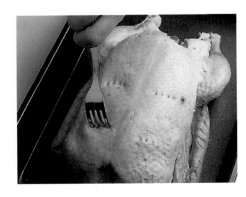

1 Preheat the oven to 200°C/400°F/
Gas 6. Place the duckling in a roasting
tin. Prick the skin well.

2 Mix the soy sauce and orange juice
together and pour over the duck. Cook
for 20 minutes.

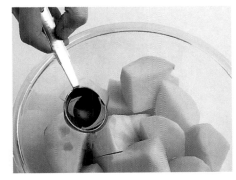

3 Place the potato chunks in a bowl
and stir in the honey, toss to mix well.
Remove the duckling from the oven and
spoon the potatoes all around and
under the duckling.

4 Roast for 35 minutes and remove
from the oven. Toss the potatoes in
the juices so the underside will be
cooked and turn the duck over. Put
back in the oven and cook for a
further 30 minutes.

5 Remove the duckling from the oven
and carefully scoop off the excess fat,
leaving the juices behind.

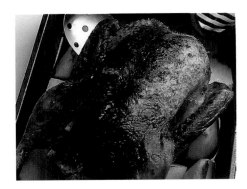

6 Sprinkle the sesame seeds over the
potatoes, season and turn the duckling
back over, breast side up, and cook for
a further 10 minutes. Remove the
duckling and potatoes from the oven
and keep warm, allowing the duck to
stand for a few minutes.

7 Pour off the excess fat and simmer
the juices on the hob for a few minutes.
Serve the juices with the carved
duckling and potatoes.

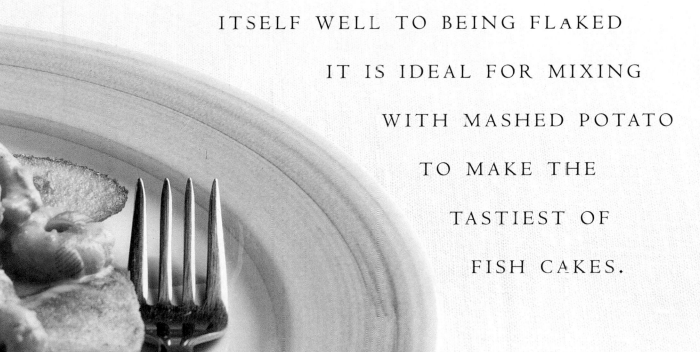

Fish Dishes

FISH TAKES ONLY A SHORT TIME TO COOK, SO
MANY OF THE RECIPES IN THIS CHAPTER USE
POTATOES READY-COOKED OR VERY FINELY
SLICED. TRY JANSSON'S TEMPTATION, A
CLASSIC SWEDISH DISH MADE WITH
MATCHSTICK POTATOES AND LAYERED WITH
ANCHOVIES AND ONIONS. SINCE FISH LENDS
ITSELF WELL TO BEING FLAKED
IT IS IDEAL FOR MIXING
WITH MASHED POTATO
TO MAKE THE
TASTIEST OF
FISH CAKES.

SMOKED SALMON QUICHE <u>WITH</u> POTATO PASTRY

THE INGREDIENTS IN THIS LIGHT BUT RICHLY-FLAVOURED QUICHE PERFECTLY COMPLEMENT THE MELT-IN-THE-MOUTH PASTRY MADE WITH POTATOES.

SERVES SIX

INGREDIENTS
For the pastry
   115g/4oz floury maincrop
     potatoes, diced
   225g/8oz/2 cups plain flour, sifted
   115g/4oz/8 tbsp butter, diced
   ½ egg, beaten
   10ml/2 tsp chilled water
For the filling
   275g/10oz smoked salmon
   6 eggs, beaten
   150ml/¼ pint/⅔ cup full cream milk
   300ml/½ pint/1¼ cups double cream
   30–45ml/2–3 tbsp chopped fresh dill
   30ml/2 tbsp capers, chopped
   salt and ground black pepper
   salad leaves and chopped fresh dill,
     to serve

1 Boil the potatoes in a large saucepan of lightly salted water for 15 minutes or until tender. Drain well through a colander and return to the pan. Mash the potatoes until smooth and set aside to cool completely.

VARIATIONS
These quantities can also be used to make six individual quiches, which are an ideal size to serve as a starter or a light lunch. Prepare them as above, but reduce the cooking time by about 15 minutes. For extra piquancy, sprinkle some finely grated fresh Parmesan cheese over the top of each quiche before baking in the oven.

2 Place the flour in a bowl and rub in the butter to form fine crumbs. Beat in the potatoes and egg. Bring the mixture together, adding chilled water if needed.

3 Roll the pastry out on a floured surface and use to line a deep 23cm/9in round, loose-based, fluted flan tin. Chill for 1 hour.

4 Preheat the oven to 200°C/400°F/ Gas 6. Place a baking sheet in the oven to preheat it. Chop the salmon into bite-size pieces and set aside.

5 For the filling, beat the eggs, milk and cream together. Then stir in the dill and capers and season with pepper. Add in the salmon and stir to combine.

6 Remove the pastry case from the fridge, prick the base well and pour the mixture into it. Bake on a baking sheet for 35–45 minutes. Serve warm with mixed salad leaves and some more dill.

COOK'S TIPS
To ensure the base cooks through it is vital to preheat a baking sheet in the oven first. Make the most of smoked salmon offcuts for this quiche, as they are much cheaper.

COD, BASIL, TOMATO AND POTATO PIE

NATURAL AND SMOKED FISH MAKE A GREAT COMBINATION, ESPECIALLY WITH THE HINT OF TOMATO AND BASIL. SERVED WITH A GREEN SALAD, IT MAKES AN IDEAL DISH FOR LUNCH OR A FAMILY SUPPER.

2 Melt 75g/3oz/6 tbsp of the butter in a large pan, add the onion and cook for about 5 minutes until softened and tender but not browned. Sprinkle over the flour and half the chopped basil. Gradually add the reserved fish cooking liquid, adding a little more milk if necessary to make a fairly thin sauce, stirring constantly to make a smooth consistency. Bring to the boil, season with salt and pepper, and add the remaining basil.

3 Remove the pan from the heat, then add the fish and tomatoes and stir gently to combine. Pour into an ovenproof dish.

SERVES EIGHT

INGREDIENTS
   1kg/2¼lb smoked cod
   1kg/2¼lb white cod
   900ml/1½ pint/3¾ cups milk
   1.2litres/2 pints/5 cups water
   2 basil sprigs
   1 lemon thyme sprig
   150g/5oz/10 tbsp butter
   1 onion, chopped
   75g/3oz/⅔ cup plain flour
   30ml/2 tbsp chopped fresh basil
   4 firm plum tomatoes, peeled
    and chopped
   12 medium main crop floury potatoes
   salt and ground black pepper
   crushed black pepper corns,
    to garnish
   lettuce leaves, to serve

1 Place both kinds of fish in a roasting tin with 600ml/1 pint/2½ cups of the milk, the water and the herb sprigs. Bring to a simmer and cook gently for about 3–4 minutes. Leave the fish to cool in the liquid for about 20 minutes. Drain the fish, reserving the cooking liquid for use in the sauce. Flake the fish, removing any skin and bone.

4 Preheat the oven to 180°C/350°F/ Gas 4. Cook the potatoes in boiling water until tender. Drain then add the remaining butter and milk, and mash. Season to taste and spoon over the fish mixture, using a fork to create a pattern. You can freeze the pie at this stage. Bake for 30 minutes until the top is golden. Sprinkle with the crushed pepper corns and serve hot with lettuce.

CLASSIC FISH PIE

ORIGINALLY A FISH PIE WAS BASED ON THE "CATCH OF THE DAY". NOW WE CAN CHOOSE EITHER THE FISH WE LIKE BEST, OR THE VARIETY THAT OFFERS BEST VALUE FOR MONEY.

SERVES FOUR

INGREDIENTS
   butter, for greasing
   450g/1lb mixed fish, such as
     cod or salmon fillets and
     peeled prawns
   finely grated rind of 1 lemon
   450g/1lb floury potatoes
   25g/1oz/2 tbsp butter
   salt and ground black pepper
   1 egg, beaten
For the sauce
   15g/½oz/1 tbsp butter
   15ml/1 tbsp plain flour
   150ml/¼ pint/⅔ cup milk
   45ml/3 tbsp chopped fresh parsley

1 Preheat the oven to 220°C/425°F/ Gas 7. Grease an ovenproof dish and set aside. Cut the fish into bite-sized pieces. Season the fish, sprinkle over the lemon rind and place in the base of the prepared dish. Allow to sit while you make the topping.

2 Cook the potatoes in boiling salted water until tender.

3 Meanwhile make the sauce. Melt the butter in a saucepan, add the flour and cook, stirring, for a few minutes. Remove from the heat and gradually whisk in the milk. Return to the heat and bring to the boil then reduce the heat and simmer, whisking all the time, until the sauce has thickened and achieved a smooth consistency. Add the parsley and season to taste. Pour over the fish mixture.

4 Drain the potatoes well and then mash with the butter.

5 Pipe or spoon the potatoes on top of the fish mixture. Brush the beaten egg over the potatoes. Bake for 45 minutes until the top is golden brown. Serve hot.

COOK'S TIP
If using frozen fish defrost it very well first, as lots of water will ruin your pie.

TUNA AND MASCARPONE BAKE

A ONE-DISH MEAL IDEAL FOR INFORMAL ENTERTAINING THAT MARRIES THE SMOKY FLAVOUR OF SEARED TUNA WITH A SWEET AND HERBY ITALIAN SAUCE.

SERVES FOUR

INGREDIENTS
   4 x 175g/6oz tuna steaks
   400g/14oz can chopped
    tomatoes, drained
   2 garlic cloves, crushed
   30ml/2 tbsp chopped fresh basil
   250g/9oz/generous 1 cup
    mascarpone cheese
   3 large potatoes
   25g/1oz/2 tbsp butter, diced
   salt and ground black pepper

VARIATION
This dish can easily be made into a side dish, simply leave out the tuna and prepare the other ingredients as before.

1 Preheat the oven to 200°C/400°F/ Gas 6. Heat a griddle pan on the hob and sear the fish steaks for 2 minutes on each side, seasoning with a little black pepper. Set aside while you prepare the sauce.

2 Mix the tomatoes, garlic, basil and cheese together in a bowl and season to taste.

3 Grate half the potatoes and dice the other half. Blanch in separate pans of lightly salted water for 3 minutes. Drain.

4 Grease a 1.75 litre/3 pint/7½ cup ovenproof dish. Spoon a little sauce and some grated potato into it. Lay the tuna over with more sauce and the remaining grated potato. Scatter the diced butter and potatoes. Bake for 30 minutes.

POTATO AND SMOKED MUSSEL BAKE

THIS RECIPE USES SMOKED MUSSELS, WHICH HAVE A CREAMY TEXTURE AND RICH FLAVOUR, DELICIOUS WITH SOURED CREAM AND CHIVES. YOU CAN EASILY SUBSTITUTE SMOKED OYSTERS FOR THE MUSSELS.

SERVES FOUR

INGREDIENTS
   2 large maincrop potatoes,
    cut in half
   butter, for greasing
   2 shallots, finely diced
   2 x 85g/3¼oz tins smoked mussels
   1 bunch chives, snipped
   300ml/½ pint/1¼ cups soured cream
   175g/6oz/1½ cups mature Cheddar
    cheese, grated
   salt and ground black pepper
   mixed vegetables, to serve

COOK'S TIP
To serve this dish for a dinner party, rather than serve it in a large dish, once it has cooked, stamp out rounds using a 5cm/2in cutter and serve on a bed of salad leaves.

1 Preheat the oven to 180°C/350°F/ Gas 4. Cook the potatoes in a large saucepan of lightly salted boiling water for 15 minutes until they are just tender. Drain and leave to cool slightly. When cool enough to handle cut the potatoes into even 3mm/⅛in slices.

2 Grease the base and sides of a 1.2 litre/2 pint/5 cup casserole dish. Lay a few potato slices over the base of the dish. Scatter a few shallots over and season well.

3 Drain the oil from the mussels into a bowl. Slice the mussels and add them again to the reserved oil. Stir in the chives and soured cream with half of the cheese. Spoon a little of the sauce over the layer of potatoes.

4 Continue to layer the potatoes, shallots and the sauce. Finish with a layer of potatoes and sprinkle over the remainder of the cheese.

5 Bake for 30–45 minutes. Remove from the oven and serve while hot with a selection of mixed vegetables.

SMOKED HADDOCK AND NEW POTATO PIE

SMOKED HADDOCK HAS A SALTY FLAVOUR AND CAN BE BOUGHT EITHER DYED OR UNDYED. THE DYED FISH HAS A STRONG YELLOW COLOUR WHILE THE OTHER IS ALMOST CREAMY IN COLOUR.

SERVES FOUR

INGREDIENTS
  450g/1lb smoked haddock fillet
  475ml/16fl oz/2 cups
    semi-skimmed milk
  2 bay leaves
  1 onion, quartered
  4 cloves
  450g/1lb new potatoes
  butter, for greasing
  30ml/2 tbsp cornflour
  60ml/4 tbsp double cream
  30ml/2 tbsp chopped fresh chervil
  salt and ground black pepper
  mixed vegetables, to serve

VARIATIONS
Instead of using all smoked haddock for this pie, use half smoked and half fresh. Cook the two types together, as described in Step 1. A generous handful of peeled prawns is a good addition to this pie is you want to make it even more filling.

COOK'S TIP
The fish gives out liquid as it cooks, so it is best to start with a slightly thicker sauce than you might think is necessary.

1 Preheat the oven to 200°C/400°F/Gas 6. Place the haddock in a deep-sided frying pan. Pour the milk over and add the bay leaves.

2 Stud the onion with the cloves and place it in the pan with the fish and milk. Cover the top and leave to simmer for about 10 minutes or until the fish starts to flake.

3 Remove the fish with a slotted spoon and set aside to cool. Strain the liquid from the pan into a separate saucepan and set aside.

4 To prepare the potatoes, cut them into fine slices, leaving the skins on.

5 Blanch the potatoes in a large saucepan of lightly salted water for 5 minutes. Drain.

6 Grease the base and sides of a 1.2 litre/2 pint/5 cup ovenproof dish. Then using a knife and fork, carefully flake the fish.

7 Reheat the milk in the saucepan. Mix the cornflour with a little water to form a paste and stir in the cream and the chervil. Add to the milk in the pan and cook until thickened.

8 Arrange one-third of the potatoes over the base of the dish and season with pepper. Lay half of the fish over. Repeat layering, finishing with a layer of potatoes on top.

9 Pour the sauce over the top, making sure that it sinks down through the mixture. Cover with foil and cook for 30 minutes. Remove the foil and cook for a further 10 minutes to brown the surface. Serve with a selection of mixed vegetables.

BAKED MUSSELS <u>AND</u> POTATOES

THIS IMAGINATIVE BAKED CASSEROLE USES SOME OF THE BEST ITALIAN FLAVOURS — TOMATOES, GARLIC, BASIL AND, OF COURSE, PLUMP, JUICY MUSSELS.

SERVES TWO TO THREE

INGREDIENTS
  750g/1¾lb large mussels, in
    their shells
  225g/8oz small firm potatoes
  75ml/5 tbsp olive oil
  2 garlic cloves, finely chopped
  8 fresh basil leaves, torn into pieces
  2 medium tomatoes, peeled and
    thinly sliced
  45ml/3 tbsp breadcrumbs
  ground black pepper
  basil leaves, to garnish

1 Cut off the "beards" from the mussels. Scrub and soak in several changes of cold water. Discard any with broken shells or ones that are open.

2 Place the mussels with a cupful of water in a large saucepan over a medium heat. As soon as they open, lift them out. Remove and discard the empty half shells, leaving the mussels in the other half. (Discard any mussels that do not open at this stage.) Strain any cooking liquid remaining through a layer of kitchen paper, and reserve to add at the final stage.

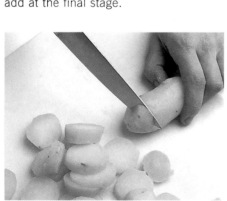

3 Cook the potatoes in a large saucepan of boiling water until they are almost tender. Drain and leave to cool. When they are cool enough to handle, peel and slice them.

4 Preheat the oven to 180°C/350°F/ Gas 4. Spread 30ml/2 tbsp of the olive oil in the bottom of a shallow ovenproof dish. Cover with the potato slices in one layer. Add the mussels in their half shells in one layer. Sprinkle with the garlic and basil. Cover with the tomato slices in one layer.

5 Sprinkle with breadcrumbs and black pepper, the reserved mussel cooking liquid and the remaining olive oil. Bake for about 20 minutes until the tomatoes are soft and the breadcrumbs are golden. Serve hot directly from the baking dish, and garnish with basil.

COD FILLET BAKED <u>WITH</u> SLICED POTATOES

COD FILLET BAKES PERFECTLY, ITS MILD FLAVOUR ENHANCED BY THE HERBS AND ITS JUICES GIVING FLAVOUR TO THE SLICED POTATOES UNDERNEATH.

SERVES FOUR

INGREDIENTS
2 large potatoes, sliced
600ml/1 pint/2½ cups water or
 fish stock
900g/2lb cod fillet, skinned and
 cut into 4 pieces
1 small bunch dill
1 small leek, shredded
50g/2oz/4 tbsp butter
olive oil, to drizzle
salt and ground black pepper
For the sauce
150ml/¼ pint/⅔ cup single cream
shredded leek, to garnish
snipped dill, to garnish

COOK'S TIP
The thicker the fillet of cod, the longer it
will take to cook.

1 Preheat the oven to 200°C/400°F/
Gas 6. Cook the potatoes in the water or
fish stock for 7–10 minutes or until
tender. Drain and reserve the stock.

2 Season the cod pieces. Divide the
potatoes into four portions. Arrange
each one in an overlapping fan shape
on a greased non-stick roasting tin.

3 Season the potatoes and snip some
of the dill over each fan, reserving a
little for the sauce. Scatter over the
leeks, reserving some for the sauce and
add a knob of the butter.

4 Lay the fish over the potatoes.
Scatter the remaining leeks and sliced
potatoes on top of the fish and drizzle
with the olive oil. Bake uncovered for
15–20 minutes.

5 Meanwhile, to make the sauce,
rapidly boil the reserved stock in a
saucepan for 10 minutes or until
reduced by two-thirds. Stir in the
cream and the remaining dill. Boil for
5 minutes to thicken slightly.

6 Remove the fish from the oven and
garnish with dill. Place the individual
portions on plates and serve with
the sauce.

JANSSON'S TEMPTATION

THIS IS ONE OF SWEDEN'S MOST FAMOUS DISHES. LAYERED WITH ANCHOVIES AND ONIONS AND BAKED WITH CREAM, THE POTATOES TAKE ON A WONDERFUL FLAVOUR.

SERVES SIX

INGREDIENTS

1kg/2¼lb potatoes
2 very large onions
2–3 tins anchovy fillets
ground black pepper
150ml/¼ pint/⅔ cup single cream
25g/1oz/2 tbsp butter, finely diced, plus extra for greasing
150ml/¼ pint/⅔ cup double cream

COOK'S TIP
To make this recipe in individual portions, pile all the ingredients except for the double cream on to large squares of buttered foil. Gather up the edges and bring them together. Bake for 40 minutes, then complete according to the recipe.

1 Preheat the oven to 220°C/425°F/ Gas 7. Peel the potatoes and cut into matchsticks. Slice the onions into rings.

2 Grease a 1.75 litre/3 pint/7½ cup casserole dish. Layer half the potatoes and onions in it. Drain the anchovies into a bowl, reserving the oil and lay the fillets over the potatoes, then layer the remaining potatoes and onions. Season.

3 Mix the anchovy oil and single cream together. Then pour evenly over the potatoes. Dot the surface with butter.

4 Cover the potatoes with foil and tightly seal the edges. Bake for 1 hour in the oven. Remove from the oven, taste and adjust the seasonings if necessary. Pour the double cream over and serve immediately.

INDONESIAN PRAWNS <u>WITH</u> SLICED POTATOES

WITH A FRESH TASTING COMBINATION OF PRAWNS AND THINLY SLICED POTATOES MADE IN INDONESIAN STYLE WITH SATAY SAUCE, THIS DISH IS SURPRISINGLY RICH AND FILLING.

SERVES FOUR

INGREDIENTS

2 large waxy maincrop potatoes, peeled and cut in half
120ml/4fl oz/½ cup vegetable oil
1 bunch spring onions, finely sliced
2 red chillies, seeded and diced
450g/1lb peeled cooked prawns
45ml/3 tbsp crunchy peanut butter
200ml/7fl oz/⅞ cup coconut cream
15ml/1 tbsp dark soy sauce
1 bunch chopped fresh coriander
salt

COOK'S TIP
For a more luxurious version, replace the cooked, peeled prawns with fresh raw, shelled king prawns.

1 Cook the potatoes in lightly salted boiling water for 15 minutes until tender. Drain and when cool enough to handle cut into 3mm/⅛in slices. Heat the oil in a frying pan and sauté the potatoes for 10 minutes, turning occasionally until browned. Drain on kitchen paper and keep hot.

2 Drain off almost all of the oil from the pan and fry the spring onions and half the chillies in the pan for 1 minute. Add the prawns and toss for a few seconds.

3 Beat together the peanut butter, coconut cream, soy sauce and remaining chilli. Add this sauce to the prawns and cook for a further minute or two until thoroughly heated through.

4 Lightly grease a large oval platter and arrange the prepared potatoes evenly around the base. Spoon the prawn mixture over until the potatoes are mostly covered over. Top with the coriander.

CLASSIC FISH AND CHIPS

NOTHING BEATS A PIECE OF COD COOKED TO A CRISP WITH FRESHLY MADE CHIPS ON THE SIDE. THE BATTER SHOULD BE LIGHT AND CRISP, BUT NOT TOO GREASY AND THE FISH SHOULD MELT IN THE MOUTH. SERVE WITH LIME WEDGES IF YOU REALLY WANT TO TART IT UP. THE SECRETS OF COOKING FISH AND CHIPS SUCCESSFULLY ARE TO MAKE SURE THE OIL IS FRESH AND CLEAN. HEAT THE OIL TO THE CORRECT TEMPERATURE BEFORE COOKING THE CHIPS AND AGAIN BEFORE ADDING THE FISH. SERVE THE DISH IMMEDIATELY, WHILE STILL CRISP AND PIPING HOT.

SERVES FOUR

INGREDIENTS
　450g/1lb potatoes
　groundnut oil for deep fat frying
　4 x 175g/6oz cod fillets, skinned
　　and any tiny bones removed
For the batter
　75g/3oz/⅔ cup plain flour
　1 egg yolk
　10ml/2 tsp oil
　salt
　lemon wedges, to garnish

1　Cut the potatoes into 5mm/¼in thick slices. Cut each slice again to make 5mm/¼in chips.

2　Heat the oil in a deep fat fryer to 180°C/350°F. Add the chips to the fryer and cook for 3 minutes, then remove from the pan and shake off all fat. Set to one side.

3　To make the batter, sift the flour into a bowl and add the remaining ingredients with a pinch of salt. Beat well until smooth. Set aside until ready to use.

4　Cook the chips again in the fat for a further 5 minutes or so until they are really nice and crisp. Drain on kitchen paper and season with salt. Keep hot in a low oven while you cook the pieces of fish.

VARIATION
Although cod is the traditional choice for fish and chips, you can also use haddock. Rock salmon, sometimes sold as huss or dogfish, also has a good flavour. It has a central bone which cannot be removed before cooking otherwise the pieces of fish will fall apart, but can be easily prized out once the fish is served.

5　Dip the fish into the batter, making sure they are evenly coated and shake off any excess.

6　Carefully lower the fish into the fat and cook for 5 minutes. Drain on kitchen paper. Serve with lemon wedges and the chips.

COOK'S TIP
Use fresh rather than frozen fish for the very best texture and flavour. If you have to use frozen fish, defrost it thoroughly and make sure it is dry before coating with batter.

CARIBBEAN CRAB CAKES

CRAB MEAT MAKES WONDERFUL FISH CAKES, AS EVIDENCED WITH THESE GUTSY MORSELS. SERVED WITH A RICH TOMATO DIP, THEY BECOME GREAT PARTY FOOD TOO, ON "STICKS".

MAKES ABOUT FIFTEEN

INGREDIENTS

225g/8oz white crab meat (fresh, frozen or canned)
115g/4oz cooked floury potatoes, mashed
30ml/2 tbsp fresh herb seasoning
2.5ml/½ tsp mild mustard
2.5ml/½ tsp ground black pepper
½ fresh hot chilli pepper, finely chopped
5ml/1 tsp fresh oregano
1 egg, beaten
plain flour, for dredging
vegetable oil, for frying
lime wedges and coriander sprigs, to garnish
fresh whole chilli peppers, to garnish
For the tomato dip
15g/½oz/1 tbsp butter or margarine
½ onion, finely chopped
2 canned plum tomatoes, chopped
1 garlic clove, crushed
150ml/¼ pint/⅔ cup water
5–10ml/1–2 tsp malt vinegar
15ml/1 tbsp chopped fresh coriander
½ hot fresh chilli pepper, chopped

1 To make the crab cakes, mix together the crab meat, potatoes, herb seasoning, mustard, peppers, oregano and egg in a large bowl. Chill the mixture in the bowl for at least 30 minutes.

2 Meanwhile, make the tomato dip to accompany the crab cakes. Melt the butter or margarine in a small pan over a medium heat.

3 Add the onion, tomatoes and garlic and sauté for about 5 minutes until the onion is tender. Add the water, vinegar, coriander and hot chilli pepper. Bring to the boil then reduce the heat and simmer for 10 minutes.

4 Transfer the mixture to a food processor or blender and blend to a smooth purée. Pour into a bowl. Keep warm or chill as wished.

5 Using a spoon, shape the crab into rounds and dredge with flour, shaking off the excess. Heat a little oil in a frying pan and fry, a few at a time, for 2–3 minutes on each side. Drain on kitchen paper and keep warm in a low oven while cooking the remainder.

6 Serve with the tomato dip and garnish with lime wedges, coriander sprigs and whole chillies.

PILCHARD AND LEEK POTATO CAKES

THIS IS A SIMPLE SUPPER USING A SELECTION OF BASIC STORE CUPBOARD INGREDIENTS. USING
PILCHARDS IN TOMATO SAUCE GIVES A GREATER DEPTH OF FLAVOUR TO THE FINISHED DISH.

SERVES SIX

INGREDIENTS
    225g/8oz potatoes, diced
    425g/15oz can pilchards in tomato
      sauce, boned and flaked
    1 small leek, very finely diced
    5ml/1 tsp lemon juice
    salt and ground black pepper
For the coating
    1 egg, beaten
    75g/3oz/1½ cups fresh white
      breadcrumbs
    vegetable oil for frying
    salad leaves, cucumber and lemon
      wedges, to garnish
    mayonnaise, to serve

1 Cook the potatoes in lightly salted boiling water for 10 minutes or until tender. Drain, mash, and cool.

2 Add the pilchards and their tomato sauce, leeks and lemon juice. Season with salt and pepper and then beat well until you have formed a smooth paste. Chill for 30 minutes.

3 Divide the mixture into six pieces and shape into cakes. Dip each cake in the egg and then the breadcrumbs.

4 Heat the oil and shallow fry the fish cakes on each side for 5 minutes. Drain on kitchen paper and garnish with salad leaves, cucumber ribbons and lemon wedges. Serve with mayonnaise.

TUNA AND CORN FISH CAKES

DEFINITELY ONE FOR YOUNGER MEMBERS OF THE FAMILY WHO LIKE THE SWEET TASTE OF CORN.
THEY MAY EVEN HELP YOU MAKE SOME FISHY-SHAPED CAKES.

SERVES FOUR

INGREDIENTS
   300g/11oz mashed potatoes
   200g/7oz can tuna fish in
     soya oil, drained
   115g/4oz/¾ cup canned or frozen
     sweetcorn
   30ml/2 tbsp chopped fresh parsley
   50g/2oz/1 cup fresh white or brown
     breadcrumbs
   salt and ground black pepper
   grilled baby plum tomatoes and
     salad potatoes, to serve

VARIATIONS
For simple storecupboard variations,
try using canned sardines, red or pink
salmon, or smoked mackerel in place of
the tuna and instant mash when you're
in a real hurry!

1 Preheat the grill. Place the mashed
potatoes in a large bowl and stir in the
tuna fish, sweetcorn and chopped
fresh parsley.

2 Season the mixture to taste with salt
and pepper and mix together
thoroughly, then shape into eight
patty shapes.

3 Lightly coat the fish cakes in the
breadcrumbs, pressing to adhere, then
place on a baking sheet.

4 Cook the fish cakes under the hot
grill until crisp and golden brown on
both sides, turning once. Serve hot with
grilled baby plum tomatoes and small
salad potatoes.

SWEET POTATO, PUMPKIN AND PRAWN CAKES

THIS UNUSUAL ASIAN COMBINATION MAKES A DELICIOUS DISH WHICH NEEDS ONLY A FISH SAUCE OR
SOY SAUCE TO DIP INTO. SERVE WITH NOODLES OR FRIED RICE FOR A LIGHT MEAL.

SERVES FOUR

INGREDIENTS
   200g/7oz/1⅔ cups strong white
     bread flour
   2.5ml/½ tsp salt
   2.5ml/½ tsp dried yeast
   175ml/6fl oz/¾ cup warm water
   1 egg, beaten
   200g/7oz fresh prawn tails, peeled
   225g/8oz pumpkin, peeled, seeded
     and grated
   150g/5oz sweet potato, grated
   2 spring onions, chopped
   50g/2oz water chestnuts, chopped
   2.5ml/½ tsp chilli sauce
   1 garlic clove, crushed
   juice of ½ lime
   vegetable oil, for deep-frying
   lime wedges, to serve

1 Sift together the flour and salt into a
large bowl and make a well in the
centre. In a separate container dissolve
the yeast in the water until creamy then
pour into the centre of the flour and salt
mixture. Pour in the egg and set aside
for a few minutes until bubbles appear.
Mix to form a smooth batter.

2 Place the prawns in a saucepan
with just enough water to cover. Bring
to the boil then reduce the heat and
simmer for about 10 minutes. Drain,
rinse in cold water and drain again
well. Roughly chop then place in a
bowl along with the pumpkin and
sweet potato.

3 Add the spring onions, water
chestnuts, chilli sauce, garlic and lime
juice and mix well. Fold into the batter
mixture carefully until evenly mixed.

4 Heat a 1cm/½in layer of oil in a large
frying pan until really hot. Spoon in the
batter in heaps, leaving space between
each one, and fry until golden on both
sides. Drain on kitchen paper and serve
with the lime wedges.

SWEET POTATO FISH ROLLS

*THE SWEETNESS OF THE POTATOES IS OFFSET PERFECTLY BY THE TARTNESS OF THE LEMON BUTTER
SAUCE SERVED OVER THE FISH ROLLS.*

SERVES FOUR

INGREDIENTS
    2 large sweet potatoes
    450g/1lb cod fillet
    300ml/½ pint/1¼ cups milk
    300ml/½ pint/1¼ cups water
    30ml/2 tbsp chopped parsley
    rind and juice of 1 lemon
    2 eggs, beaten
For the coating
    175g/6oz/3 cups fresh white
       breadcrumbs
    5ml/1 tsp Thai 7-spice seasoning
    vegetable oil, for frying
For the sauce
    50g/2oz/4 tbsp butter
    150ml/¼ pint/⅔ cup single cream
    15ml/1 tbsp chopped fresh dill
    lemon zest, to serve

3 Place the cod fillet in a large frying
pan and pour over the milk and water.
Cover and poach for 10 minutes or until
the fish starts to flake.

4 Drain and discard the milk, and then
remove the skin and the bones from
the fish.

6 Divide and shape the mixture into
8 oval sausages. Dip each in egg. Mix
the breadcrumbs with the seasoning.
Roll the dipped fish rolls in the
breadcrumbs.

7 Heat the oil and shallow fry in
batches for about 7 minutes, carefully
rolling the rolls to brown evenly.
Remove from the pan and drain on
kitchen paper. Keep hot.

1 Scrub the sweet potatoes and cook
them in their skins in plenty of lightly
salted boiling water for 45 minutes or
until very tender. Drain and cool.

5 Flake the fish into the potatoes in a
large bowl, stir in the parsley, the rind
and juice of ½ of the lemon and 1 egg.
Chill for 30 minutes.

COOK'S TIP
Make sure the mixture is chilled
thoroughly before you begin shaping and
cooking. This helps to hold the
ingredients together.

8 To make the sauce, melt the butter
in a small pan and add the remaining
lemon juice and rind and allow the
mixture to sizzle for a few seconds.

9 Remove from the heat and add the
cream and dill. Whisk well to prevent
the sauce from curdling and serve with
the fish rolls.

2 When the potatoes are cool, peel the
skins and mash the flesh.

Vegetarian Dishes

GIVE THE CLASSIC JACKET POTATO A NEW TWIST WITH A CHOICE OF INTERESTING TOPPINGS. USE POTATOES TO TOP A PIZZA, OR ADD THEM TO A RICH CHEESY BAKE OR A SPICY, GARLIC-FLAVOURED CASSEROLE. MANY COUNTRIES HAVE THEIR OWN SIGNATURE DISHES, SUCH AS GREEK TOMATO AND POTATO BAKE, WHERE CHUNKS OF POTATO ARE SLOW COOKED WITH MEDITERRANEAN RIPENED TOMATOES AND GARLIC — SIMPLY DELICIOUS.

POTATO AND CABBAGE RISSOLES

ORIGINALLY MADE ON MONDAYS WITH LEFTOVER POTATOES AND CABBAGE FROM THE SUNDAY LUNCH, THESE RISSOLES ARE QUICK TO MAKE AND GREAT FOR ANY LIGHT MEAL. OR MAKE THEM FOR BRUNCH TEAMED WITH FRIED EGGS, GRILLED TOMATOES AND MUSHROOMS.

SERVES FOUR

INGREDIENTS
450g/1lb mashed potato
225g/8oz steamed or boiled cabbage
  or kale, shredded
1 egg, beaten
115g/4oz/1 cup Cheddar cheese,
  grated
freshly grated nutmeg
plain flour, for coating
vegetable oil, for frying
salt and ground black pepper
lettuce, to serve

COOK'S TIP
If you want to flavour the rissoles with a stronger tasting cheese, try a blue, such as Stilton or Shropshire Blue.

1 Mix the potato with the cabbage or kale, egg, cheese, nutmeg and seasoning. Divide and shape into eight small sausage shapes.

2 Chill for an hour or so, if possible, as this enables the rissoles to become firm and makes them easier to fry. Dredge them in the flour, shaking off the excess.

3 Heat a 1cm/½in layer of oil in a frying pan until it is really hot. Carefully slide the rissoles into the oil and fry in batches on each side for about 3 minutes until golden and crisp.

4 Remove the rissoles from the pan and drain on kitchen paper. Serve piping hot with fresh lettuce leaves.

POTATO, MOZZARELLA AND GARLIC PIZZA

NEW POTATOES, SMOKED MOZZARELLA AND GARLIC MAKE THIS PIZZA UNIQUE. YOU COULD ADD SLICED SMOKED PORK SAUSAGE OR PASTRAMI TO MAKE IT EVEN MORE SUBSTANTIAL.

SERVES TWO TO THREE

INGREDIENTS
350g/12oz small new or
  salad potatoes
45ml/3 tbsp olive oil
2 garlic cloves, crushed
1 pizza base, 25–30cm/
  10–12 in diameter
1 red onion, thinly sliced
150g/5oz/1¼ cups smoked mozzarella
  cheese, grated
10ml/2 tsp chopped fresh rosemary
  or sage
salt and ground black pepper
30ml/2 tbsp freshly grated Parmesan
  cheese, to garnish

1 Preheat the oven to 220°C/425°F/ Gas 7. Cook the potatoes in boiling salted water for 5 minutes. Drain well and leave to cool. Peel and slice thinly.

2 Heat 30ml/2 tbsp of the oil in a frying pan. Add the sliced potatoes and garlic and fry for 5–8 minutes turning frequently until tender.

3 Brush the pizza base with the remaining oil. Scatter the onion over, then arrange the potatoes on top.

4 Sprinkle over the mozzarella and rosemary or sage and plenty of black pepper. Bake for 15–20 minutes until golden. Remove from the oven, sprinkle with Parmesan and more black pepper.

BAKED POTATOES AND THREE FILLINGS

POTATOES BAKED IN THEIR SKINS UNTIL THEY ARE CRISP ON THE OUTSIDE AND FLUFFY IN THE MIDDLE MAKE AN EXCELLENT AND NOURISHING MEAL ON THEIR OWN. BUT FOR AN EVEN BETTER TREAT, ADD ONE OF THESE DELICIOUS AND EASY TOPPINGS.

SERVES FOUR

INGREDIENTS
    4 medium baking potatoes
    olive oil
    sea salt
    filling of your choice (see below)

COOK'S TIP
Choose potatoes which are evenly sized and have undamaged skins, and scrub them thoroughly. If they are done before you are ready to serve them, take them out of the oven and wrap them up in a warmed cloth until they are needed.

1 Preheat the oven to 200°C/400°F/ Gas 6. Score the potatoes with a cross and rub all over with the olive oil.

2 Place on a baking sheet and cook for 45 minutes to 1 hour until a knife inserted into the centres indicates they are cooked. Or cook in the microwave according to your manufacturer's instructions.

3 Cut the potatoes open along the score lines and push up the flesh. Season and fill with your chosen filling.

STIR-FRY VEG
    45ml/3 tbsp groundnut or sunflower oil
    2 leeks, thinly sliced
    2 carrots, cut into sticks
    1 courgette, thinly sliced
    115g/4oz baby corn, halved
    115g/4oz/1½ cup button mushrooms, sliced
    45ml/3 tbsp soy sauce
    30ml/2 tbsp dry sherry or vermouth
    15ml/1 tbsp sesame oil
    sesame seeds, to garnish

1 Heat the groundnut or sunflower oil in a wok or large frying pan until really hot. Add the leeks, carrots, courgette and baby corn and stir-fry together for about 2 minutes, then add the mushrooms and stir-fry for a further minute. Mix the soy sauce, sherry or vermouth and sesame oil and pour over the vegetables. Heat through until just bubbling and scatter the sesame seeds over.

RED BEAN CHILLIES
    425g/15oz can red kidney beans, drained
    200g/7oz/scant 1 cup low-fat cottage or cream cheese
    30ml/2 tbsp mild chilli sauce
    5ml/1 tsp ground cumin

1 Heat the beans in a pan or microwave and stir in the cottage or cream cheese, chilli sauce and cumin.

2 Serve topped with more chilli sauce.

CHEESE AND CREAMY CORN
    425g/15oz can creamed corn
    115g/4oz/1 cup hard cheese, grated
    5ml/1 tsp mixed dried herbs
    fresh parsley sprigs, to garnish

1 Heat the corn gently with the cheese and mixed herbs until well blended.

2 Use to fill the potatoes and garnish with fresh parsley sprigs.

TRUFFADE

BAKED UNTIL MELTINGLY SOFT, THIS WARMING CHEESE AND POTATO SUPPER IS THE PERFECT SLOW BAKE TO COME HOME TO. IN FRANCE, WHERE IT ORIGINATED, IT WOULD BE MADE WITH A TOMME OR CANTAL CHEESE WHICH ARE NOW READILY AVAILABLE.

SERVES FOUR TO SIX

INGREDIENTS
    a little sunflower oil or melted butter
    1 large onion, thinly sliced
    675g/1½lb baking potatoes, very
        thinly sliced
    150g/5oz/1¼ cups grated hard
        cheese, such as Tomme, Cantal or
        mature Cheddar
    freshly grated nutmeg
    salt and ground black pepper
    mixed salad leaves, to serve

VARIATION
In France, they make a non-vegetarian version of this dish, which is cooked with diced streaky bacon (lardons) and the cheese is chopped, not grated. The ingredients are mixed and cooked slowly in a little lard in a pan on top of the stove.

1 Preheat the oven to 180°C/350°F/ Gas 4. Lightly grease the base of a shallow baking dish or roasting tin with the oil or melted butter.

2 Arrange a layer of onions over the bottom of the dish and then add a layer of potatoes over them, and a sprinkling of cheese. Finish with a layer of potatoes.

3 Brush the top layer of potatoes with oil or melted butter and season with nutmeg, salt and pepper.

4 Top the dish with a layer of cheese. Bake for 1 hour 5 minutes until the vegetables are tender and the top is golden brown. Leave the dish to stand for about 5 minutes, then serve in wedges with a salad.

POTATOES BAKED <u>WITH</u> TOMATOES

THIS SIMPLE, HEARTY DISH FROM THE SOUTH OF ITALY IS BEST WHEN TOMATOES ARE IN SEASON AND BURSTING WITH FLAVOUR, BUT IT CAN ALSO BE MADE WITH CANNED PLUM TOMATOES.

SERVES SIX

INGREDIENTS
    2 large red or yellow onions,
        thinly sliced
    1kg/2¼lb baking potatoes,
        thinly sliced
    450g/1lb tomatoes, fresh or canned,
        sliced, with their juice
    90ml/6 tbsp olive oil
    115g/4oz/1 cup Parmesan
        or Cheddar cheese,
        freshly grated
    a few fresh basil leaves
    50ml/2fl oz/¼ cup water
    salt and ground black pepper

1 Preheat the oven to 180°C/350°F/ Gas 4. Brush a large baking dish generously with oil.

2 Arrange a layer of some onions in the base of the dish, followed by layers of some potatoes and tomatoes alternating them to make the dish look colourful. Pour a little of the oil over the surface, and sprinkle with some of the cheese. Season with salt and ground black pepper.

3 Continue to layer the vegetables in the dish until they are used up, ending with an overlapping layer of potatoes and tomatoes. Tear the basil leaves into small pieces, and add them here and there among the vegetables, saving a few for garnish. Sprinkle the top with the remaining grated cheese and oil.

4 Pour the water over the dish. Bake in the oven for 1 hour until the vegetables are tender.

5 Check the potato dish towards the end of cooking and if the top begins to brown too much, place a sheet of foil or greaseproof paper, or a flat baking tray on top of the dish. Garnish the dish with the remaining fresh basil, once it is cooked, and serve hot.

TURKISH-STYLE NEW POTATO CASSEROLE

HERE'S A MEAL IN A POT THAT'S SUITABLE FOR FEEDING LARGE NUMBERS OF PEOPLE. IT'S LIGHTLY SPICED AND HAS PLENTY OF GARLIC — WHO COULD REFUSE?

SERVES FOUR

INGREDIENTS

  60ml/4 tbsp olive oil
  1 large onion, chopped
  2 small–medium aubergines, cut into
    small cubes
  4 courgettes, cut into small chunks
  1 green pepper, seeded and chopped
  1 red or yellow pepper, seeded
    and chopped
  115g/4oz/1 cup fresh or frozen peas
  115g/4oz French beans
  450g/1lb new or salad
    potatoes, cubed
  2.5ml/½ tsp cinnamon
  2.5ml/½ tsp ground cumin
  5ml/1 tsp paprika
  4–5 tomatoes, skinned
  400g/14oz can chopped tomatoes
  30ml/2 tbsp chopped fresh parsley
  3–4 garlic cloves, crushed
  350ml/12fl oz/1½ cups
    vegetable stock
  salt and ground black pepper
  black olives, to garnish
  fresh parsley, to garnish

1 Preheat the oven to 190°C/375°F/ Gas 5. Heat 45ml/3 tbsp of the oil in a heavy-based pan, add the onion and fry until golden. Add the aubergines, sauté for about 3 minutes and then add the courgettes, green and red or yellow peppers, peas, beans and potatoes, together with the spices and seasoning.

2 Continue to cook for 3 minutes, stirring all the time. Transfer to a shallow ovenproof dish.

3 Halve, seed and chop the fresh tomatoes and mix with the canned tomatoes, parsley, garlic and the remaining olive oil in a bowl.

4 Pour the stock over the aubergine mixture and then spoon over the prepared tomato mixture.

5 Cover and bake the dish for 30–45 minutes until the vegetables are tender. Serve hot, garnished with black olives and parsley.

POTATO GNOCCHI

GNOCCHI ARE LITTLE ITALIAN DUMPLINGS MADE EITHER WITH MASHED POTATO AND FLOUR, OR WITH SEMOLINA. TO ENSURE THAT THEY ARE LIGHT AND FLUFFY, TAKE CARE NOT TO OVERMIX THE DOUGH.

4 Divide the dough into 4 pieces. On a lightly floured surface, form each into a roll about 2cm/¾in in diameter. Cut the rolls crossways into pieces about 2cm/¾in long.

5 Hold an ordinary table fork with tines sideways, leaning on the board. Then one by one, press and roll the gnocchi lightly along the tines of the fork towards the points, making ridges on one side, and a depression from your thumb on the other.

6 Bring a large pan of salted water to a fast boil, then drop in about half the prepared gnocchi

7 When the gnocchi rise to the surface, after 3–4 minutes they are done. Lift them out with a slotted spoon, drain well, and place in a warmed serving bowl. Dot with butter. Cover to keep warm while cooking the remainder. As soon as they are cooked, toss the gnocchi with the butter, garnish with Parmesan shavings and fresh basil leaves, and serve at once.

SERVES FOUR TO SIX

INGREDIENTS
 1kg/2¼lb waxy potatoes
 250–300g/9–11oz/2¼–2¾ cups
  plain flour, plus more
  if necessary
 1 egg
 pinch of freshly grated nutmeg
 25g/1oz/2 tbsp butter
 salt
 fresh basil leaves, to garnish
 Parmesan cheese cut in shavings,
  to garnish

COOK'S TIP
Gnocchi are also excellent served with a heated sauce, such as Bolognese.

1 Cook the potatoes in their skins in a large saucepan of boiling salted water until tender but not falling apart. Drain and peel while the potatoes are still hot.

2 Spread a layer of flour on a work surface. Pass the hot potatoes through a food mill, dropping them directly on to the flour. Sprinkle with about half of the remaining flour and mix in very lightly. Break the egg into the mixture.

3 Finally add the nutmeg to the dough and knead lightly, adding more flour if the mixture is too loose. When the dough is light to the touch and no longer moist t is ready to be rolled.

PUMPKIN GNOCCHI <u>WITH A</u> CHANTERELLE PARSLEY CREAM

ITALIANS LOVE PUMPKIN AND OFTEN INCORPORATE IT INTO THEIR DUMPLINGS AND OTHER TRADITIONAL PASTA DISHES AS IT ADDS A SLIGHT SWEET RICHNESS. THESE GNOCCHI ARE SUPERB ON THEIR OWN BUT THEY ARE ALSO GREAT SERVED WITH MEAT OR GAME.

SERVES FOUR

INGREDIENTS
  450g/1lb floury potatoes
  450g/1lb pumpkin, peeled, seeded
    and chopped
  2 egg yolks
  200g/7oz/1¾ cups plain flour, plus
    more if necessary
  pinch of ground allspice
  1.5ml/¼ tsp cinnamon
  pinch of freshly grated nutmeg
  finely grated rind of ½ orange
  salt and ground pepper
For the sauce
  30ml/2 tbsp olive oil
  1 shallot, finely chopped
  175g/6oz/2½ cups fresh chanterelles,
    sliced, or 15g/½oz/½ cup dried,
    soaked in warm water for
    20 minutes, then drained
  10ml/2 tsp almond butter
  150ml/¼ pint/⅔ cup crème fraîche
  a little milk or water
  75ml/5 tbsp chopped fresh parsley
  50g/2oz/½ cup Parmesan cheese,
    freshly grated

1 Cook the potatoes in a large saucepan of boiling salted water for 20 minutes. Drain and set aside.

2 Place the pumpkin in a bowl, cover and microwave on full power for 8 minutes. Alternatively, wrap the pumpkin in foil and bake at 180°C/ 350°F/Gas 4 for 30 minutes. Drain well.

3 Pass the pumpkin and potatoes through a food mill into a bowl. Add the egg yolks, flour, spices, orange rind and seasoning and mix well to make a soft dough. If you find that the mixture is too loose you can add a little more flour to stiffen it up.

4 Bring a large pan of salted water to a fast boil. Meanwhile, spread a layer of flour on a clean work surface. Spoon the prepared gnocchi mixture into a piping bag fitted with a 1cm/½in plain nozzle.

VARIATION
Turn these gnocchi into a main meal for vegetarians by serving them with a rich home-made tomato sauce. If you want to make the dish more special, serve the gnocchi with a side dish of ratatouille made from courgettes, peppers and aubergines, cooked gently with tomatoes, plenty of garlic and really good extra virgin olive oil.

5 Pipe directly on to the flour to make a 15cm/6in sausage. Roll in flour and cut crossways into 2.5cm/1in pieces. Repeat to make more sausage shapes and pieces. Mark each lightly with the tines of a fork and drop into the boiling water. When they rise to the surface, after 3–4 minutes, they are done.

6 Meanwhile make the sauce. Heat the oil in a non-stick frying pan, add the shallot and fry until soft but not coloured. Add the chanterelles and cook briefly, then add the almond butter. Stir to melt and stir in the crème fraîche. Simmer briefly and adjust the consistency with milk or water. Add the parsley and season to taste.

7 Lift the gnocchi out of the water with a slotted spoon, drain well, and turn into bowls. Spoon the sauce over the top, sprinkle with grated Parmesan, and serve at once.

COOK'S TIPS
If planning ahead, gnocchi can be shaped, ready for cooking, up to 8 hours in advance. Almond butter is available from health food shops.

POTATO CAKES WITH GOAT'S CHEESE

GRILLED GOAT'S CHEESE MAKES A DELICATELY TANGY AND GENTLY BUBBLING TOPPING FOR THESE HERBY POTATO CAKES. SERVE WITH A FLAVOURSOME SALAD.

<u>SERVES TWO TO FOUR</u>

INGREDIENTS
    450g/1lb floury potatoes
    10ml/2 tsp chopped fresh thyme
    1 garlic clove, crushed
    2 spring onions (including the green
        parts), finely chopped
    30ml/2 tbsp olive oil
    50g/2oz/4 tbsp unsalted butter
    2 x 65g/2½oz firm goat's cheese
    salt and ground black pepper
    salad leaves, such as curly endive,
        radicchio and lamb's lettuce, tossed
        in walnut dressing, to serve
    thyme sprigs, to garnish

COOK'S TIP
These potato cakes make great party snacks. Make them half the size and serve warm on a large platter.

1 Coarsely grate the potatoes. Using your hands, squeeze out as much of the thick starchy liquid as possible, then gently combine with the chopped thyme, garlic, spring onions and seasoning.

2 Heat half the oil and butter in a non-stick frying pan. Add two large spoonfuls of the potato mixture, spacing them well apart, and press firmly down with a spatula. Cook for 3–4 minutes on each side until golden.

3 Drain the potato cakes on kitchen paper and keep warm in a low oven. Heat the remaining oil and butter and fry two more potato cakes in the same way with the remaining mixture. Meanwhile preheat the grill.

4 Cut the cheese in half horizontally and place one half, cut side up, on each potato cake. Grill for 2–3 minutes until lightly golden. Serve on plates and arrange the salad leaves around them. Garnish with thyme sprigs.

WILD MUSHROOM GRATIN WITH BEAUFORT CHEESE, NEW POTATOES AND WALNUTS

THIS IS ONE OF THE SIMPLEST AND MOST DELICIOUS WAYS OF COOKING MUSHROOMS. SERVE THIS DISH AS THE SWISS DO, WITH NEW POTATOES AND GHERKINS.

<u>SERVES FOUR</u>

INGREDIENTS
    900g/2lb small new or
        salad potatoes
    50g/2oz/4 tbsp unsalted butter or
        60ml/4 tbsp olive oil
    350g/12oz/5 cups assorted wild and
        cultivated mushrooms, thinly sliced
    175g/6oz Beaufort or Fontina cheese,
        thinly sliced
    50g/2oz/½ cup broken walnuts,
        toasted
    salt and ground black pepper
    12 gherkins and mixed green salad
        leaves, to serve

1 Cook the potatoes in boiling salted water for 20 minutes until tender. Drain and return to the pan. Add a knob of butter or oil and cover to keep warm.

2 Heat the remaining butter or the oil in a frying pan over a medium-high heat. Add the mushrooms and fry until their juices appear, then increase the heat and fry until most of their juices have cooked away. Season.

3 Meanwhile preheat the grill. Arrange the cheese on top of the mushroom slices, place the pan under the grill and grill until bubbly and golden brown. Scatter the gratin with walnuts and serve at once with the buttered potatoes and sliced gherkins. Serve a side dish of mixed green salad to complete this meal.

SPICY POTATO STRUDEL

WRAP UP A TASTY MIXTURE OF VEGETABLES IN A SPICY, CREAMY SAUCE WITH CRISP FILO PASTRY. SERVE WITH A GOOD SELECTION OF CHUTNEYS OR A YOGURT SAUCE.

SERVES FOUR

INGREDIENTS
1 onion, chopped
2 carrots, coarsely grated
1 courgette, chopped
350g/12oz firm potatoes,
 finely chopped
65g/2½oz/5 tbsp butter
10ml/2 tsp mild curry paste
2.5ml/½ tsp dried thyme
150ml/¼ pint/⅔ cup water
1 egg, beaten
30ml/2 tbsp single cream
50g/2oz/½ cup Cheddar
 cheese, grated
8 sheets filo pastry, thawed if frozen
sesame seeds, for sprinkling
salt and ground black pepper

1 In a large frying pan cook the onion, carrots, courgette and potatoes in 25g/1oz/2 tbsp of the butter for 5 minutes tossing frequently so they cook evenly. Add the curry paste and stir in. Continue to cook, the vegetables for a further minute or so.

2 Add the thyme, water and seasoning. Bring to the boil then reduce the heat and simmer for 10 minutes until tender, stirring occasionally.

3 Remove from the heat and leave to cool. Transfer the mixture into a large bowl and then mix in the egg, cream and cheese. Chill until ready to fill the filo pastry.

4 Melt the remaining butter and lay out four sheets of filo pastry, slightly overlapping them to form a fairly large rectangle. Brush with some melted butter and fit the other sheets on top. Brush again.

5 Preheat the oven to 190°C/375°F/ Gas 5. Spoon the filling along one long side, then roll up the pastry. Form it into a circle and set on a baking sheet. Brush again with the last of the butter and sprinkle over the sesame seeds.

6 Bake the strudel in the oven for about 25 minutes until golden and crisp. Stand for 5 minutes before cutting.

PEPPER AND POTATO TORTILLA

TORTILLA IS TRADITIONALLY A SPANISH DISH LIKE A THICK OMELETTE, BEST EATEN COLD IN CHUNKY WEDGES. IT MAKES IDEAL PICNICKING FOOD. USE A HARD SPANISH CHEESE, LIKE MAHÓN, OR A GOAT'S CHEESE, ALTHOUGH SHARP CHEDDAR MAKES A GOOD SUBSTITUTE.

SERVES FOUR

INGREDIENTS

    2 medium firm potatoes
    45ml/3 tbsp olive oil, plus more
      if necessary
    1 large onion, thinly sliced
    2 garlic cloves, crushed
    2 peppers, one green and one red,
      seeded and thinly sliced
    6 eggs, beaten
    115g/4oz/1 cup sharp cheese, grated
    salt and ground black pepper

VARIATION
You can add any sliced and lightly cooked vegetable, such as mushrooms, courgette or broccoli, to this tortilla instead of the green and red peppers. Cooked pasta or brown rice are both excellent alternatives to the potatoes.

1 Par-boil the potatoes in boiling water for about 10 minutes. Drain and leave to cool slightly. Slice them thickly. Preheat the grill.

2 In a large non-stick or well-seasoned frying pan, heat the oil over a medium heat. Add the onion, garlic and peppers and cook for 5 minutes until softened.

3 Add the potatoes and continue frying, stirring occasionally, until the potatoes are tender.

4 Pour in half the beaten eggs, sprinkle half the cheese over this and then the remainder of the egg. Season. Finish with a layer of cheese. Reduce the heat to low and continue to cook without stirring, half covering the pan with a lid to help set the eggs.

5 When the tortilla is firm, place the pan under the hot grill to seal the top just lightly. Leave the tortilla in the pan to cool. Serve at room temperature, cut into wedges.

CHINESE POTATOES WITH CHILLI BEANS

EAST MEETS WEST IN THIS AMERICAN-STYLE DISH WITH A CHINESE FLAVOUR — THE SAUCE IS PARTICULARLY TASTY. TRY IT AS A QUICK SUPPER WHEN YOU FANCY A MEAL WITH A LITTLE ZING!

SERVES FOUR

INGREDIENTS
    4 medium firm or waxy potatoes,
      cut into thick chunks
    30ml/2 tbsp sunflower or
      groundnut oil
    3 spring onions, sliced
    1 large fresh chilli, seeded and sliced
    2 garlic cloves, crushed
    400g/14oz can red kidney
      beans, drained
    30ml/2 tbsp soy sauce
    15ml/1 tbsp sesame oil
    15ml/1 tbsp sesame seeds,
      to garnish
    chopped fresh coriander or parsley,
      to garnish
    salt and ground black pepper

1 Cook the potatoes in boiling water until they are just tender. Take care not to overcook them. Drain and reserve.

2 Heat the oil in a large frying pan or wok over a medium-high heat. Add the spring onions and chilli and stir-fry for about 1 minute, then add the garlic and stir-fry for a few seconds longer.

3 Add the potatoes, stirring well, then the beans and finally the soy sauce and sesame oil.

4 Season to taste and continue to cook the vegetables until they are well heated through. Sprinkle with the sesame seeds and the coriander or parsley and serve hot.

GREEK TOMATO AND POTATO BAKE

AN ADAPTATION OF A CLASSIC GREEK DISH, WHICH IS USUALLY COOKED ON THE HOB. THIS RECIPE HAS A RICHER FLAVOUR AS IT IS STOVE COOKED FIRST AND THEN BAKED IN THE OVEN.

SERVES FOUR

INGREDIENTS
    120ml/4fl oz/½ cup olive oil
    1 large onion, finely chopped
    3 garlic cloves, crushed
    4 large ripe tomatoes, peeled,
      deseeded and chopped
    1kg/2¼lb even-size main crop
      waxy potatoes
    salt and freshly ground black pepper
    flat leaf parsley, to garnish

COOK'S TIP
Make sure that the potatoes are completely coated in the oil for even cooking.

1 Preheat the oven to 180°C/350°F/ Gas 4. Heat the oil in a flameproof casserole. Fry the onion and garlic for 5 minutes until softened and just starting to brown.

2 Add the tomatoes to the pan, season and cook for 1 minute. Cut the potatoes into wedges. Add to the pan. Cook for 10 minutes. Season again and cover with a tight fitting lid.

3 Place the covered casserole on the middle shelf of the oven and cook for 45 minutes–1 hour. Garnish with flat leaf parsley.

CHILLI CHEESE TORTILLA WITH FRESH TOMATO SALSA

GOOD WARM OR COLD, THIS IS LIKE A SLICED POTATO QUICHE WITHOUT THE PASTRY BASE, WELL SPIKED WITH CHILLI. THE SALSA CAN BE MADE WITHOUT THE CHILLI IF YOU PREFER.

SERVES FOUR

INGREDIENTS
    45ml/3 tbsp sunflower or olive oil
    1 small onion, thinly sliced
    2–3 fresh green jalapeño chillies,
       seeded and sliced
    200g/7oz cold cooked potato,
       thinly sliced
    120g/4¼oz/generous 1 cup cheese,
       grated (use a firm but not hard
       cheese, such as Double Gloucester,
       Monterey Jack or Manchego)
    6 eggs, beaten
    salt and ground black pepper
    fresh herbs, to garnish
For the salsa
    500g/1¼lb fresh flavoursome
       tomatoes, peeled, seeded and
       finely chopped
    1 fresh mild green chilli, seeded and
       finely chopped
    2 garlic cloves, crushed
    45ml/3 tbsp chopped fresh coriander
    juice of 1 lime
    2.5ml/½ tsp salt

1 To make the salsa, put the tomatoes in a bowl and add the chopped chilli, garlic, coriander, lime juice and salt. Mix well and set aside.

2 Heat 15ml/1 tbsp of the oil in a large omelette pan and gently fry the onion and jalapeños for 5 minutes, stirring until softened. Add the potato and cook for 5 minutes until lightly browned, keeping the slices whole.

3 Using a slotted spoon, transfer the vegetables to a warm plate. Wipe the pan with kitchen paper, then add the remaining oil and heat until really hot. Return the vegetables to the pan. Scatter the cheese over the top. Season.

4 Pour in the beaten eggs, making sure that they seep under the vegetables. Cook the tortilla over a low heat, without stirring, until set. Serve hot or cold, cut into wedges, garnished with fresh herbs and with the salsa on the side.

POTATO AND RED PEPPER FRITTATA

FRITTATA IS LIKE A LARGE OMELETTE, THIS TASTY VERSION IS FILLED WITH POTATOES AND PLENTY OF HERBS. DO USE FRESH MINT IN PREFERENCE TO DRIED IF YOU CAN FIND IT.

2 Whisk together the eggs, mint and seasoning in a bowl, then set aside. Heat the oil in a large frying pan.

3 Add the onion, garlic, peppers and potatoes to the pan and cook, stirring occasionally, for 5 minutes.

4 Pour the egg mixture over the vegetables in the frying pan and stir gently.

5 Push the mixture towards the centre of the pan as it cooks to allow the liquid egg to run on to the base. Meanwhile preheat the grill.

6 When the frittata is lightly set, place the pan under the hot grill for 2–3 minutes until the top is a light golden brown colour.

7 Serve hot or cold cut into wedges piled high on a serving dish and garnished with sprigs of mint.

SERVES THREE TO FOUR

INGREDIENTS
   450g/1lb small new or
    salad potatoes
   6 eggs
   30ml/2 tbsp chopped fresh mint
   30ml/2 tbsp olive oil
   1 onion, chopped
   2 garlic cloves, crushed
   2 red peppers, seeded and
    roughly chopped
   salt and ground black pepper
   mint sprigs, to garnish

1 Cook the potatoes in their skins in boiling salted water until just tender. Drain and leave to cool slightly, then cut into thick slices.

POTATOES WITH BLUE CHEESE AND WALNUTS

FIRM SMALL POTATOES, SERVED IN A CREAMY BLUE CHEESE SAUCE WITH THE CRUNCH OF WALNUTS, MAKE A GREAT SIDE DISH TO A SIMPLE ROAST MEAL. FOR A CHANGE, SERVE IT AS A LUNCH DISH OR A LIGHT SUPPER WITH A GREEN SALAD.

SERVES FOUR

INGREDIENTS
  450g/1lb small new or
    salad potatoes
  1 small head of celery, sliced
  1 small red onion, sliced
  115g/4oz/1 cup blue cheese, mashed
  150ml/¼ pint/⅔ cup single cream
  50g/2oz/½ cup walnut pieces
  30ml/2 tbsp chopped fresh parsley
  salt and ground black pepper

COOK'S TIP
Use a combination of blue cheeses, such as Dolcelatte and Roquefort, or go for the distinctive flavour of Stilton on its own. If walnuts are not available, blue cheeses marry equally well with hazelnuts.

1 Cook the potatoes in their skins in a large saucepan with plenty of boiling water for about 15 minutes or until tender, adding the sliced celery and onion to the pan for the last 5 minutes or so of cooking.

2 Drain the vegetables well through a colander and put them into a shallow serving dish.

3 In a small saucepan, slowly melt the cheese in the cream, stirring occasionally. Do not allow the mixture to boil but heat it until it scalds.

4 Check the sauce and season to taste. Pour it evenly over the vegetables in the dish and scatter over the walnut pieces and fresh parsley. Serve hot, straight from the dish.

RACLETTE WITH NEW POTATOES

TRADITIONAL TO BOTH SWITZERLAND AND FRANCE, RACLETTE MELTS TO A VELVETY CREAMINESS AND WARM GOLDEN COLOUR AND HAS A SAVOURY TASTE WITH A HINT OF SWEETNESS.

SERVES FOUR

INGREDIENTS
For the pickle
  2 red onions, sliced
  5ml/1 tsp sugar
  90ml/6 tbsp red wine vinegar
  2.5ml/½ tsp salt
  generous pinch of dried dill
For the potatoes
  500g/1¼lb new or salad potatoes,
    halved if large
  250g/9oz raclette cheese slices
  salt and ground black pepper

1 To make the pickle spread out the onions in a glass dish, pour over boiling water to cover and leave until cold.

2 Meanwhile mix the sugar, vinegar, salt and dill in a small pan. Heat gently, stirring, until the sugar has dissolved, then set aside to cool.

3 Drain the onions and return them to the dish, pour the vinegar mixture over, cover and leave for at least 1 hour, preferably overnight.

4 Cook the potatoes in their skins in boiling water until tender, then drain and place in a roasting tin. Preheat the grill. Season the potatoes and arrange the raclette on top. Place the tin under the grill until the cheese melts. Serve hot. Drain the excess vinegar from the red onion pickle and serve the pickle with the potatoes.

COOK'S TIP
To speed up the process look for ready-sliced raclette for this dish. It is available from most large supermarkets and specialist cheese shops.

LAYERED VEGETABLE TERRINE

A COMBINATION OF VEGETABLES AND HERBS LAYERED AND BAKED IN A SPINACH-LINED LOAF TIN. DELICIOUS SERVED HOT OR WARM WITH A SIMPLE SALAD GARNISH.

SERVES SIX

INGREDIENTS
   3 red peppers, halved
   450g/1lb main crop waxy potatoes
   115g/4oz spinach leaves, trimmed
   25g/1oz/2 tbsp butter
   pinch grated nutmeg
   115g/4oz/1 cup vegetarian Cheddar
      cheese, grated
   1 medium courgette, sliced
      lengthways and blanched
   salt and ground black pepper

1 Preheat the oven to 180°C/350°F/ Gas 4. Place the peppers in a roasting tin and roast, cores in place, for 30–45 minutes until charred. Remove from the oven. Place in a plastic bag to cool. Peel the skins and remove the cores. Halve the potatoes and boil in lightly salted water for 10–15 minutes.

2 Blanch the spinach for a few seconds in boiling water. Drain and pat dry on kitchen paper. Line the base and sides of a 900g/2lb loaf tin, making sure the leaves overlap slightly.

3 Slice the potatoes thinly and lay one-third of the potatoes over the base, dot with a little of the butter and season with salt, pepper and nutmeg. Sprinkle a little cheese over.

4 Arrange 3 of the peeled pepper halves on top. Sprinkle a little cheese over and then a layer of courgettes. Lay another one-third of the potatoes on top with the remaining peppers and some more cheese, seasoning as you go. Lay the final layer of potato on top and scatter over any remaining cheese. Fold the spinach leaves over. Cover with foil.

5 Place the loaf tin in a roasting tin and pour boiling water around the outside, making sure the water comes halfway up the sides of the tin. Bake for 45 minutes–1 hour. Remove from the oven and turn the loaf out. Serve sliced with lettuce and tomatoes.

BAKED SCALLOPED POTATOES WITH FETA CHEESE AND OLIVES

THINLY SLICED POTATOES ARE COOKED WITH GREEK FETA CHEESE AND BLACK AND GREEN OLIVES IN OLIVE OIL. THIS DISH IS A GOOD ONE TO SERVE WITH TOASTED PITTA BREAD.

SERVES FOUR

INGREDIENTS
  900g/2lb main crop potatoes
  150ml/¼ pint/⅔ cup olive oil
  1 sprig rosemary
  275g/10oz/2½ cups feta cheese,
    crumbled
  115g/4oz/1 cup pitted black and
    green olives
  300ml/½ pint/1¼ cups hot
    vegetable stock
  salt and ground black pepper

COOK'S TIP
Make sure you choose Greek feta cheese, which has a completely different texture to Danish.

1 Preheat the oven to 200°C/400°F/Gas 6. Cook the potatoes in plenty of boiling water for 15 minutes. Drain and cool slightly. Peel the potatoes and cut into thin slices.

2 Brush the base and sides of a 1.5 litre/2½ pint/6¼ cup rectangular ovenproof dish with some of the olive oil.

3 Layer the potatoes in the dish with the rosemary, cheese and olives. Drizzle with the remaining olive oil and pour over the stock. Season the whole with salt and plenty of ground black pepper.

4 Cook for 35 minutes, covering with foil to prevent the potatoes from getting too brown. Serve hot, straight from the dish.

Breads and Scones

POTATOES PLAY AN ESSENTIAL PART IN MANY LOCAL AND REGIONAL BREAD AND SCONE DISHES. TRY MAKING HERB POTATO SCONES AND BE SURPRISED AT THEIR LIGHT TEXTURE AND WONDERFUL FLAVOUR. FOR A CONTRAST IN FLAVOURS, SERVE STEAMING HOT BOWLS OF SOUP WITH SWEET POTATO AND HONEY BREAD ROLLS, SPICED WITH THE DELICATE FLAVOUR OF CUMIN.

GRATED CHEESE AND ONION POTATO BREAD

A PLAITED LOAF WITH A CRISP CHEESE AND ONION TOPPING. IDEALLY YOU SHOULD SERVE THIS BREAD BY PULLING CHUNKS OFF THE LOAF RATHER THAN SLICING, SO THAT YOU GET MASSES OF TOPPING WITH EACH BITE. THIS BREAD IS PARTICULARLY DELICIOUS SERVED WARM.

MAKES A 900G/2LB LOAF

INGREDIENTS
    225g/8oz floury potatoes
    350g/12oz/3 cups strong white flour
    7.5ml/1½ tsp easy-blend dried yeast
    25g/1oz/2 tbsp butter, diced
    50g/2oz/½ cup pitted green or
        black olives
For the topping
    30ml/2 tbsp olive oil
    1 onion, sliced into rings
    50g/2oz/½ cup mature Cheddar
        cheese, grated
    salt and ground black pepper

3 Bring the mixture together with a round-bladed knife and then turn out on to a floured surface. Knead for about 5 minutes. Return the dough to a bowl and cover with a damp cloth. Leave to rise for 1 hour or until doubled in size. Turn the dough out onto a floured surface and knock back to remove any air bubbles. Carefully knead in the olives. Cut the dough into three even pieces.

5 Meanwhile, for the topping, preheat the oven to 220°C/425°F/Gas 7. Heat the oil in a saucepan and fry the onions for 10 minutes until golden.

6 Remove the onions from the pan and drain on kitchen paper.

7 Scatter the onions and grated cheese over the bread and bake in the oven for 20 minutes.

1 Chop the potatoes and cook in a large saucepan with plenty of salted boiling water for 15–20 minutes or until tender.

2 Meanwhile, sift the flour into a bowl, add the yeast and a little salt. Rub in the butter to form fine crumbs. Drain the potatoes and mash well. Add to the dry ingredients with 300ml/½ pint/1¼ cups lukewarm water.

4 Roll each piece out to a long thick sausage. Twist the sausages over each other to form a plait (see Cook's Tip, below). Lift on to a greased baking sheet. Cover with a damp cloth and leave to rise for 30 minutes or until doubled in size.

COOK'S TIP
To plait a loaf successfully, lay the three lengths of dough side by side. Plait the dough from one end to the centre and repeat with the other end. This will give an even loaf with a professional looking touch to it.

SWEET POTATO AND HONEY BREAD ROLLS

A SWEET ROLL THAT TASTES AS DELICIOUS SERVED WITH CONSERVES AS WITH A SAVOURY SOUP.

MAKES TWELVE

INGREDIENTS
1 large sweet potato
225g/8oz/2 cups strong white flour
5ml/1 tsp easy-blend dried yeast
pinch ground nutmeg
pinch cumin seeds
5ml/1 tsp runny honey
200ml/7fl oz/scant 1 cup
  lukewarm milk
oil, for greasing

1 Cook the potato in plenty of boiling water for 45 minutes or until very tender. Preheat the oven to 220°C/425°F/Gas 7.

2 Meanwhile, sift the flour into a large bowl, add the yeast, ground nutmeg and cumin seeds. Give the ingredients a good stir.

3 Mix the honey and milk together. Drain the potato and peel the skin. Mash the potato flesh and add to the flour mixture with the liquid.

4 Bring the mixture together and knead for 5 minutes on a floured surface. Place the dough in a bowl and cover with a damp cloth. Leave to rise for 30 minutes.

5 Turn the dough out and knock back to remove any air bubbles. Divide the dough into 12 pieces and shape each one into a round.

6 Place the rolls on a greased baking sheet. Cover with a damp cloth and leave to rise in a warm place for 30 minutes or until doubled in size.

7 Bake for 10 minutes. Remove from the oven and drizzle with more honey and cumin seeds before serving.

COOK'S TIP
This dough is quite sticky, so use plenty of flour on the surface when you are kneading and rolling it.

SWEET POTATO BREAD <u>WITH</u> CINNAMON <u>AND</u> WALNUTS

A WONDERFUL BRUNCH DISH, AND COMPLETELY DELICIOUS SERVED WITH CRISPY BACON.

3 Drain the potatoes and cool in cold water, then peel the skins. Mash the potatoes with a fork and mix into the dry ingredients with the nuts.

4 Make a well in the centre and pour in the milk. Bring the mixture together with a round-bladed knife, place on to a floured surface and knead for 5 minutes.

5 Return the dough to a bowl and cover with a damp cloth. Leave to rise for 1 hour or until doubled in size. Turn the dough out and knock back to remove any air bubbles. Knead again for a few minutes. If the dough feels sticky add more flour to the mixture. Shape into a ball and place the bread in an oiled and base-lined 900g/2lb loaf tin. Cover with a damp cloth and leave to rise in a warm place for 1 hour or until doubled in size.

MAKES A 900G/2LB LOAF

INGREDIENTS
  1 medium sweet potato
  5ml/1 tsp ground cinnamon
  450g/1lb/4 cups strong white flour
  5ml/1 tsp easy-blend dried yeast
  50g/2oz/½ cup walnut pieces
  300ml/½ pint/1¼ cups warmed milk
  salt and ground black pepper
  oil, for greasing

COOK'S TIP
For an extra-crispy loaf, after the bread is cooked, remove from the tin and return the bread to the oven placing it upside down on the oven rack. Continue to cook for a further 5 minutes.

1 Boil the whole potato in its skin for 45 minutes or until tender.

2 Meanwhile, sift the cinnamon and flour together into a large bowl. Stir in the dried yeast.

6 Preheat the oven to 200°C/400°F/ Gas 6. Bake on the middle shelf of the oven for 25 minutes. Turn out and tap the base; if it sounds hollow the bread is cooked. Cool on a wire rack.

POTATO BREAD WITH CARAMELISED ONIONS AND ROSEMARY

THE ROSEMARY AND ONIONS INCORPORATED INTO THIS BREAD GIVE IT A MEDITERRANEAN FEEL. IT IS DELICIOUS SERVED WARM WITH A SIMPLE VEGETABLE SOUP.

MAKES A 900G/2LB LOAF

INGREDIENTS
450g/1lb/4 cups strong white flour
5ml/1 tsp easy-blend dried yeast
a pinch of salt, for the dough
15g/½oz/1 tbsp butter
325ml/11fl oz/1⅓ cups warmed milk
15ml/1 tbsp olive oil
2 medium onions, sliced into rings
115g/4oz maincrop potatoes, grated
1 sprig rosemary, chopped
2.5ml/½ tsp sea salt
oil, for greasing and to serve

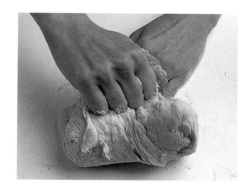

1 Sift the flour into a large bowl. Make a well in the centre and stir in the yeast and a pinch of salt. Rub in the butter until the mixture resembles fine breadcrumbs and then gradually pour in the lukewarm milk.

2 Stir the mixture with a round-bladed knife and then once the wet ingredients have become incorporated, bring it together with your fingers.

3 Turn the dough out and knead on a surface dusted with flour for 5 minutes or until the dough is smooth and elastic. Return the bread to a clean bowl and cover with a damp cloth. Leave to rise in a warm place for 45 minutes or until the dough has doubled in size.

4 Meanwhile, heat the oil in a saucepan and add the onions, stir over a low heat and cook for about 20 minutes until the onions are golden brown and very soft. Set aside.

5 Bring a saucepan of lightly salted water to the boil and add the grated potatoes to the pan. Cook for 5 minutes or until just tender. Drain and plunge into cold water.

VARIATION
For a more piquant flavour, add some bottled sundried tomatoes, drained of their oil and chopped, and a scattering of pitted black olives to the onion layers. Try fresh thyme for a subtle herby tang.

6 Turn the dough out of the bowl and knock back. Roll out on a lightly floured surface. Drain the potatoes and scatter half over the surface with a little rosemary and half the onions. Carefully roll the dough up into a sausage shape.

7 Lift the dough into an oiled 23 x 23cm/9 x 9in tin. Using the palms of your hands flatten the dough out, making sure that the dough fits the tin neatly. Scatter the remaining potatoes and onions over the top with the sea salt and rosemary.

8 Cover again with a damp cloth and leave to rise for 20 minutes.

9 Meanwhile, preheat the oven to 220°C/425°F/Gas 7. Bake the bread for 15–20 minutes. Serve warm drizzled with a little extra olive oil.

COOK'S TIP
If you don't like your onions very crisp, cover the loaf with foil after 10 minutes to prevent the surface from over-browning. Use the largest grater setting available on the food processor for the potatoes, to keep them from becoming too sticky when blanched.

RUSSIAN POTATO BREAD

POTATOES ARE PART OF THE STAPLE DIET IN RUSSIA AND ARE OFTEN USED TO REPLACE SOME OF THE FLOUR IN BREAD RECIPES. THE RESULT IS A LOVELY, MOIST LOAF WHICH IS DELICIOUS JUST SERVED WITH BUTTER. THIS EASY-TO-MAKE BREAD ALSO KEEPS REALLY WELL.

MAKES ONE LOAF

INGREDIENTS
    butter, for greasing
    225g/8oz floury potatoes, diced
    6g/¼oz sachet easy-blend
        dried yeast
    350g/12oz/3 cups unbleached white
        bread flour
    115g/4oz/1 cup wholemeal
        bread flour, plus extra for spinkling
    2.5ml/½ tsp caraway seeds, crushed
    10ml/2 tsp salt
    25g/1oz/2 tbsp butter, diced

1 Lightly grease a baking sheet. Cook the potatoes in boiling water until tender. Drain well, reserving 150ml/ ¼ pint/⅔ cup of the cooking water. Mash and sieve the potatoes and leave to cool.

2 Mix together the yeast, white bread flour, wholemeal bread flour, caraway seeds and salt in a large bowl. Add the butter, cut into small pieces and rub in to form a breadcrumb consistency.

3 Mix together the reserved potato water and sieved potatoes. Gradually work this mixture into the flour mixture to form a soft dough.

4 Turn out on to a lightly floured surface and knead for 8–10 minutes until smooth and elastic.

5 Place the dough in a large, lightly oiled bowl, cover with lightly oiled clear film and leave to rise, in a warm place, for about 1 hour, or until it has doubled in size.

VARIATION
Omit the caraway seeds and knead 115g/4oz/1 cup grated or crumbled Cheddar, Red Leicester or blue cheese into the dough before shaping.

6 Turn out on to a lightly floured surface, knock back and knead gently. Shape into a plump oval loaf about 18cm/7in long. Place on the prepared baking sheet and sprinkle with a little wholemeal bread flour.

7 Cover with lightly oiled clear film and leave to rise, in a warm place, for 30 minutes, or until doubled in size.

8 Meanwhile preheat the oven to 200°C/400°F/Gas 6. Using a sharp knife, slash the top with 3–4 diagonal cuts to make a criss-cross effect.

9 Bake for 30–35 minutes until golden and hollow sounding when tapped on the base. Transfer to a wire rack to cool.

KARTOFFELBROT

THIS IS AN ADAPTATION OF THE CLASSIC GERMAN-STYLE BREAD, THIS VERSION IS MADE WITH STRONG WHITE FLOUR AND FLOURY POTATOES.

MAKES A 450G/1LB LOAF

INGREDIENTS
    butter, for greasing
    225g/8oz/2 cups strong white flour
    10ml/2 tsp baking powder
    5ml/1 tsp salt
    175g/6oz potatoes, cooked
     and mashed
    15ml/1 tbsp vegetable oil
    paprika, for dusting
    mustard-flavoured butter, to serve

COOK'S TIP
This bread is best eaten warm with lashings of mustard-flavoured butter.

1 Preheat the oven to 230°C/450°F/ Gas 8. Grease and line a 450g/1lb loaf tin.

2 Sift the flour into a large bowl and mix together with baking powder and the salt.

3 Rub the mashed potato into the dry ingredients making sure you achieve an even mixture.

4 Stir in the oil and 200ml/7fl oz/scant 1 cup lukewarm water. Turn the dough into the tin and dust with the paprika. Bake in the oven for 25 minutes. Turn out on to a wire rack to cool. Cut the bread into thick chunks and serve with mustard-flavoured butter.

SAVOURY CRANBERRY AND POTATO BREAD SLICE

AN INTERESTING COMBINATION OF CRANBERRIES WITH BACON AND POTATOES. THE CRANBERRIES COLOUR THE BREAD SLICES, GIVING IT A VERY FESTIVE FEEL.

MAKES A 450G/1LB LOAF

INGREDIENTS
450g/1lb/4 cups strong white flour
5ml/1 tsp easy-blend dried yeast
5ml/1 tsp salt
25g/1oz/2 tbsp butter, diced
325ml/11fl oz/1⅓ cups
  lukewarm water
75g/3oz/¾ cup fresh or frozen
  cranberries, thawed
oil, for greasing
225g/8oz floury potatoes, halved
6 rashers rindless streaky
  bacon, chopped
30ml/2 tbsp runny honey
salt and ground black pepper

1 Sift the flour into a bowl, stir in the yeast and 5ml/1 tsp salt. Rub in the butter to form breadcrumbs. Make a well in the centre and stir in the water.

2 Bring the mixture together with a round-bladed knife and then turn out on to a floured surface. Knead for 5 minutes. Place the dough in a bowl and cover with a damp cloth. Leave to rise for 1 hour or until doubled in size.

COOK'S TIP
If you can't find fresh or frozen cranberries, substitute them with sweetcorn niblets.

3 Turn the dough out and knock back to remove the air bubbles. Knead for a few minutes. Carefully knead the cranberries into the bread. Roll the dough out to a rectangle and place in an oiled 23 x 23cm/9 x 9in flan tin. Push the dough into the corners and cover with a damp cloth. Leave to rise in a warm place for 30 minutes.

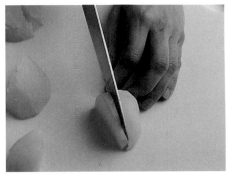

4 Preheat the oven to 220°C/425°F/ Gas 7. Meanwhile, boil the potatoes in plenty of salted water for 15 minutes or until just tender. Drain and when cool enough to handle, slice thinly.

5 Scatter the potatoes and bacon over the risen bread dough, season, then drizzle with the honey and bake for 25 minutes, covering the bread loosely with foil after 20 minutes to prevent burning.

6 Remove the bread from the oven and transfer to a wire rack. Return to the oven for 5 minutes to crisp the base. Leave to cool on the wire rack.

CHEESE AND POTATO BREAD TWISTS

A COMPLETE "PLOUGHMAN'S LUNCH", WITH THE CHEESE COOKED RIGHT IN THE BREAD. IT MAKES AN EXCELLENT BASE FOR A FILLING OF SMOKED SALMON WITH LEMON JUICE.

MAKES EIGHT

INGREDIENTS
    225g/8oz potatoes, diced
    225g/8oz/2 cups strong
      white flour
    5ml/1 tsp easy-blend
      dried yeast
    150ml/¼ pint/⅔ cup
      lukewarm water
    175g/6oz/1½ cups red Leicester
      cheese, finely grated
    10ml/2 tsp olive oil, for greasing
    salt

1 Cook the potatoes in a large saucepan with plenty of lightly salted boiling water for 20 minutes or until tender. Drain through a colander and return to the pan. Mash until smooth and set aside to cool.

2 Meanwhile, sift the flour into a large bowl and add the yeast and a good pinch of salt. Stir in the potatoes and rub with your fingers to form a crumb consistency.

3 Make a well in the centre and pour in the lukewarm water. Start by bringing the mixture together with a round-bladed knife, then use your hands. Knead for 5 minutes on a well-floured surface. Return the dough to the bowl. Cover with a damp cloth and leave to rise in a warm place for 1 hour or until doubled in size.

4 Turn the dough out and knock back the air bubbles. Knead again for a few seconds.

5 Divide the dough into 12 pieces and shape into rounds.

6 Scatter the cheese over a baking sheet. Take each ball of dough and roll it in the cheese.

7 Roll each cheese-covered roll on a dry surface to a long sausage shape. Fold the two ends together and twist the bread. Lay the bread twists on an oiled baking sheet.

8 Cover with a damp cloth and leave the bread to rise in a warm place for 30 minutes. Preheat the oven to 220°C/425°F/Gas 7. Bake the bread for 10–15 minutes.

VARIATION
Any hard, well-flavoured cheese can be used. Mature Cheddar is the traditional choice for a ploughman's lunch, or you could try a smoked cheese, or a variety with added herbs, such as sage Lancashire. For a substantial filling, use slices of ham from the bone, rashers of crisply grilled streaky bacon with avocado slices, or a helping of egg mayonnaise.

COOK'S TIP
These bread twists stay moist and fresh for up to 3 days if stored in airtight food bags.

SWEET POTATO SCONES

THESE ARE SCONES WITH A DIFFERENCE. A SWEET POTATO GIVES THEM A PALE ORANGE COLOUR AND THEY ARE MELTINGLY SOFT IN THE CENTRE, JUST WAITING FOR A KNOB OF BUTTER.

2 In a separate bowl, mix the mashed sweet potatoes with the milk and melted butter or margarine. Beat well to blend.

3 Add the flour to the sweet potato mixture and stir to make a dough. Turn out on to a lightly floured surface and knead until soft and pliable.

MAKES ABOUT TWENTY-FOUR

INGREDIENTS
  butter, for greasing
  150g/5oz/1¼ cups plain flour
  20ml/4 tsp baking powder
  5ml/1 tsp salt
  15g/½oz/1 tbsp soft light
    brown sugar
  150g/5oz mashed sweet potatoes
  150ml/¼ pint/⅔ cup milk
  50g/2oz/4 tbsp butter or margarine,
    melted

1 Preheat the oven to 230°C/450°F/ Gas 8. Grease a baking sheet. Sift together the flour, baking powder and salt into a bowl. Mix in the sugar.

4 Roll or pat out the dough to a 1cm/½in thickness. Cut into rounds using a 4cm/1½in cutter.

5 Arrange the rounds on the baking sheet. Bake for about 15 minutes until risen and lightly golden. Serve warm.

IRISH GRIDDLE SCONES

THESE ARE ALSO CALLED POTATO CAKES OR GRIDDLE CAKES, BUT WHATEVER YOU CALL THEM THEY ARE DELICIOUS SERVED HOT WITH BUTTER AND JAM, OR WITH BACON FOR A HEARTY BREAKFAST.

MAKES SIX

INGREDIENTS
    225g/8oz floury potatoes, cut into
      uniform chunks
    115g/4oz/1 cup plain flour
    2.5ml/½ tsp salt
    2.5ml/½ tsp baking powder
    50g/2oz/4 tbsp butter, diced
    25ml/1½ tbsp milk
    bacon rashers, to serve
    butter, for greasing

1 Cook the potatoes in a saucepan of boiling water until tender.

4 Add the mashed potatoes and mix thoroughly with a fork. Make a well in the centre and pour in the milk. Mix to form a smooth dough.

5 Turn out on to a lightly floured surface and knead gently for about 5 minutes until soft and pliable. Roll out to a round 5mm/¼ in thick. Cut in half, then cut each half into three wedges.

6 Before you cook the scones, fry a batch of bacon rashers to serve with them. Keep warm in a low oven, until the scones are ready.

7 Grease a griddle or frying pan with a little butter and heat until very hot. Add the cakes and fry for 3–4 minutes until golden brown on both sides turning once. Serve hot with the bacon rashers.

2 Drain the potatoes and return them to the pan over a high heat. Using a wooden spoon, stir the potatoes for 1 minute until all traces of moisture have evaporated. Remove from the heat. Mash well, making sure there are no lumps.

3 Sift together the flour, salt and baking powder into a bowl. Rub in the butter with your fingertips until it has the consistency of fine breadcrumbs.

DILL <u>AND</u> POTATO SCONES

POTATO SCONES FLAVOURED WITH DILL ARE QUITE SCRUMPTIOUS AND CAN BE SERVED WARM JUST WITH BUTTER. OR IF YOU WANT TO MAKE THEM SUBSTANTIAL ENOUGH FOR A LIGHT SUPPER, SERVE THEM TOPPED WITH FLAKED SALMON, KIPPER OR MACKEREL.

MAKES ABOUT TEN

INGREDIENTS
   oil, for greasing
   225g/8oz/2 cups self-raising flour
   40g/1½oz/3 tbsp butter, softened
   pinch of salt
   15ml/1 tbsp finely chopped fresh dill
   175g/6oz mashed potato,
     freshly made
   30–45ml/2–3 tbsp milk

COOK'S TIP
If you don't have any dill you can replace it with the herb of your choice. Try fresh parsley or basil as an alternative.

1 Preheat the oven to 230°C/450°F/ Gas 8. Grease a baking sheet. Sift the flour into a bowl, and rub in the butter with your fingertips. Add the salt and dill and stir.

2 Add the mashed potato to the mixture and enough milk to make a soft, pliable dough.

3 Turn out the dough on to a well-floured surface and roll out until it is fairly thin. Cut into rounds using a 7.5cm/3in cutter.

4 Place the scones on the prepared baking sheet, leaving space between each one, and bake for 20–25 minutes until risen and golden. Serve warm.

SAVOURY POTATO DROP SCONES

A LIGHT SCONE WITH A MILD MUSTARD AND CHEESE FLAVOUR, THESE MAKE A DELICIOUS BREAKFAST DISH SERVED WITH SCRAMBLED EGGS AND GRILLED TOMATOES.

MAKES SIXTEEN

INGREDIENTS
   175g/6oz floury potatoes, diced
   115g/4oz/1 cup self-raising flour
   5ml/1 tsp mustard powder
   1 egg, beaten
   25g/1oz/¼ cup Cheddar cheese,
     grated
   150ml/¼ pint/⅔ cup milk
   oil, for frying and greasing
   salt and freshly ground black pepper
   butter, to serve

COOK'S TIP
It is best to use a flat griddle rather than a ridged one for this recipe as the scones are quite small and thin.

1 Cook the potatoes in plenty of boiling salted water for 20 minutes or until tender. Drain the potatoes and then mash them well.

2 Spoon the mashed potato from the saucepan into a large mixing bowl and then add the flour, mustard powder, egg, cheese and milk.

3 Beat well until the mixture comes together. Season.

4 Heat a griddle pan and brush with oil. Drop tablespoonfuls of the mixture on to the griddle and cook for 1–2 minutes. Flip the scones over and cook the second side. Repeat to make 16 scones. Serve warm with butter.

SWEET POTATO MUFFINS WITH RAISINS

MUFFINS HAVE BEEN A PART OF THE AMERICAN BREAKFAST FOR MANY YEARS. THIS VARIETY MIXES THE GREAT COLOUR AND FLAVOUR OF SWEET POTATOES WITH THE MORE USUAL INGREDIENTS.

2 Meanwhile, preheat the oven to 220°C/425°F/Gas 7. Sift the flour and baking powder over the potatoes with a pinch of salt and beat in the egg.

3 Stir the butter and milk together and pour into the bowl. Add the raisins and sugar and mix the ingredients until everything has just come together.

MAKES TWELVE

INGREDIENTS
  1 large sweet potato
  350g/12oz/3 cups plain flour
  15ml/1 tbsp baking powder
  1 egg, beaten
  225g/8oz/1 cup butter, melted
  250ml/8fl oz/1 cup milk
  50g/2oz/scant ½ cup raisins
  50g/2oz/¼ cup caster sugar
  salt
  12 paper muffin cases
  icing sugar, for dusting

1 Cook the sweet potato in plenty of boiling water for 45 minutes or until very tender. Drain the potato and when cool enough to handle peel off the skin. Place in a large bowl and mash well.

4 Spoon the mixture into muffin cases set in a muffin tin.

5 Bake for 25 minutes until golden. Dust with icing sugar and serve warm.

THREE HERB POTATO SCONES

THESE FLAVOURSOME SCONES ARE PERFECT SERVED WARM AND SPLIT IN TWO WITH HAND-CARVED HAM AND PARMESAN SHAVINGS AS A FILLING.

MAKES TWELVE

INGREDIENTS
    225g/8oz/2 cups self-raising flour
    5ml/1 tsp baking powder
    pinch of salt
    50g/2oz/4 tbsp butter, diced
    25g/1oz potato flakes
    15ml/1 tbsp chopped fresh parsley
    15ml/1 tbsp chopped fresh basil
    15ml/1 tbsp chopped fresh oregano
    150ml/¼ pint/⅔ cup milk
    oil, for greasing

1 Preheat the oven to 180°C/350°F/ Gas 4. Sift the flour into a bowl with the baking powder. Add a pinch of salt. Rub in the butter with your fingertips to form crumbs. Place the potato flakes in bowl and pour over 200ml/7fl oz/scant 1 cup boiling water. Beat well and cool slightly.

2 Stir the potatoes into the dry ingredients with the herbs and milk.

3 Bring the mixture together to form a soft dough. Turn out on to a floured surface and knead the dough very gently for a few minutes, until soft and pliable.

COOK'S TIP
Don't be tempted to overseason the mixture, as once cooked the baking powder can also increase the salty flavour of the finished scone and this can overpower the taste of the herbs.

4 Roll the dough out on a floured surface to about 4cm/1½in thickness and stamp out rounds using a 7.5cm/3in cutter. Reshape any remaining dough and re-roll for more scones. Place the scones on to a greased baking dish and brush the surfaces with a little more milk.

5 Cook for 15–20 minutes and serve warm. They can be eaten plain, or with a filling.

CHOCOLATE POTATO CAKE

THIS IS A VERY RICH, MOIST CHOCOLATE CAKE, TOPPED WITH A THIN LAYER OF CHOCOLATE ICING. USE A GOOD-QUALITY DARK CHOCOLATE FOR BEST RESULTS AND SERVE WITH WHIPPED CREAM.

MAKES A 23CM/9IN CAKE

INGREDIENTS
 oil, for greasing
 200g/7oz/1 cup sugar
 250g/9oz/1 cup and 2 tbsp butter
 4 eggs, separated
 275g/10oz dark chocolate
 75g/3oz/¾ cup ground almonds
 165g/5½ oz mashed potato
 225g/8oz/2 cups self-raising flour
 5ml/1 tsp cinnamon
 45ml/3 tbsp milk
 white and dark chocolate shavings,
  to garnish
 whipped cream, to serve

1 Preheat the oven to 180°C/350°F/ Gas 4. Grease and base-line a 23cm/9in round cake tin with a circle of baking parchment.

2 In a large bowl, cream together the sugar and 225g/8oz/1 cup of the butter until light and fluffy. Then beat the egg yolks into the creamed mixture one at a time until it is smooth and creamy.

3 Finely chop or grate 175g/6oz of the chocolate and stir it into the creamed mixture with the ground almonds. Pass the mashed potato through a sieve or ricer and stir it into the creamed chocolate mixture.

4 Sift together the flour and cinnamon and fold into the mixture with the milk.

COOK'S TIP
Chocolate can be melted very successfully in the microwave. Place the pieces of chocolate in a plastic measuring jug or bowl. The chocolate may scorch if placed in a glass bowl. Microwave on high for 1 minute, stir, and then heat again for up to 1 minute, checking halfway through to see if it is done.

5 Whisk the egg whites until they hold stiff but not dry peaks, and fold into the cake mixture.

6 Spoon into the prepared tin and smooth over the top, but make a slight hollow in the middle to help keep the surface of the cake level during cooking. Bake in the oven for 1¼ hours until a wooden toothpick inserted in the centre comes out clean. Allow the cake to cool slightly in the tin, then turn out and cool on a wire rack.

7 Meanwhile break up the remaining chocolate into a heatproof bowl and stand it over a saucepan of hot water. Add the remaining butter in small pieces and stir well until the chocolate has melted and the mixture is smooth and glossy.

8 Peel off the lining paper and trim the top of the cake so that it is level. Smooth over the chocolate icing and allow to set. Decorate with white and dark chocolate shavings and serve with lashings of whipped cream.

INDEX

potatoes baked with
tomatoes, 212

ACKNOWLEDGEMENTS

Of the many people and organisations who have patiently answered my persistent questioning by phone, fax or email Alex Barker and the publishers would like to thank the following:
Three Countries Potatoes, (David Chappel of Newport, Norman Hosking of Penzance, Morrice Innes of Aberdeenshire and Andrew McQueen of Shrewsbury) – especially for providing so many potato samples for photography; Alan Wilson (Agronomist and Potato Specialist to Waitrose) and *The Story of the Potato* by Alan Wilson published by Alan Wilson; Alan Romans – and his *Guide to Seed Potato Varieties* published by the Henry Doubleday Research Organisation, Ryton Organic Gardens, Coventry CV8 3LG UK; David Turnbull and Stuart Carnegie at the Scottish Agricultural Science Agency; Nicola Bark of Vegfed, Huddart Parker Building, Post Office Square, PO Box 10232, Wellington, New Zealand Tel 644472 3795 Fax 644471 2861 www.vegfed.co.nz; Lori Wing, The Potato Association of America, University of Maine, 5715 Coburn Hall, #6 Orono, ME 04469 5715; Kathleen

Haynes @asrr.arsusda.gov, Dr Alvin Reeves REEVES@ MAINE.MAINE.EDU; Carl Duivenvoorden, New Brunswick Agriexport Inc., 850 Lincoln Rd PO Box 1101, Station "A", Fredericton, New Brunswick, Canada E3B 5C2 Tel 506 453 2890 Fax 506 453 7170; Peter Boswall, Prince Edward Island Agriculture & Forestry, PO Box 1600, Charlottetown, Prince Edward Island, Canada CIA 7N3 Tel 902 368 5600 Fax 902 368 5729; An Bord Glas, 8-11 Lower Baggot Street, Dublin 2; Dr F Ezeta and Christine Graves, The International Potato Centre, Lima, Peru; The British Potato Council, 4300 Nash Court, John Smith Drive, Oxford Business Park, South, Oxford OX4 2RT; Phil Harlock at Covent Garden Supply Co., A24-29 New Covent Garden Market, London SW8 5LR; Colin Randel, Mr Fothergill's Seeds, Kentford, Newmarket, Suffolk CB8 7QB Tel 01638 751 161 Fax 01638 751 624. Not forgetting the many other companies, farmers, producers and experts worldwide who have helped answer my numerous questions.

For potato samples for photography:
Glens of Antrim Potatoes, Red

Bay, Cushendall, Co Antrim, BT44 0SH; ASDA; J Sainsbury plc; Waitrose

For the generous loan of photographic props:
David Mellor, 4 Sloane Square, London SW1 Tel 0171 730 4259; Divertimenti, 139-141 Fulham Rd, London SW3 6SD Mail Order 0181 246 4300; Elizabeth David Cookshop, Covent Garden, London WC2 Tel 0171 836 9167; Kenwood Ltd, New Lane, Havant, Hampshire PO9 2NH Tel 01705 476 000; Magimix UK Ltd, 115A High Street, Godalming, Surrey GU7 1AQ Tel 01483 427 411

For her styling, hand modelling and days of telephone researching – Stephanie England – Thank you.

Useful reference publications:
The Netherlands Catalogue of Potato Varieties 1997, published by NIVAA
The Potato Variety Handbook published by NIAB (The National Institute of Agricultural Botany) Huntingdon Rd, Cambridge CB3 OLE OK
Potato Varieties in Canada 1997, produced by the New Brunswick Department of Agriculture, Canada

Classification of Potato Varieties in the Reference Collection at East Craigs, Edinburgh, by Douglas M Macdonald, published by the Scottish Office Agriculture and Fisheries Department
Atlantic Canada Potato Guide published by authority of the Atlantic Provinces Agriculture Services Co-ordinating Committee, New Brunswich, Canada
EC Common Catalogue Vol 40, (Plant Varieties and Seeds Gazette) from The Stationery Office Ltd, 51 Nine Elms, London SW8 4DR
North American Potato Varieties Handbooks published by the Potato Association of America

Picture Credits:
All pictures taken by Steve Moss (potatoes and techniques), Sam Stowell (recipes) and Walt Chrynwski (US potatoes) except for the following: p. 6 (top and bottom, p. 7 (top), p. 8 E.T. Archive; p. 7 (bottom) Illustrated London News; p. 9 (bottom) The British Potato Council; p. 10 (middle and bottom) The International Potato Centre, Peru.